ERP: Making It Happen

The Implementers' Guide to Success with Enterprise Resource Planning

Thomas F. Wallace
Michael H. Kremzar

John Wiley & Sons, Inc.

New York • Chichester • Weinheim • Brisbane • Singapore • Toronto

Published by John Wiley & Sons, Inc.
Published simultaneously in Canada.

This publication is designed to provide accurate and authoritative
information in regard to the subject matter covered. It is sold with
the understanding that the publisher is not engaged in rendering
professional services. If professional advice or other expert assistance
is required, the services of a competent professional person
should be sought.

Library of Congress Cataloging-in-Publication Data:
Wallace, Thomas F.
ERP : making it happen : the implementers' guide to success with
enterprise resource planning / Thomas F. Wallace, Michael H. Kremzar.
p. cm.
Includes bibliographical references and index.
ISBN 0-471-39201-4 (cloth : alk. paper)
1. Production planning.   2. Manufacturing resource planning.
I. Kremzar, Michael H.   II. Title.
TS176.W333 2001
658.5—dc21
2001017644

Printed in the United States of America.
10 9 8 7 6 5 4 3 2 1

Contents

Acknowledgments

There are so many people to acknowledge when a book like this is complete. All of those who contributed to the earlier MRPII book certainly played a role, albeit indirect, in this new effort. Many others who are active in the field provided insight through their books, papers, or talks. For sake of brevity, we are going to focus on this book and hope that all of those who built the foundation of the earlier works will still feel ownership for this one.

As the final draft developed, we asked a handful of people to help us with input on the quality of our effort. Their insightful feedback has been extremely important.

Gary Abyad
Chief Operating Officer
Clopay Plastic Products
    Company

Mike Friedman
Director of Product Supply
The Procter & Gamble
    Company

Mike Landrigan
Chief Financial Officer
Innotek, Inc.

Jerry Clement
Principal
The Oliver Wight
    Companies

Chris Gray
Principal
Gray Research

Jim Rice
Leader, MIT Integrated
    Supply Management
        Program

Travis Rushing
Director, Commercial
Products Product Supply
The Procter & Gamble
  Company

Bob Stahl
Principal
Partners In Excellence

Our sincere thanks go to all of you for taking the time to pour over the manuscript and pouring your insights into comments—sometimes painful but always helpful. Thanks also to the folks at the APICS Region III Officers Meeting in January, 2001 for their valuable feedback.

There are two individuals who need to be highlighted since they did so much to pave the way for what all of us are doing today. The late Oliver Wight must be credited for developing most of the concepts in resource planning still in use today. Ollie certainly was an inspiration for much that has followed. Also, Darryl Landvater developed the Detailed MRPII Implementation Plan that was featured in the earlier works and now continues to be utilized in this book. We owe much to these two as well as many others at the Oliver Wight Companies who have done such good work in developing the widespread understanding of resource planning.

In this book, we quote from an excellent work by Thomas H. Davenport, *Mission Critical—Realizing the Promise of Enterprise Systems.* For those digging more deeply into issues related to enterprise-wide software, we highly recommend this book. Also, Professor Jeanne W. Ross, Center for Information Systems Research at MIT, shared her thoughts with us on ERP. Both of these sources were helpful as we wrestled with how best to present the software side of the ERP equation.

We need to recognize our families for their support and comfort during this effort. Marilyn Kremzar has been putting up with the frustrations of living with Mike throughout his entire career with P&G and now during this book as well. Yes, Marilyn, Mike will retire one of these days! Tom acknowledges the enormous contributions of his wife of 38 years, Evelyn, in this and so many other projects during that time. She died during the writing of this book.

Last, and most assuredly not least, we're deeply indebted to the users, the people in manufacturing companies who've made resource planning work. The early implementers in particular displayed great vision and courage to persevere, to take two steps forward and then maybe one step back, to keep the faith and to make it happen. Thanks largely to them, a trial-and-error approach to implementing ERP is no longer necessary.

Thomas F. Wallace
Michael H. Kremzar
Cincinnati, Ohio

How to Use This Book

The intended audience for this book comes primarily from companies in two categories:

Companies that recognize the need for better decision-making processes, enhanced coordination, and greater responsiveness both internally and within their extended supply chain

Companies that have installed an enterprise-wide software system and now realize that they need to change their businesses processes to gain major benefits from their investment in software.

The people who should read all or part of this book include:

The executive in charge of the entire business unit (general manager, president, chief executive officer): Read at a minimum Chapters 1, 2, and 3 to understand the basic concepts of ERP and the scope of the project. It should prove helpful to read Chapter 8 on Sales & Operations Planning and Chapter 13 on an implementation approach called Quick Slice. Finish with Chapter 16 for some insight into the full potential of ERP, which is enormous.

The chair of the executive steering committee (described in Chapter 6): Read all chapters.

Members of the executive steering committee (described in Chapter 6): Read Chapters 1, 2, 5, 6, and 7 and the part of Chapter 11 that deals with implementing Sales & Operations Planning. Further, if implementation is being done on a Quick-Slice basis (defined in Chapter 2), they should read Chapters 13 and 14. Here also, Chapter 16 should prove to be of interest.

All members of the ERP Project Team: Read all chapters.

We prepared this book to be useful either as selective reading for those who need only specific pieces of information, or as a virtual checklist for those who need to know every step. Those of us who have been through ERP implementations with the Second Edition of this book have found that it was the book most often referred to. Even after the project is well underway, we suspect you'll probably find yourself opening this book and referring to specific subjects.

Lastly, while this book does cover every aspect of implementing ERP, it does not tell you every step, every report, or every piece of data required. You will need more than this one book to do the entire project. Our job here has been to give you the working knowledge to know what needs to be done. Each company will design the details of the project to reflect its individual business, people, and challenges but the implementation path described here is for every company.

Go make it happen!

PART I

Introduction

Chapter 1

Enterprise Resource Planning

This is not a book about software. One more time: This is not a book about how to select software and install it on your computers. Rather, it's a book about how to implement superior business processes in your company—processes that yield a competitive advantage.

Right now you might be thinking: "Wait a minute. The name of this book is ERP. How can it not be about software?"

The answer is that Enterprise Resource Planning (ERP) is not software. One more time: ERP is not software. There's a lot of sloppy terminology flying around today in the business press, and one misnomer is to label enterprise-wide transaction processing software systems as ERP. These software packages support effective resource planning and make much of it feasible, but they don't truly do it. Plus these packages contain many business processes other than resource planning.

Therefore, we need to trot out another acronym that does refer to software: ES. This stands for Enterprise System or Enterprise Software. In his book *Mission Critical*,[i] author Thomas H. Davenport describes enterprise systems as "packages of computer applications that support many, even most, aspects of a company's information needs."

That makes sense to us. Now for another distinction: Not all ERP business functions are contained in the typical Enterprise Software

3

Figure 1-1
ERP Processes

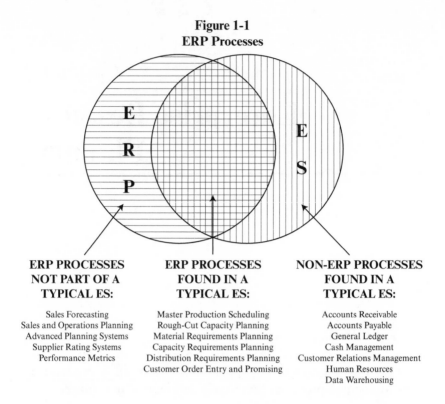

ERP PROCESSES NOT PART OF A TYPICAL ES:	ERP PROCESSES FOUND IN A TYPICAL ES:	NON-ERP PROCESSES FOUND IN A TYPICAL ES:
Sales Forecasting	Master Production Scheduling	Accounts Receivable
Sales and Operations Planning	Rough-Cut Capacity Planning	Accounts Payable
Advanced Planning Systems	Material Requirements Planning	General Ledger
Supplier Rating Systems	Capacity Requirements Planning	Cash Management
Performance Metrics	Distribution Requirements Planning	Customer Relations Management
	Customer Order Entry and Promising	Human Resources
		Data Warehousing

(ES) suite. Similarly, the typical ES contains software support for business processes that are not a part of ERP. In Figure 1-1, we can see that distinction graphically. Please note the three areas on that diagram. The rightmost part of the figure refers to those functions contained within a typical ES that are not part of ERP; the leftmost area is for those ERP functions not normally supported by an ES; the area of overlap in the center references those ERP functions typically supported by Enterprise Software.

Now let's take a look at just what this ERP thing is all about.

WHAT IS ENTERPRISE RESOURCE PLANNING AND WHAT DOES IT DO?

Enterprise Resource Planning (ERP)—and its predecessor, Manufacturing Resource Planning (MRP II)—is helping to transform our industrial landscape. It's making possible profound improvements in the way manufacturing companies are managed. It is a strong contributor to America's amazing economic performance of the 1990s and the emergence of the New Economy. A half century from now, when the definitive industrial history of the twentieth century is written, the evolution of ERP will be viewed as a watershed event. Let's describe Enterprise Resource Planning as:

An enterprise-wide set of management tools that balances demand and supply,

containing the ability to link customers and suppliers into a complete supply chain,

employing proven business processes for decision-making, and

providing high degrees of cross-functional integration among sales, marketing, manufacturing, operations, logistics, purchasing, finance, new product development, and human resources, thereby

enabling people to run their business with high levels of customer service and productivity, and simultaneously lower costs and inventories; and providing the foundation for effective e-commerce.

Here are some descriptions of ERP, not definitions but certainly good examples.

Enterprise Resource Planning is a company increasing its sales by 20 percent in the face of an overall industry decline. Discussing how this happened, the vice president of sales explained: "We're capturing lots of business from our competitors. We can out-deliver 'em. Thanks to (ERP), we can now ship quicker than our competition, and we ship on time."

Enterprise Resource Planning is a Fortune 50 corporation achieving enormous cost savings and acquiring a significant competitive advantage. The vice president of logistics stated: "ERP has provided the key to becoming a truly global company. Decisions can be made with accurate data and with a process that connects demand and supply across borders and oceans. This change is worth billions to us in sales worldwide."

Enterprise Resource Planning is a purchasing department generating enormous cost reductions while at the same time increasing its ability to truly partner with its suppliers. The director of purchasing claimed: "For the first time ever, we have a good handle on our future requirements for components raw and materials. When our customer demand changes, we—ourselves and our suppliers—can manage changes to our schedules on a very coordinated and controlled basis. I don't see how any company can do effective supply chain management without ERP."

That's ERP. Here's how it came to be.

The Evolution of Enterprise Resource Planning

Step One—Material Requirements Planning (MRP)

ERP began life in the 1960s as Material Requirements Planning (MRP), an outgrowth of early efforts in bill of material processing. MRP's inventors were looking for a better method of ordering material and components, and they found it in this technique. The logic of material requirements planning asks the following questions:

- What are we going to make?
- What does it take to make it?
- What do we have?
- What do we have to get?

This is called the universal manufacturing equation. Its logic applies wherever things are being produced whether they be jet aircraft, tin cans, machine tools, chemicals, cosmetics . . . or Thanksgiving dinner.

Material Requirements Planning simulates the universal manufacturing equation. It uses the master schedule (What are we going to make?), the bill of material (What does it take to make it?), and inventory records (What do we have?) to determine future requirements (What do we have to get?).

For a visual depiction of this and the subsequent evolutionary steps, please see Figure 1-2, a modified version of a diagram in Carol Ptak's recent book on ERP.[ii]

Figure 1-2

EVOLUTION OF ERP

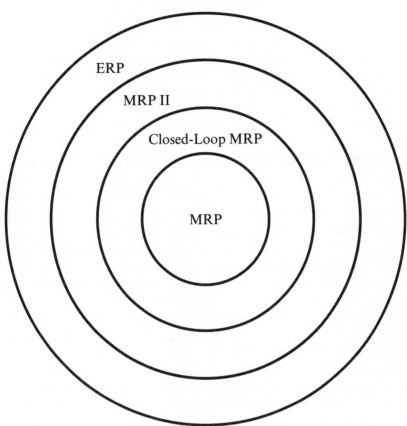

Step Two—Closed-Loop MRP

MRP quickly evolved, however, into something more than merely a better way to order. Early users soon found that Material Requirements Planning contained capabilities far greater than merely giving better signals for reordering. They learned this technique could help to *keep* order due dates valid *after* the orders had been released to production or to suppliers. MRP could detect when the *due date* of an order (when it's scheduled to arrive) was out of phase with its *need* date (when it's required).

Figure 1-3
Priority vs. Capacity

Priority	Capacity
Which ones?	Enough?
Sequence	Volume
Scheduling	Loading

This was a breakthrough. For the first time ever in manufacturing, there was a formal mechanism for keeping priorities valid in a constantly changing environment. This is important, because in a manufacturing enterprise, change is not simply a possibility or even a probability. It's a certainty, the only constant, the only sure thing. The function of keeping order due dates valid and synchronized with these changes is known as *priority planning.*

So, did this breakthrough regarding priorities solve all the problems? Was this all that was needed? Hardly. The issue of priority is only half the battle. Another factor—capacity—represents an equally challenging problem. (See Figure 1-3.)

Techniques for helping plan capacity requirements were tied in with Material Requirements Planning. Further, tools were developed to support the planning of aggregate sales and production levels (Sales & Operations Planning); the development of the specific build schedule (master scheduling); forecasting, sales planning, and customer-order promising (demand management); and high-level resource analysis (Rough-Cut Capacity Planning). Systems to aid in executing the plan were tied in: various plant scheduling techniques for the inside factory and supplier scheduling for the outside factory — the suppliers. These developments resulted in the second step in this evolution: closed-loop MRP. (See Figure 1-4.)

Closed-loop MRP has a number of important characteristics:

It's a series of functions, not merely material requirements planning.

It contains tools to address both priority and capacity, and to support both planning and execution.

It has provisions for feedback from the execution functions back to the planning functions. Plans can then be altered when necessary, thereby keeping priorities valid as conditions change.

Figure 1-4

CLOSED-LOOP MRP

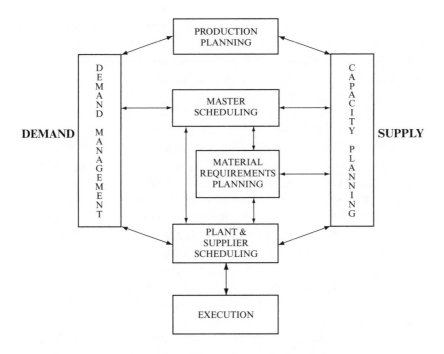

Step Three—Manufacturing Resource Planning (MRP II)

The next step in this evolution is called Manufacturing Resource Planning or MRP II (to distinguish it from Material Requirements Planning, MRP). A direct outgrowth and extension of closed-loop MRP, it involves three additional elements:

1. Sales & Operations Planning—a powerful process to balance demand and supply at the volume level, thereby providing top management with far greater control over operational aspects of the business.

2. Financial interface—the ability to translate the operating plan (in pieces, pounds, gallons, or other units) into financial terms (dollars).

3. Simulation—the ability to ask "what-if" questions and to obtain actionable answers—in both units and dollars. Initially

this was done only on an aggregate, "rough-cut" basis, but today's advanced planning systems (APS) enable effective simulation at very detailed levels.

Now it's time to define Manufacturing Resource Planning. This definition, and the one to follow, come from APICS—The Educational Society for Resource Management. APICS is the leading professional society in this field, and its dictionary has set the standard for terminology over the years.

MANUFACTURING RESOURCE PLANNING (MRP II)— A method for the effective planning of all resources of a manufacturing company. Ideally, it addresses operational planning in units, financial planning in dollars, and has a simulation capability to answer "what-if" questions. It is made up of a variety of functions, each linked together: business planning, sales and operations planning, production planning, master scheduling, material requirements planning, capacity requirements planning, and the execution support systems for capacity and material. Output from these systems is integrated with financial reports such as the business plan, purchase commitment report, shipping budget, and inventory projections in dollars. Manufacturing resource planning is a direct outgrowth and extension of closed-loop MRP.[iii]

Step Four—Enterprise Resource Planning (ERP)

The latest step in this evolution is Enterprise Resource Planning (ERP). The fundamentals of ERP are the same as with MRP II. However, thanks in large measure to enterprise software, ERP as a set of business processes is broader in scope, and more effective in dealing with multiple business units. Financial integration is even stronger. Supply chain tools, supporting business across company boundaries, are more robust. For a graphical view of ERP, see Figure 1-5.

Let's now look at a complete definition of ERP, based on the description we saw a few pages back:

ENTERPRISE RESOURCE PLANNING (ERP) predicts and balances demand and supply. It is an enterprise-wide set of forecasting, planning, and scheduling tools, which:

Figure 1-5

ENTERPRISE RESOURCE PLANNING

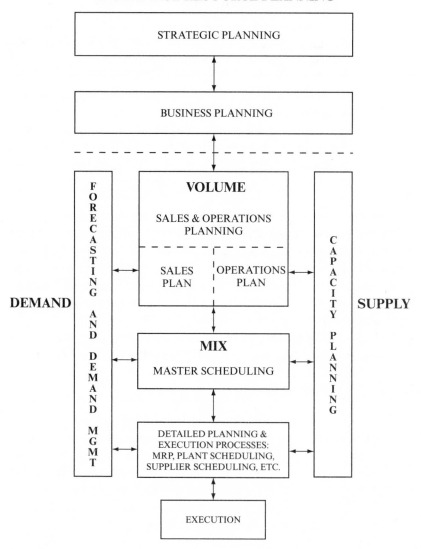

- links customers and suppliers into a complete supply chain,

- employs proven processes for decision-making, and

- coordinates sales, marketing, operations, logistics, purchasing, finance, product development, and human resources.

Its goals include high levels of customer service, productivity, cost reduction, and inventory turnover, and it provides the foundation for effective supply chain management and e-commerce. It does this by developing plans and schedules so that the right resources—manpower, materials, machinery, and money—are available in the right amount when needed.

Enterprise Resource Planning is a direct outgrowth and extension of Manufacturing Resource Planning and, as such, includes all of MRP II's capabilities. ERP is more powerful in that it: a) applies a single set of resource planning tools across the entire enterprise, b) provides real-time integration of sales, operating, and financial data, and c) connects resource planning approaches to the extended supply chain of customers and suppliers.

The primary purpose of implementing Enterprise Resource Planning is to run the business, in a rapidly changing and highly competitive environment, far better than before. How to make that happen is what this book is all about.

The Applicability of ERP

ERP and its predecessor, MRP II, have been successfully implemented in companies with the following characteristics:

- Make-to-stock

- Make-to-order

- Design-to-order

- Complex product

- Simple product

- Multiple plants
- Single plant
- Contract manufacturers
- Manufacturers with distribution networks
- Sell direct to end users
- Sell through distributors
- Businesses heavily regulated by the government
- Conventional manufacturing (fabrication and assembly)
- Process manufacturing
- Repetitive manufacturing
- Job shop
- Flow shop
- Fabrication only (no assembly)
- Assembly only (no fabrication)
- High-speed manufacturing
- Low-speed manufacturing

Within the universe of companies that make things—manufacturing enterprises—ERP has virtually universal application. This book deals with how to implement ERP in any of the above environments. Some people struggle with this applicability issue; they sometimes say: "We're different, we're unique, it won't work for us." We've heard that a lot over the years. What we have *never* heard is: "We're different, we're unique, Generally Accepted Accounting Principles (GAAP) won't work for us." Well, ERP is the *logistics analog* of GAAP. It's a defined body of knowledge that contains the standard best practices for managing that part of the business. The main difference between the two is that ERP and its predecessors have been with us for about four decades; double-entry bookkeeping and its offshoots have been around for four centuries. More on this later.

ERP AS A FOUNDATION

Today, there are a wide variety of tools and techniques that have been designed to help companies and their people produce their products better and more efficiently. These include Lean Manufacturing, Six Sigma Quality, Employee Involvement, Factory Automation, Design for Manufacturability, and many more. These are excellent tools with enormous potential.

But . . . none of them will ever yield their full potential unless they're coupled with *effective forecasting, planning, and scheduling processes.* Here's why:

It's not good enough to be extremely efficient . . . if you're making the wrong stuff.

It's not good enough to make items at a very high level of quality . . . if they're not the ones needed.

It's not good enough to reduce setup times and cut lot sizes . . . if bad schedules prevent knowing what's really needed and when.

Back in the early 1980s, a new way of thinking about manufacturing came out of Japan, and it was truly revolutionary. In this country we've called it Just-In-Time (JIT), and more recently it has evolved into Lean Manufacturing.[1]

As with most new tools and processes, its early adherents promoted JIT with a missionary zeal—and rightly so. This is great stuff. Some of them, however, took the approach that MRP/MRP II was no longer necessary for companies doing JIT. The MRP establishment pushed back and the result was a raging debate that generated a lot of heat and not much light.

Today we can see the situation much more clearly, and we feel this view has been best articulated by Chris Gray, president of Gray Research in Wakefield, NH. Chris says that improvements to business processes take one of three forms:

1. Improving process reliability. Six Sigma and other Total Quality tools are predominant here.

[1] Also called Agile Manufacturing or Synchronous Flow Manufacturing.

2. Reducing process complexity. Lean Manufacturing is heavily used here.

3. Coordinating the individual elements of the overall set of business processes. ERP lives here.

Enterprise Resource Planning, when operating at a high level of effectiveness, will do several things for a company. First, it will enable the company's people to generate enormous benefits. Many companies have experienced, as a direct result of ERP (or MRP II) dramatic increases in responsiveness, productivity, on-time shipments and sales, along with substantial decreases in lead times, purchase costs, quality problems, and inventories.

Further, ERP can provide the foundation upon which additional productivity and quality enhancements can be built—an environment where these other tools and techniques can reach their full potential.

Effective forecasting, planning and scheduling—knowing routinely what is needed and when via the formal system—is fundamental to productivity. ERP is the vehicle for getting valid plans and schedules, but not just of materials and production. It also means valid schedules of shipments to customers, of personnel and equipment requirements, of required product development resources, and of cash flow and profit. Enterprise Resource Planning has proven itself to be the foundation, the bedrock, for supply chain management. It's the glue that helps bind the company together with its customers, distributors, and suppliers—all on a coordinated, cooperative basis.

MORE ABOUT SOFTWARE

Now that we've kicked the ERP topic around a bit, let's double back on the software issue. Software for ERP is like a set of golf clubs. You could give the greatest, most expensive set of golf clubs ever made to either one of your friendly authors, but they wouldn't break 120. Why? It's simple; neither of us knows how to play golf.

On the other hand, let's say we send Tiger Woods out on the pro tour with only a four-wood and a sand wedge. Would Tiger win any tournaments? Not a chance. He'd never even make the cut. The reason: To be competitive at the highest levels of the game, you need a full set of clubs in the bag.

Two principles flow from this analogy:

1. The acquisition of the tools, of and by itself, will not make you proficient in their use and thus will *not* provide a competitive advantage.

2. To be truly competitive, you need a good and reasonably complete set of tools.

Too many companies have bought an extremely expensive set of "golf clubs" (an enterprise software system) but haven't learned how to play golf. That's why we read about so many "ERP failures" in the business press. The fact of the matter is that ERP hasn't failed at all in those cases; it hasn't even been attempted. Saying that ERP failed in these cases is like saying that *golf failed* because one of your authors bought a $2,000 set of golf clubs and didn't break 120. Golf failed? Makes no sense.

THE ABCs OF IMPLEMENTATION

Let's look at the ABCs of implementing Enterprise Resource Planning. The concept is derived from the basic ABC approach to inventory control, in turn derived from Pareto's law. In that technique, the A items are considered very significant, costly, important, etc. Hence, they deserve the most attention and the most careful planning and control. The B items are of less significance than the A items, and, hence, less time is devoted to each of them. The C items, while essential, are of least overall significance and are given proportionate attention.

This ABC approach, applied to implementation, states that *Item C is the computer,* both the hardware and software. It's essential since ERP can't be done manually, but it's of lesser significance overall than the other elements.

Item B is the data: the inventory records, the bills of material, the routings, etc. They are more significant and require more of the company's overall attention and managerial emphasis.

Item A is the people, the most important element in making it happen. If the people part of the implementation process is managed properly, the people will understand the objectives and how to get there. They'll take care of getting and keeping the data accurate. They won't allow the "computer tail" to wag the "company dog," as has been the case far too often. People are the key.

CLASS ABCD

At the risk of getting into what might look like alphabet soup, we need to introduce another concept based on the letters A, B, and C plus one more. Here goes.

By the mid-1970s the term MRP had become a buzzword. Almost everyone, it seemed, was "doing MRP." Many companies weren't happy with their results. On the other hand, some companies were achieving spectacular results. Companies' reactions to MRP ranged from: "It hasn't helped us at all." to "It's terrific; we couldn't run the business without it."

It became obvious that there were profound differences in how well companies were using this set of tools. To help focus on this issue, Oliver Wight, the leading pioneer in this field, developed the ABCD classification. (See Figure 1-6.)

Figure 1-6

Class A	Effectively used company-wide; generating significant improvements in customer service, productivity, and costs.
Class B	Supported by top management; used by middle management to achieve measurable quality improvements.
Class C	Operated primarily as better methods for ordering materials; contributing to better inventory management.
Class D	Information inaccurate and poorly understood by users; providing little help in running the business.

Class D installations have often been viewed as "another computer failure." This strikes us as a bum rap for the computer, because the computer is the only element that's doing its job. Has the computer failed? No, it's working. Has ERP failed? Not really; it hasn't had a chance. What has failed? The *people* in the company. They've failed to implement and operate this set of tools successfully.

Class C means a company has reduced its inventories, in some cases substantially, and probably is better able to manage engineering changes. The return on investment (ROI) for Class C typically is very good. However, the company really hasn't changed the way it runs the business.

The company operating ERP at a Class B level has dramatically improved its ability to deliver the product on time to its customers, minimize shortages in the plant, avoid unplanned overtime, reduce inventories, and cope with the myriad of changes that typically confront a manufacturing organization.

Class A yields all of the Class B benefits and more. The business is managed with one consistent set of numbers, from top management's sales & operations plans down through the detailed schedules for the plant floor, the suppliers, the distribution centers and, most important, the customers. Financial plans and reports are developed from the highly accurate operational numbers used to run the business on a day-to-day basis. Extensive use is made of simulation, performing what-if analyses using the ERP data base, in both units and dollars.

To evaluate their performance, many companies have used the *Oliver Wight ABCD Checklist for Operational Excellence* (Fifth edition, 2000, John Wiley & Sons, New York, NY). This checklist is a series of questions which an organization can self-administer to determine how effectively it's using the tools of ERP, and this process results in a letter grade (A,B, C, or D) and helps to determine the path for improvement.

IMPLEMENTERS AND RE-IMPLEMENTERS

This book deals with how to implement ERP at a Class A level. Further, it applies to both first-time implementers and to *re-implementers,* companies whose first implementation resulted in Class C or D results and who now want to get the full bang for their buck. For those of you who'll be re-implementing, be of good cheer: Many companies now getting Class A results got there via re-implementation. The steps involved in a re-implementation are virtually identical to a first-time implementation; the main difference is that some of the necessary steps may have already been accomplished satisfactorily.

Many companies today need to re-implement. Some of these are companies who, as we saw earlier, thought they were implementing ERP, but actually were only installing enterprise software. Their motivations were largely software-driven: Y2K compliance, legacy systems becoming unworkable, multiple hardware platforms supporting too many operational systems, etc. The problem is that, in many cases, the new software was installed but not much else changed.

Many companies' ERP implementations in the past started out with the best intentions in the world. Company S, for example, wanted to re-engineer and improve processes, to improve the way they managed the business, and to give far better customer service to an increasingly demanding customer base. During the implementation, however, they were overwhelmed by the software. Enterprise software tends to be highly complex, and complexity can make it very difficult to install. As the implementation project took longer and longer, and cost more and more, top management became more and more impatient. The result: a decision to forget about implementing better business processes and just get the software running.

Thus, Company S has new software but is still running the business in much the same old way, and thus they need to re-implement.[2] If you're in this category, this book is intended for you every bit as much as for the company implementing for the first time.

THE IMPLEMENTERS' DILEMMA

In the chapters to come, we'll talk a lot about the "Proven Path," which is the implementation approach we recommend. The company that follows the Proven Path can be virtually assured of a successful implementation. The dilemma is that some companies may not be able to follow the Proven Path, and the reason has to do with software.

Let's look at the three types of companies wanting to implement enterprise resource planning:

---

[2] Some call this a "second wave" implementation.

The first type of company has already installed enterprise software. Now it wants to improve its business processes by implementing ERP, and thus capitalizing on the ES investment. The Proven Path will work very nicely for this company, probably in the Quick Slice variant discussed in Chapters 13 and 14.

The second category of company has not yet installed a complete set of enterprise software (although it may have installed a few modules of an ES). ERP is a higher priority than ES; thus software issues will be subordinated to the ERP initiative. This company has what we call a "clean sheet of paper" and the Proven Path applies completely.

In the third case, the company has already begun installing enterprise software or is about to do so. ES is the priority. This company may not be able to simultaneously implement ERP using the Proven Path. Here's the dilemma: workload. Installing enterprise software can be an enormous task. Even with lots of people from outside consulting firms, the time requirements for the company's people are very large.

Later we'll discuss in detail why implementing ERP cannot be subcontracted to outsiders. For now, take it on faith: An ERP implementation is a do-it-yourself project; it requires intimate knowledge of your business. The essence of implementing ERP is to acquire better business processes, and these must be implemented by the people operating the business.

That said, if these folks are pretty much overwhelmed with a) doing their day-to-day jobs and b) participating heavily in an ES installation, they won't have the time or mental energy necessary to do the hard work involved in implementing ERP. Thus this company *will not be able to follow the Proven Path.* They may pay it lip service. They may pretend they're following it. But they can't. They don't have the horses.

We call these companies "dilemma companies" and our advice to them is simple: Don't try to implement ERP simultaneously with installing an enterprise software system if you aren't convinced that your people have the time to do it justice. Rather, we recommend that you:

- recognize the dilemma,

- complete the ES installation,

- start to make a limited number of process improvements during the ES installation, ones that won't consume large amounts of peoples' time. (One excellent process that applies here is Sales & Operations Planning, covered in Chapter 8. Another opportunity is data integrity, discussed in Chapter 10.) As you make these improvements, recognize that you are not following the Proven Path, but rather that you are doing things that are consistent with it and that will make the task easier when you begin an ERP implementation.

Then, following the ES installation, you will have ceased being a dilemma company and have migrated to the Type 1 company previously identified. You have implemented ES software, and are now in a position to initiate a Proven Path implementation of ERP. Bob Stahl, a highly successful ERP consultant based in Attleboro, MA, says it well:

The Proven Path was sound 15 years ago, before the onset of enterprise software. It's every bit as sound today. However, given today's very complex, hard-to-install software, it's more important than ever to follow the Proven Path correctly and with the right timing.

Coming up in the next chapter: a closer look at the Proven Path.

Q & A WITH THE AUTHORS

TOM: Mike, you were one of the key players at Procter & Gamble's very successful implementations of ERP (which I think you called MRP II). When you got started with MRP II, had P&G already implemented enterprise software, or were you a "clean sheet of paper company," or were you in the dilemma category of having just too much on your plates for a Proven Path implementation?

MIKE: We were all of these. SAP (our enterprise software package) in Europe was 80 percent installed before MRP II got started. In North America, we started with business process improvements, one being Sales & Operations Planning, and the SAP installation came a bit later. Latin America was pretty much a clean sheet of paper. On the other hand, Asia was certified as Class A before we ever heard of SAP or other enterprise software packages.

One last point: Our selection of SAP as the software supplier was influenced somewhat by the fact that an older version of it (R-2) was almost totally installed in Europe. We might have been happy with a number of other software packages, but our European folks had been working with SAP for some time and were comfortable with them. We felt it was important not to require them to change unless there was a compelling reason to do so.

NOTES

[i] *Mission Critical—Realizing the Promise of Enterprise Systems,* 2000, Harvard Business School Press, Boston, MA.

[ii] *ERP—Tools, Techniques, and Applications for Integrating the Supply Chain,* 1999, St.Lucie Press/APICS, Falls Church, VA.

[iii] APICS Dictionary, Ninth Edition, 1998, APICS—The Educational Society for Resource Management, Falls Church, VA.

Chapter 2

The Implementation Challenge

CATCH-22

There's an apparent catch-22 involved in implementing Enterprise Resource Planning successfully. It goes like this:

1. It's a lot of work.

Implementing ERP as a new set of decision-making processes is a major undertaking involving many people throughout the company, including general management. In essence, the entire company must learn how to deal with demand and supply issues in a new way. The speed of information flow with enterprise software combined with ERP's new approach to all of the planning and execution systems represents a major shift in company thinking—and that means a lot of work.

2. It's a do-it-yourself project.

Successful implementations are done internally. In other words, virtually all of the work involved must be done by the company's own people. The responsibility can't be turned over to outsiders, such as consultants or software suppliers. That's been tried repeatedly, and hasn't worked well at all. Consultants can have a real role in providing expertise but only company people know the company well enough and have the authority to change how things are done.

When implementation responsibility is de-coupled from operational responsibility, who can be legitimately accountable for results? If results aren't forthcoming, the implementers can claim the users aren't operating it properly, while the users can say that it wasn't implemented correctly. Almost without exception, the companies who have become Class A or B and have achieved the greatest bottom-line benefits are the ones where the users implemented ERP themselves.

Therefore, a key principle of implementation is:

IMPLEMENTERS = USERS

The people who implement the various tools within Enterprise Resource Planning need to be the same folks who will operate those tools after they're implemented.

3. *It's not priority number one.*

The problem is, the people who need to do it are already very busy with their first priority: getting customer orders, making shipments, meeting payroll, keeping the equipment operating, running the business. All other activities must be subordinate. Implementing ERP can't be priority number one, but it does need to be pegged as a high priority within the company, preferably the number two priority, right below running the business.

Well, who runs the business? People do. People starting with general managers[1] as well as department leaders in sales, manufacturing, finance, and marketing. Virtually everyone in the company has a stake, including those who plan, produce, and sell the product at every level in the business.

---

[1] Throughout this book, we'll use the term General Manager to refer to the senior executive in charge of the business unit. In this context, general manager can be synonymous with President, Chief Executive Officer, or Managing Director. It is the person to whom all the major disciplines report: Sales & Marketing, Operations, Product Development, Finance.

This catch-22 is one of the reasons why many companies that implement ERP never get beyond Class C. Other reasons include:

It's people-intensive.

ERP is commonly misperceived as a computer system. Not so. It's a *people* system made possible by the computer software and hardware.

It requires top management leadership and participation.

If the goal is truly to run the business better, then the general manager and staff must be deeply involved because they and they alone have the real leverage over how the business is to be managed. Changes made at a lower level in the organization won't matter much if it's business as usual at the top. Bob Stahl says: "I find that priority comes from a leadership who understands that ERP is tied to their future success. It becomes part of their defined 'strategic imperatives.'"

It involves virtually every department within the company.

It's not enough for just the manufacturing or logistics or materials departments to be on board. Virtually all departments in the company must be deeply involved in implementing ERP; those mentioned, plus marketing, engineering, sales, finance, and human resources.

It requires people to do their jobs differently.

Most companies implementing ERP must undergo massive behavior change to be successful. ERP requires a new set of values. Many things must be done differently, and this kind of transformation is never easy to achieve.

Many people in general management will assume that a massive software change such as an ES is sufficient to achieve major results. In fact, this system simply moves more information faster and deeper in the company. If the actual work processes don't change, then bad information moves more quickly and with dangerous momentum across the company. ERP provides the work and people process to make sense out of this rapid flow of data.

Experienced users say implementing ERP is more difficult than building a new plant, introducing a new product, or entering a whole new market. Breaking through the catch-22, overcoming the people problems, making it happen—these are the challenges.

That's the bad news.

The good news is there's a way to meet these challenges. There's no mystery involved. Implementing ERP successfully can be almost a sure thing—if it's done right. Yes, it is a lot of work. However, ERP has never failed to work, not once, when correctly implemented. It will work and users will realize enormous benefits.

Doing it right involves two major elements:

1. An aggressive implementation schedule, focused on achieving maximum benefits in minimum time.

2. The *Proven Path*. A set of steps that, if followed, will ensure a successful implementation.

AN AGGRESSIVE IMPLEMENTATION SCHEDULE

The question arises: "How long should it take to implement all of the functions of Enterprise Resource Planning throughout the entire company, from when we start until we're fully implemented?" First of all, it's difficult to implement all of ERP, company wide, in less than a year. Some companies have achieved Class A status in less than 12 months, but not many. Why? Simply because so many things need to be done: massive education, data integrity, changing the way the business is run. And, all the while, it's not the number one priority.

On the other hand, for an average-sized or smaller company (division, business unit), if it's taking longer than two years, it's probably not being done correctly. As a matter of fact, if a given business unit takes longer than two years to implement, the odds for achieving superior results decrease sharply. It becomes more and more difficult to maintain the intensity, the enthusiasm, the drive and dedication necessary, and thus it's harder to keep ERP pegged as a very high priority. The world is simply changing too fast.

Therefore, plan on the full implementation of Enterprise Resource Planning for a given business unit to take longer than one year, but less than two. For purposes of simplicity and consistency, let's routinely refer to an 18-month implementation. Now 18 months is a fairly long time. Therefore, during that period, early successes are important, and thus we recommend that they be identified and aggressively pursued. The most important early win is typically Sales & Operations Planning (to be covered in Chapter 8), and another is inventory record accuracy (Chapter 10).

On the other hand, some people feel an 18-month time frame is too aggressive or ambitious. It's not. It's a very practical matter, and also necessary. Here's why:

Intensity and enthusiasm.

Because ERP will be implemented by the people running the business, their first priority *must* be running the business, which is a full-time job in itself. Now their responsibilities for implementing ERP will require more work and more hours above and beyond running the business.

With a long, extended project, these people will inevitably become discouraged. The payoff is too far in the future. There's no light at the end of the tunnel.

However, with an aggressive schedule, these people can see progress being made early on. They can expect improvement within a relatively short time. In our experience, the operating people— sales and marketing people, foremen, buyers, engineers, planners, etc.—respond favorably to tangible gains.

Priority.

It's quite unlikely ERP can hold the necessary high priority over three or four years. (Companies are like people; their attention spans are limited.) As the project's priority drops, so do the odds for success. The best approach is to establish ERP as a very high priority; implement it quickly and successfully. And then capitalize on it. Build on it. Use it to help run the business better and better.

Unplanned change.

Unforeseen changes come in two forms: changes in people and changes in operating environment. Each type represents a threat to the ERP project.

Regarding people changes, take the case of a division whose general manager is ERP-knowledgeable, enthusiastic, and leading the implementation effort. Suppose this person is suddenly promoted to the corporate office. The new general manager is an unknown entity. That person's reaction to ERP will have a major impact on the project's chances for success. He or she may not be supportive of ERP (usually because of a lack of understanding), and the entire implementation effort will be at risk.

Environmental change includes factors such as a sharp increase in business ("We're too busy to work on ERP"), a sharp decrease in business ("We can't afford ERP"), competitive pressures, new governmental regulations, etc.

While such changes can certainly occur during a short project, they're much more likely to occur over a long, stretched-out time period.

Schedule slippage.

In a major project like implementing ERP, it's easy for schedules to slip. If the enterprise software is being installed at the same time, software installation deadlines might suggest pushing back the planning portion of ERP. Throughout this book, we'll discuss ways to minimize slippage. For now, let us just point out an interesting phenomenon: In many cases, tight, aggressive schedules are actually less likely to slip than loose, casual, non-aggressive schedules.

Benefits.

Taking longer than necessary to implement defers realizing the benefits. The lost-opportunity cost of only a one-month delay can, for many companies, exceed $100,000. A one-year delay could easily range into the millions. An aggressive implementation schedule, therefore, is very desirable. But . . . is it practical? Yes, almost always. To understand how, we need to understand the concept of the three knobs.

The Three Knobs

In project management, there are three primary variables: the amount of *work* to be done; the amount of *time* available (calendar time, not person-years); and the amount of *resources* available to accomplish the work. Think of these as three knobs, which can be adjusted (as shown in Figure 2-1).

It's possible to hold any two of these knobs constant by varying the third. For example, let's assume the following set of conditions:

1. The workload is considered to be a constant, a given. There is a certain amount of work that simply has to be done to implement ERP.

2. The time can also be considered a constant, and, in this example, let's say it's fixed at about 18 months.

3. The variable then becomes the resource knob. By adjusting it, by providing resources at the appropriate level, the company can accomplish the necessary amount of work in the defined time. (Developing a proper cost-benefit analysis can put the resource issue into clearer focus, and we'll return to that issue in Chapter 5.)

But, what if a company can't increase the resource knob? Sometimes, it's simply not possible. Maybe there's not enough money, or the organization is stretched so thin already that consuming large blocks of employee time on an implementation just isn't in the cards.

Well, there's good news. Within the Proven Path, provisions are made for:

Figure 2-1
Work, Time, and Resources

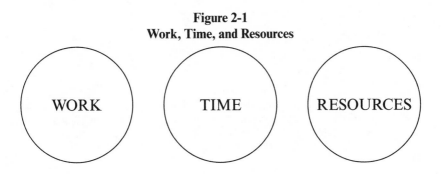

- Company-wide implementation: total company project; all ERP functions implemented; time frame one to two years.

- Quick-Slice ERP implementation: confined to one or several Pareto[2] high-impact product lines; most, but not all, ERP functions implemented; time frame three to five months.

With Quick-Slice ERP, the resources are considered a constant, because they are limited. Further, the time is considered fixed and is a very short, aggressive period. Thus the variable becomes the amount of work to be done. The principle of urgency applies here also; since only a portion of the products/company will be cutting over to ERP, it should be done quickly. This is because the company will need to move aggressively to the next step, which may be to do another Quick-Slice implementation on the next product family or perhaps to convert to a company-wide implementation.

Resource constraints are only one reason why companies elect to begin implementation on a Quick-Slice basis. For other reasons, and for a detailed description of the Quick-Slice implementation process via the Proven Path, see Chapters 13 and 14. For now, let's examine the Proven Path methodology, realizing that either implementation approach—company-wide or Quick Slice—applies.

THE PROVEN PATH

Today there is a tested, proven way to implement Enterprise Resource Planning. Thirty or so years ago, no one could say that. Back then, people said:

It should work.

We really believe it'll work.

It stands a good chance of working.

It certainly ought to work.

---

[2] Pareto's law refers to the principle of the "vital few—trivial many." For example, in many companies, 30 to 60 percent of their sales comes from 5 to 10 percent of their products. Pareto's law is also the basis for ABC inventory analysis, and is used extensively within Total Quality Management and Lean Manufacturing/Just-In-Time.

No more. There's no longer any mystery about how to implement ERP. There is a well-defined set of steps, which guarantees a highly successful implementation in a short time frame, if followed faithfully and with dedication.[3] These steps are called the Proven Path.

If you do it right, it will work. *Period.* And you can take that to the bank.

How can we be so certain? How did this become such a sure thing? The main reason centers on some executives and managers in certain North American manufacturing companies. They had several things in common: a dissatisfaction with the status quo, a belief that better tools to manage their business could be developed, and an ample supply of courage. These early implementers led the way.

Naturally, they had some help. Consultants and educators were key to developing theory and practice. Computer companies, in the early days, developed generalized software packages for material requirements planning, capacity requirements planning, and plant floor control. But, fundamentally, the users did it themselves.

Over the past 35 years, thousands of companies have implemented MRP/MRPII/ERP. Many have implemented very successfully (Class A or B); even more companies less so (Class C or D). By observing a great variety of these implementation attempts and their results, it's become very clear what works and what doesn't. The methods that have proven unworkable have been discarded. The things that work have been refined, developed, and synthesized into what we call the Proven Path. Today's version of the Proven Path is an evolutionary step over the prior ones; it has been refined for ERP but it is true to the history of proven success over a quarter century.

The Proven Path isn't theory; it's not blue sky or something dreamed up over a long weekend in Colorado Springs, where the air's really thin. Rather, it's a product of the school of hard knocks—built out of sweat, scar tissue, trial and error, learning, testing, refining.

Surprising? Not really. The Proven Path evolved the same way ERP did—in a pragmatic, practical, and straightforward manner. It wasn't created in an ivory tower or a laboratory, but on the floors of our factories, in our purchasing departments, in our sales and marketing departments, and on our shipping docks.

---

[3] *Faithfully* and *with dedication* are important words. They mean that this is not a pick-and-choose kind of process. They mean skip no steps.

This evolution has continued, right into the twenty-first century, triggered by three factors:

1. New opportunities for improvement.

2. Common goals and processes.

3. Time pressures to make improvements quickly.

Keep in mind, when the original Proven Path was developed by Darryl Landvater in the mid-1970s, what was then called closed-loop MRP was close to being "the only game in town" for major improvements in manufacturing companies. Quality? In the United States that was viewed as the job of the quality control department, and people like W. Edwards Deming and others had to preach the gospel of Total Quality Control in other parts of the world. Just-in-Time, and its successor, Lean Manufacturing hadn't yet hit the North American continent in any meaningful way. Other important tools like Design for Manufacturability, Activity-Based Costing, and Gainsharing, hadn't been invented yet or existed in small and relatively unpublicized pockets of excellence.

Today, it's a very different world. It is no longer good enough to implement any one major initiative and then stop. Tools like Enterprise Resource Planning, Lean Manufacturing, Total Quality Management, and others are all essential. Each one alone is insufficient. Companies must do them all, and do them very well, to be competitive in the global marketplace of the 2000s. Winning companies will find themselves constantly in implementation mode, first one initiative, then another, then another. Change, improvement, implementation—these have become a way of life.

As competitive pressures have increased, so has the urgency to make rapid improvement. Time frames are being compressed, necessary not only for the introduction of new products, but also for new *processes* to improve the way the business is run.

The current Proven Path reflects all three of the aforementioned factors. It is broader and more flexible. It incorporates the learning from the early years and includes new knowledge gleaned from ERP. Further, it offers an option on timing. The original Proven Path dealt with implementation on a company-wide basis only: all products, all components, all departments, and all functions to be addressed in one major implementation project. However, as we've just seen, the current Proven Path also includes the Quick-Slice implementation route,[4] which can enable a company to make major improvements in a short time.

The Proven Path consists of a number of discrete steps that will be covered one at a time. We'll take a brief look at each of these steps now, and discuss them more thoroughly in subsequent chapters. The steps, shown graphically in Figure 2-2, are defined as follows:

- *Audit/Assessment I.*

An analysis of the company's current situation, problems, opportunities, strategies, etc. It addresses questions such as: Is Enterprise Resource Planning the best step to take now to make us more competitive? If so, what is the best way to implement: company-wide or Quick-Slice? The analysis will serve as the basis for putting together a short-term action plan to bridge the time period until the detailed project schedule is developed.

- *First-cut Education.*

A group of executives and operating managers from within the company must learn, in general terms, how Enterprise Resource Planning works; what it consists of; how it operates; and what is required to implement and use it properly. This is necessary to affirm the direction set by audit/assessment I and to effectively prepare the vision statement and cost/benefit analysis. It's essential for another reason: These leaders need to learn their roles in the process, because all significant change begins with leadership.

A word about sequence: Can first-cut education legitimately occur before audit/assessment I? Indeed it can. Should it? Possibly, in those cases where the executive team is already in "receive mode," in other words, ready to listen. Frequently, however, those folks are still in "transmit mode," not ready to listen, and audit/assessment I can help them to work through that. Further, the information gained in audit/assessment I can be used to tailor the first-cut education to be more meaningful and more relevant to the company's problems.

[4] Quick-Slice ERP will be covered later in this book.

Figure 2-2

ERP PROVEN PATH

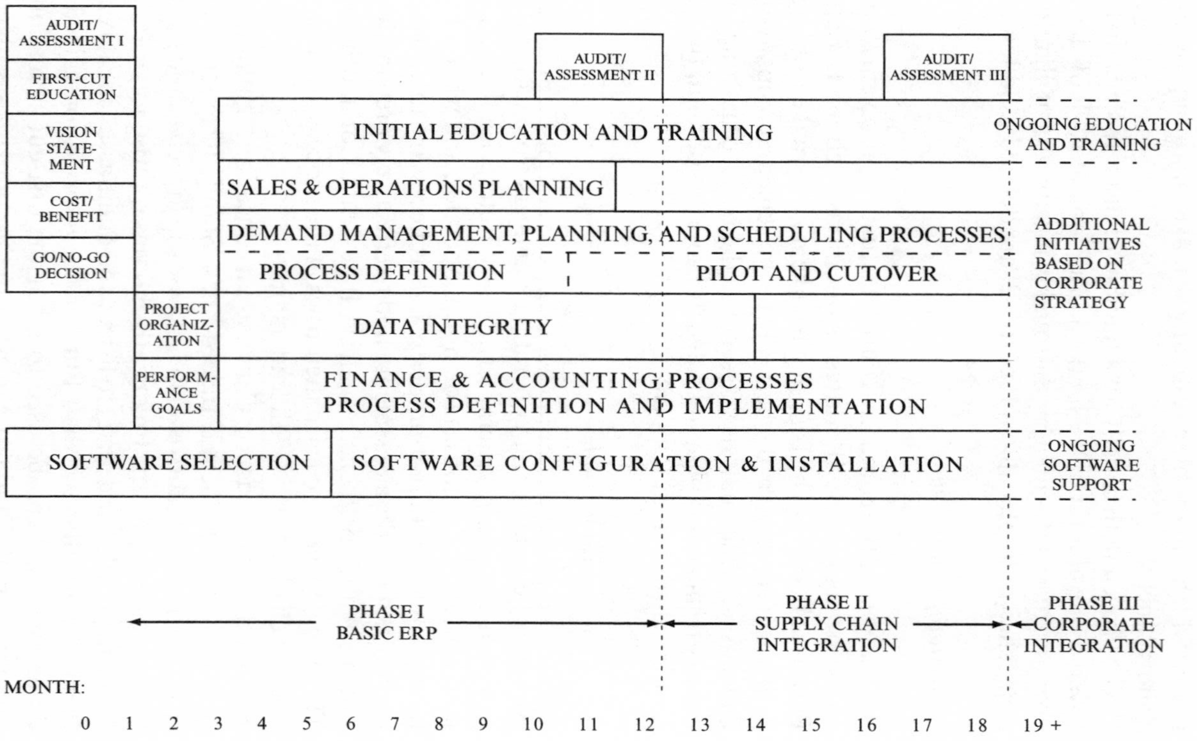

AUDIT/ASSESSMENT I

FIRST-CUT EDUCATION

VISION STATEMENT

COST/BENEFIT

GO/NO-GO DECISION

PROJECT ORGANIZATION

PERFORMANCE GOALS

SOFTWARE SELECTION

AUDIT/ASSESSMENT II

AUDIT/ASSESSMENT III

INITIAL EDUCATION AND TRAINING

SALES & OPERATIONS PLANNING

DEMAND MANAGEMENT, PLANNING, AND SCHEDULING PROCESSES

PROCESS DEFINITION

DATA INTEGRITY

PILOT AND CUTOVER

FINANCE & ACCOUNTING PROCESSES

PROCESS DEFINITION AND IMPLEMENTATION

SOFTWARE CONFIGURATION & INSTALLATION

ONGOING EDUCATION AND TRAINING

ADDITIONAL INITIATIVES BASED ON CORPORATE STRATEGY

ONGOING SOFTWARE SUPPORT

PHASE I
BASIC ERP

PHASE II
SUPPLY CHAIN INTEGRATION

PHASE III
CORPORATE INTEGRATION

MONTH: 0 1 2 3 4 5 6 7 8 9 10 11 12 13 14 15 16 17 18 19 +

- *Cost/Benefit Analysis.*

A process to generate a written document that spells out the costs of implementation and the benefits of operating Enterprise Resource Planning successfully, and results in a formal decision whether or not to proceed with ERP.

- *Go/No-Go Decision.*

It's possible—but not very likely—that your business may be so well managed and so far ahead of competition that the Cost/Benefit Analysis may not indicate that ERP is for you. If not, then that data will lead you to go on to other projects. However, if ERP's benefits are compelling, then the decision to go ahead needs to be made clear and made "official" from the top of the organization. The starter's gun should sound at the moment the leader agrees with the formal recommendation to go.

- *Vision Statement.*

A written document defining the desired operational environment to be achieved with the implementation of ERP. It answers the question: What do we want this company to look like after the implementation?

- *Performance Goals.*

Agreement as to which performance categories are expected to improve and what specific levels they are expected to reach.

- *Project Organization.*

Creation of an Executive Steering Committee; an operational-level project team, consisting mainly of the managers of operating departments throughout the company; and the selection of the full-time project leader and other people who will work full time on the project.

- *Initial Education and Training.*

Ideally 100 percent, a minimum of 80 percent, of *all* of the people in the company need to receive some education on ERP as part of the implementation process. For ERP to succeed, many things will have to change, including the way that many people do their jobs—at all levels in the company. People need to know what, why, and how these changes will affect them. People need to see the reasons why they should do their jobs differently and the benefits that will result. Remember that skipping any or all of this step results in a bigger debt later. Companies that short-change education and training almost always find that they need to double back and do it right—after seeing that the new processes aren't working properly.

- *Implementing Sales & Operations Planning.*

Sales & Operations Planning, often called "top management's handle on the business," is an essential part of ERP. In fact, it may be *the most important element* of all. ERP simply won't work well without it. Because it involves relatively few people and does not take a long time to implement, it makes sense to start this process early in the ERP implementation and to start getting benefits from it well before the other ERP processes are in place.

- *Demand Management, Planning, and Scheduling Processes.*

Sales & Operations Planning (S&OP) balances demand and supply at the *volume* level. Issues of *mix*—specific products, customers, orders, equipment—are handled in the area of demand management, planning, and scheduling.

Involved in this step of the Proven Path are two primary elements: One is to develop and define the new approaches to be used in forecasting, customer order entry, and detailed planning and scheduling. The other is to implement these new processes via a pilot and a cutover approach.

- *Data Integrity.*

ERP, to be successful, requires levels of data integrity far higher than most companies have ever achieved—or even considered. Inventory records, bills of material, formulas, recipes, routings, and other data need to become highly accurate, complete, and properly structured.

• *Finance and Accounting Processes—Process Definition and Implementation.*

Financial and accounting processes must be defined and implemented with the same rigor as the demand and planning processes. But there's good news here: For most companies, this step will be less demanding and go more smoothly than dealing with demand management, planning, and scheduling (facing). The reason is that the finance and accounting body of knowledge is more mature, more developed, better codified, and—most importantly—better understood by more people.

• *Software Selection, and Software Configuration Installation.*

Companies that have already implemented an ES will find this step to be relatively painless. There may be some additional "bolt-on" software to acquire, but typically, these are not major stumbling blocks. For companies doing a combined ERP/ES implementation, these software steps are, of course, major and must be managed very carefully to avoid having "the computer tail wag the company dog."

• *Audit/Assessment II.*

A focused evaluation of the company's situation, problems, opportunities, and strategies following the implementation. It is the driver via which the company moves into its next improvement initiative.

• *Ongoing Education.*

Initial education for new people coming into the company and refresher education for continuing employees. This is necessary so that ERP can continue to be operated very well, and made even better as the company continuously improves further in every other area.

Those companies that maintain Class A status beyond the first two years are those that have solid ongoing education programs.

WHY THE PROVEN PATH IS PROVEN

There are three main reasons why the Proven Path is so effective. The first is its tight alignment with the ABC's of ERP—people, data, computer. It mirrors those priorities, reflecting the intensive need for education to address the people issue.

The second reason also concerns alignment with the logical construct of Enterprise Resource Planning. The Proven Path methodology is in sync with ERP's structure.

Third, the Proven Path is based completely on demonstrated results. One more time: It is a lot of work but virtually no risk. If a company follows the Proven Path faithfully, sincerely, and vigorously, it will become Class A—and it won't take forever.

"Oh, really," you might be thinking, "how can you be so certain? What about all the 'ERP failures' I've heard about? You yourselves said just a few pages ago there were more Class C and D users than Class A and B. That indicates that our odds for high success are less than 50 percent."

Our response: It's up to you. If you want to have the odds for Class A or B less than 50 percent, you have that choice. On the other hand, if you want the odds for success to be near 100 percent, you can do so. Here's why. The total population of Class C and D users includes virtually zero companies who followed the Proven Path closely and faithfully. Most of them are companies who felt that ERP was a computer deal to order parts and help close the books faster, and that's what they wound up with. Others in this category tried to do it without educating their people and/or without getting their data accurate. Others got diverted by software issues. Or politics.

Here's the bottom line: Of the companies who've implemented via the Proven Path, who've sincerely and rigorously gone at it the right way, virtually all of them have achieved a Class A or high Class B level of success with ERP. And they've realized enormous benefits as a result.

There are no sure things in life. Achieving superior results with ERP, from following the Proven Path, is about as close as it gets.

Q & A WITH THE AUTHORS

TOM: What do you say, Mike, to someone wanting to skip a step—or several steps—on the Proven Path?

MIKE: Pay the bill now or pay more later. I've been astounded at how important each step is on the Proven Path. Every single time one of our organizations skipped a step, they had to go back and do it over later—at greater cost and with lost time.

PART II

Company-Wide Implementation

Chapter 3

Company-Wide Implementation—Overview

In Chapter 2 we talked about the two different implementation approaches contained within the Proven Path methodology: Company Wide and Quick Slice. We'll get into the details of Quick Slice in Chapters 12 and 13. For now, let's look at how to implement ERP on a company-wide basis. To get started, consider the following:

It's possible to swallow an elephant . . . one chunk at a time.

Be aggressive. Make deliberate haste. Implement in about 18 months or less.

Those two concepts may sound contradictory, but they're not. There's a way to "swallow the elephant one chunk at a time" and still get there in a reasonable time frame. Here's the strategy:

1. Divide the total ERP implementation project into several major phases to be done *serially*—one after another.

2. Within each phase, accomplish a variety of individual tasks *simultaneously.*

For almost any company, implementing all of ERP is simply too much to handle at one time. The sum of the chunks is too much to

Figure 3-1

ERP PROVEN PATH

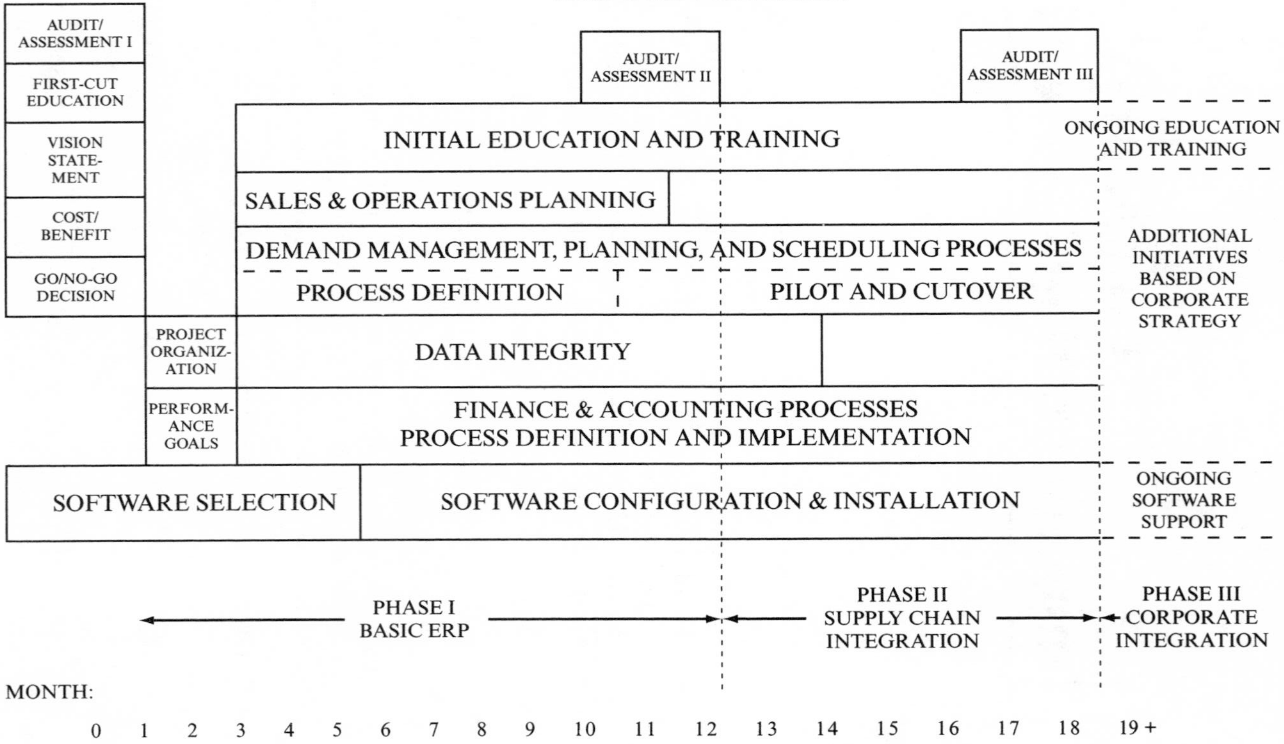

A Gantt-chart style diagram of the ERP Proven Path, with a MONTH timeline across the bottom from 0 to 19+.

Timeline tasks and activities:

- AUDIT/ASSESSMENT I
- FIRST-CUT EDUCATION
- VISION STATEMENT
- COST/BENEFIT
- GO/NO-GO DECISION
- PROJECT ORGANIZATION
- PERFORMANCE GOALS
- SOFTWARE SELECTION
- INITIAL EDUCATION AND TRAINING
- SALES & OPERATIONS PLANNING
- DEMAND MANAGEMENT, PLANNING, AND SCHEDULING PROCESSES PROCESS DEFINITION
- PILOT AND CUTOVER
- DATA INTEGRITY
- FINANCE & ACCOUNTING PROCESSES PROCESS DEFINITION AND IMPLEMENTATION
- SOFTWARE CONFIGURATION & INSTALLATION
- AUDIT/ASSESSMENT II
- AUDIT/ASSESSMENT III
- ONGOING EDUCATION AND TRAINING
- ADDITIONAL INITIATIVES BASED ON CORPORATE STRATEGY
- ONGOING SOFTWARE SUPPORT

Phases:
- PHASE I BASIC ERP
- PHASE II SUPPLY CHAIN INTEGRATION
- PHASE III CORPORATE INTEGRATION

MONTH: 0 1 2 3 4 5 6 7 8 9 10 11 12 13 14 15 16 17 18 19 +

digest all together. That's one reason for the multiphase approach. Further, in many cases, activities in the subsequent phase are dependent on the prior phase being completed.

The use of simultaneous tasks within each phase is based on the need for an aggressive implementation cycle of typically one year to 18 months for a business unit of average size. Doing each of the many tasks involved serially would simply take too long.

For the time being, let's assume a three-phase project. Let's examine what's to be done in each of the three phases:

Phase I—Basic ERP:

This includes Sales & Operations Planning, demand management, Rough-Cut Capacity Planning, master scheduling, Material Requirements Planning, plant scheduling where practical, and necessary applications for finance and accounting. Also included here are the support functions of inventory accuracy, bill of material accuracy and structure, plus activating the feedback loops from the plant floor and purchasing.

Basic ERP is not all of Enterprise Resource Planning. Of and by itself, it will produce substantial results; however, key elements remain to be implemented. This phase normally takes about nine to twelve months to complete.

Phase II—Supply Chain Integration:

Included here are the processes that extend ERP both backward and forward into the supply chain: backward to the suppliers via techniques such as supplier scheduling and Internet-based business-to-business e-commerce; forward toward the customers via distribution requirements planning and vendor managed inventories (VMI).[1] This phase usually requires three to six months, possibly more depending on the scope and intensity of the applications.

---

[1] Many people use the term VMI to refer to linking with their suppliers and refer to customer linking as Continuous Replenishment (CR). With either term, the processes are the same.

Phase III—Extensions and Enhancements to Support Corporate Strategy:

This phase covers the extension of ERP software capabilities further throughout the total organization. It can include completion of any finance and accounting elements not yet implemented, linkages to other business units within the global organization, HR applications, maintenance, product development, and so on.

Also included here may be enhancements that were identified earlier as desirable but not absolutely necessary for phases I or II to become operational. This could include full simulation capabilities, advanced planning systems (APS), manufacturing execution systems (MES), enhanced customer order entry processes, development of a supplier rating system, and so forth.

Time required for phase III could range from several months to more than a year, reflecting the fact that this phase is less defined and more "free form" than the prior two phases. In fact, there's a progression here: phase I is somewhat more structured than phase II, and phase II more so than phase III.

Let's consider elapsed time for a moment. From the above, we can see that phase I (Basic ERP) begins at time zero and continues through months 9 to 12, phase II (Supply Chain Integration) through months 12 to 18, and phase III (Extensions and Enhancements) through about months 18 to 30.

This says that the total project's time can range from a bit more than a year up to between two and three years. Why the broad time span? It's mainly a function of several things; one factor is the size and complexity of the organization, another of course, is the resources, and perhaps the most important element is the scope of the overall project, that is, how extensively the supply chain tools are to be deployed and how far extensions and enhancements will be pursued.

Here's the critical point regarding timing: Implementing Basic ERP successfully (the phase I task) will generate enormous benefits for the company. And, *if you do it right,* you can get it done in nine to twelve months. Part of *doing it right* is to avoid "scope creep," i.e., laying non-critical tasks into phase I. It's necessary here to adopt a hard-nosed attitude that says: "We're not going to tackle anything in phase I that's not necessary for Basic ERP. When we come across 'nice-to's' (opportunities that aren't essential for Basic ERP), we'll slot them into phase II or III. All we'll work on during phase I are the 'have-to's'—stuff that's essential for Basic ERP."

On occasion, people question the location of time zero—the day the clock starts ticking. Should it follow the early and preliminary steps, as shown on the phase I bar chart? Or should it be at the very beginning of audit/assessment I?

We prefer it where it is, because that facilitates the consensus building, which is so important. Some companies move through these early steps quickly, so for them the precise location of time zero is not terribly important. Other companies, however, find they need more time for these early activities than the several months implied by the chart. The principles to be considered are:

1. Take as much time as needed to learn about ERP, and build a consensus among the management team. Set the vision statement and the performance goals. Do the cost/benefit analysis. Make sure this is the direction the company wants to go. Then commit to the project.

2. Once the decision is made to go for it, pursue it aggressively.

Occasionally, people have questions on the functional content of each of the three phases, such as: "Why isn't supplier scheduling in phase I? Can we move MRP to phase II and Sales & Operations Planning to phase III?"

The timing of this implementation plan is structured to get the basic ERP planning tools in place early. For example, companies that implement advanced supplier scheduling—possibly via the Internet—before material requirements planning, may save a few bucks on reduced paperwork and get a better handle on order status, but probably not much else.

This is because most companies, prior to successful ERP, can't give their suppliers good schedules. The reason is their current systems can't generate *and maintain* valid order due dates as conditions change. (These companies schedule their suppliers via the shortage list, which is almost always wrong, contradictory, and/or incomplete.) The biggest benefit from effective supplier scheduling comes from its ability to give the suppliers valid and complete schedules—

statements of what's really needed and when. It simply can't do that without valid order due dates, which come from Material Requirements Planning (MRP).

Further, material requirements planning can't do its job without a valid master schedule, which must be in balance with the sales & operations plan. That's why these functions are in phase I, and certain "downstream" functions are in phase II.

Schedule by Function, Not Software Modules

Business functions and software modules are not the same. A business function is just that—something that needs to be done to run the business effectively. Examples include planning for future capacity needs; maintaining accurate inventory records, bills of material, and routings; customer order entry and delivery promising; and so on.

Software modules are pieces of computer software that support people in the effective execution of business functions. Frequently we see companies involved in an ERP implementation scheduling their project around tasks like: "Implement the SOE (Sales Order Entry) module," "Implement the ITP (Inventory Transaction Processing) module," or "Implement the PDC (Product Data Control) module." This is a misguided approach for two reasons: sequence and message.

Companies that build their project plan around implementing software modules often do so based on their software vendor's recommendation. This sequence may or may not be the best one to follow. In some cases, it merely slows down the project, which is serious enough. In others, it can greatly reduce the odds for success.

One such plan recommended the company first install the MRP module, then the plant floor control module, then the master scheduling module. Well, that's backward. MRP can't work properly without the master schedule, and plant floor control can't work properly without MRP working properly. To follow such a plan would have not only slowed down the project but also would have substantially decreased the odds for success.

The second problem concerns the message that's sent out when the implementation effort is focused on software modules. Concentrating on implementing software modules sends exactly the wrong message to the people in the company. The primary emphasis is on the wrong thing—the computer. ERP is *not* a computer system; it's a *people* system made possible by the computer. Implementing it is not a computer project or a systems project; it's a *management* project. The people in the company are changing the way they manage the business, so that they can manage it better than they ever could before.

Keep those ABC's of implementation firmly in mind: the C item is the computer; the B item is the data; the A item is the people.

CUT THE CLOTH TO FIT THE PATTERN

ERP is a generalized set of tools that applies to any manufacturing company. Part of the A-item implementation task is to help people break through the "we're-unique" syndrome that we talked about earlier. When people recognize that there is a well-defined, universally applicable body of knowledge in this field, they'll be able to use it to solve fundamental problems.

On the other hand, ERP is a set of tools that must be tailored to fit individual companies. The implementation project must also reflect the individual company, its environment, its people, its processes, its history, and so on. Here are some examples of special situations that can affect the specifics of implementation:

Flow shops.

Flow shop is the term we give companies with manufacturing methods that can be described as purely process (chemicals, food, plastics, etc.) or as highly repetitive (tin cans, automobiles, razor blades, etc.).

The overall concept of ERP definitely applies to these kinds of manufacturing environments. However, each and every function within ERP may not be necessary. One good example is shop floor dispatching on an operation-by-operation basis, which is typically needed only in a functional, job-shop form of organization.[2] The technique known as detailed Capacity Requirements Planning (CRP) is another. In most flow shops, all of the necessary capacity

[2] For an explanation of the job shop/flow shop differences, see Appendix B.

planning can be done at the rough-cut level. Simple output tracking can be used instead of the more complex input-output control.

A company in this situation, not needing detailed shop dispatching and CRP, should exclude them from its implementation plan. Simple plant schedules (plant sequence lists, not shop dispatch lists) can usually be generated directly from the master schedule or Material Requirements Planning as a part of phase 1. And that's good news. It'll be easier and quicker to get to Class A.

Financials already integrated.

Some companies, prior to implementing ERP, already use operational data to drive much of their financial reporting. Numbers from the operating system are converted to dollars for certain financial planning and control purposes; product costing and inventory valuation are two functions often already integrated. At a minimum, of course, the current degree of financial integration must be implemented as part of phase I, not phase III.

Companies with high degrees of financial integration, prior to ERP, are often seen in the process world (i.e., flow shops). For many of these companies, virtually all of their financial system implementation will occur in phase 1.

Re-implementers.

Some companies have already attempted to implement ERP, but it's not working properly. They have some or all of the pieces in place, yet they're not getting the results they should. Now they need to *re-implement,* but this time to do it right. Darryl Landvater said it well: "The jobs involved in *improving* an (ERP) system are the same as those in implementing it correctly." As we said earlier, the difference is that, for re-implementers, some of the tasks may already be done.

That's perhaps the good news. However, in a re-implementation, there's one big issue that makes it tougher: how to convince all the people that it'll work the second time around[3] when it didn't work

---

[3] Or third possibly? We've talked to people whose companies were in their third or fourth implementation. This gets really tough. The best number of times to implement ERP is once. Do it right the first time.

well after the first try. This will put more pressure on the education process, which we'll discuss later, and on top management's actions. Words alone won't do it. Their feet and their mouths must be moving in the same direction.

ES/No ERP.

Here are the many companies that have installed Enterprise Software but not done much about improving business processes. In most respects, they're quite similar to re-implementers: Some of the implementation tasks have been done—mostly software-related—so those steps can largely be dropped from their plans.

Multiplant.

How about a company or division with more than one plant? How should it approach implementation? Broadly, there are three choices: serial, simultaneous, or staggered.

Take the case of the Jones Company, with four plants. Each plant employs hundreds of people, and has a reasonably complete support staff. The company wants to implement ERP in all four plants.

The *serial* approach to implementation calls for implementing completely in a given plant, then starting in the second plant and implementing completely there, and so forth. The schedule would look like Figure 3-2:

Figure 3-2
Serial Approach

Plant 1	Plant 2	Plant 3	Plant 4

Month 0   15   30   45   60

This time span is not acceptable. Sixty months is five years, and that's much too long.

The *simultaneous* approach is to do them all at the same time, as shown in Figure 3-3.

Figure 3-3
Simultaneous Approach

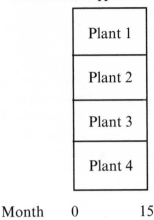

Month   0   15

This approach looks good because the entire project is finished in 15 months. However, there may be some problems. One would be availability of centralized resources such as Information Systems, overall project management, and so forth. It may be impractical to support all four plants simultaneously.

Another potential problem gets back to the catch-22 of ERP. Implementing ERP is not the first priority. Some companies may wisely conclude that implementing simultaneously in all plants could be more than they want to bite off at one time. The effort and intensity required may be more than desired.

This leads most companies to choose the *staggered* method shown in Figure 3-4.

This approach has several advantages

1. ERP gets implemented throughout the entire company fairly quickly (in this case, in slightly over two years for four plants).

2. The impact on centralized resources is lessened.

3. Only one plant is piloting and cutting over onto master scheduling (MS) and Material Requirements Planning (MRP) at a time, so the overall level of effort and intensity is reduced.

4. Plant personnel can teach each other. For example, users from

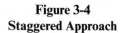

Figure 3-4
Staggered Approach

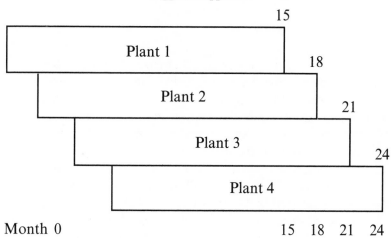

plant 2 may participate in the pilot and cutover at plant 1. In so doing, they can learn from the first plant's mistakes and avoid them. Plant 3 people can learn and help at plant 2, and so on.

One company we worked with brought all nine of its plants from time zero to Class A in less than three years. This was a very complex implementation, and the staggered method served them very well. Please note: Even though their implementation was staggered, Sales & Operations Planning was implemented *across the board* and was done early. The reasons:

1. S&OP only really works well when it operates across the entire business unit.

2. Implementing S&OP does not typically involve major resources.

3. In a combined ERP/ES implementation, S&OP can be implemented independently of software considerations. It doesn't need to "wait for the software."

4. It's an early win.

We recommend you follow this company's example, and implement S&OP across the board—early.

Multiple business units.

Many organizations have more than one business unit. These could be corporations with multiple divisions, or perhaps divisions containing more than one business. The Acme Widget company, for example, is a stand-alone corporation with three divisions: industrial, consumer, and aerospace and defense. Each division is self-contained and has its own plant.

If centralized, corporate resources will be involved in the ERP implementation, then Acme should follow the approach outlined above in the multiplant section. On the other hand, if Acme's divisions are highly self-contained with ample resources, then there may be no need for Corporate to force fit the divisions into a centralized implementation schedule. They may feel more accountability, and implement faster, if they're calling the shots on their schedule.

Obviously, it doesn't matter if Acme Widget were a stand-alone corporation or, alternatively, part of a larger corporation. The approach we've outlined here would apply in either case.

Necessary nonstandard functions.

Here, we're referring to functions necessary to run the business, but which are peculiar to a given company or industry. Some examples are:

1. The pharmaceutical industry, among many others, requires lot traceability and lot number inventory control.

2. Firms supplying the U.S. Department of Defense must adhere to special contract accounting requirements.

3. Product shelf life is a major issue in many companies producing consumer packaged goods.

There are many other examples. The message here is obvious: Look very closely at the company, its industry and marketplace, its position within them, and its overall strategy. Don't make the serious error of assuming that if a given function isn't in the software package, it's not needed for your company. The new software may need to be modified to support the function in question, ideally enabling it to be done even better. Perhaps the software will need modification merely to allow the function to be done as before. Or perhaps no software changes will be necessary for a given function.

It's important for companies to do their homework on such issues. They need to ask: "What special things are we doing today that we'll continue to do in the future after ERP is operational? Are they essential? If so, will they be handled within ERP or not? If not, how will we do them?"

Part of getting a better set of tools to run the business is to make certain that all of the necessary tools are in place.

TIME WASTERS

Nowhere on the Proven Path does one see things like:

- Document the current system in detail.
- Design the new system.

That's because these things are time wasters when done as separate activities.

Yes, it is necessary to identify those elements of today's operations that need to be blended into ERP. What's *not* necessary is to spend time doing a detailed documentation of the current system, with piles of paper and flow charts covering many square yards of wall space. After all, the current system is going to be replaced.

And, yes, it's necessary to ensure that the details of how ERP will be operated support the company's goals, operating environment, and necessary functions. What's *not* necessary is to spend time reinventing the wheel. The set of tools is already designed; it's called ERP. The issue is how, specifically and in detail, will the tools of ERP be used to run the business?

The Proven Path approach makes provisions for these things, to occur not as separate steps, but as part of an integrated, logical process of managing the implementation of ERP. The details will come in Chapters 5, 6, and 7.

Q & A with the Authors

Mike: Might some people have a problem with what we just said—the system is already designed; it's called ERP; and that the issue is how will the tools of ERP be used to run the business?

Tom: Probably, and to help with that, let's once again hop over into the wonderful world of accounting. When a company gets ready to implement a new accounting system, they don't sit down and design a new approach to accounting. They don't re-invent double-entry bookkeeping and GAAP. They recognize that there exists a defined body of knowledge in this field, and that their challenge is to utilize that body of knowledge in the best way possible.

ERP, as we said earlier, is the logistics analog of GAAP and its basic structure should be considered as a given. The focus needs to be on how to use the tools within ERP in the best way possible.

Chapter 4
Software

Back in Chapter 1, we talked about how software for ERP is like a set of golf clubs. We said that owning a fine set of clubs does not by itself make a good golfer. On the other hand, playing golf at a world-class, competitive level requires a full set of clubs, even if your name happens to be Tiger Woods. The same is true for companies: Owning good software of and by itself won't make you more competitive, but to be competitive requires a reasonably complete set of software.

The emergence of Enterprise Software over the past ten years has revolutionized not just how computers are used but the very way companies think. In the past, a typical company would design its own software for individual operations or would purchase "off the shelf" software for specific tasks. This led to a complex mix of non-matching systems that rarely communicated well and led to extensive maintenance of systems. Companies had large IS (information systems) or IT (information technology) organizations that wrote software, provided the linkages to purchased systems, and maintained the system. Because these software experts were often located inside individual business units, it sometimes happened that different units could not communicate with each other except through written reports.

The development of the Enterprise Software systems offered the clear advantage of connecting every transaction in the company to a central database that could be accessed by the appropriate corporate systems. Unloading a truckload of chemicals in any part of the com-

Figure 4-1

ERP PROVEN PATH

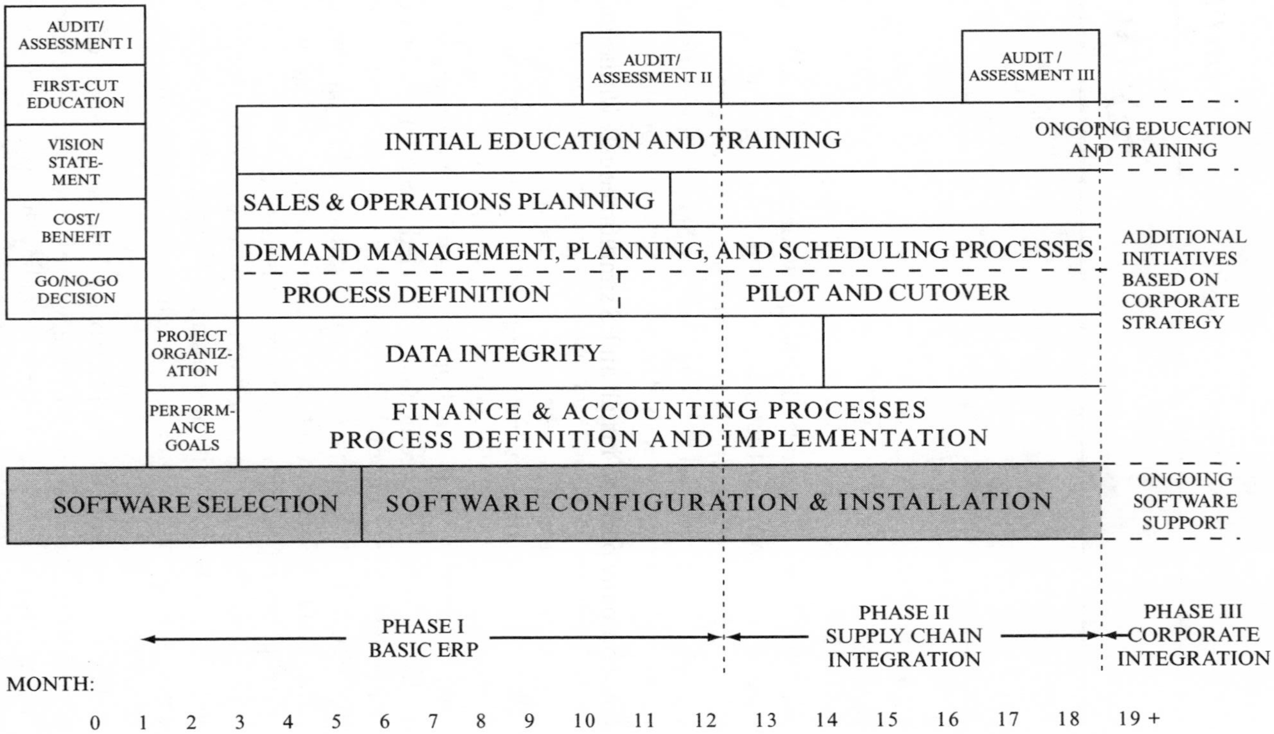

AUDIT/ ASSESSMENT I				AUDIT/ ASSESSMENT II	AUDIT / ASSESSMENT III
FIRST-CUT EDUCATION		INITIAL EDUCATION AND TRAINING			ONGOING EDUCATION AND TRAINING
VISION STATE-MENT		SALES & OPERATIONS PLANNING			ADDITIONAL INITIATIVES BASED ON CORPORATE STRATEGY
COST/ BENEFIT		DEMAND MANAGEMENT, PLANNING, AND SCHEDULING PROCESSES			
GO/NO-GO DECISION		PROCESS DEFINITION	PILOT AND CUTOVER		
	PROJECT ORGANIZ-ATION	DATA INTEGRITY			
	PERFORM-ANCE GOALS	FINANCE & ACCOUNTING PROCESSES PROCESS DEFINITION AND IMPLEMENTATION			
SOFTWARE SELECTION		SOFTWARE CONFIGURATION & INSTALLATION			ONGOING SOFTWARE SUPPORT

PHASE I
BASIC ERP

PHASE II
SUPPLY CHAIN
INTEGRATION

PHASE III
CORPORATE
INTEGRATION

MONTH:

0 1 2 3 4 5 6 7 8 9 10 11 12 13 14 15 16 17 18 19 +

pany became a corporate piece of data, not just an isolated act to be observed only locally. This also means that the company financial books can be adjusted for the cost of this transaction immediately. There is no delay for passing data from point to point or clerk to clerk. This is good stuff; it offers enormous benefits.

What has happened here is that companies are moving from a wide variety of relatively simple systems but with complex interfaces, to a single complex system with simple interfaces. This clear choice offers major benefits to the corporation but is seen as painful by each unit of the company. For most, this is the proper trade-off. However, the choice does have a major impact.

We said in Chapter 1 that this is not a software book. Then why include this chapter on software? Simply because every manufacturing company needs ERP and there are big decisions to be made about software interactions. A company implementing ERP will be in one of three categories regarding software:

The Enterprise System software (ES) has already been installed. Now the company wants to improve its business processes by implementing ERP.

The company plans to install an ES simultaneously with implementing ERP.

The company has no ES and presently has no plans to install one. It wants to implement ERP, perhaps using a legacy system or possibly by acquiring low-cost software to support the core ERP functions of demand management, master scheduling, Material Requirements Planning, and so on.

We'll look at each one of these conditions individually and then, towards the end of this chapter, we'll discuss the issue of "bolt-ons." This is software from outside the ES, which performs certain specific functions.

CATEGORY 1: ES ALREADY INSTALLED

The typical company in this category has, with substantial pain and expense, installed an Enterprise System and not gotten much back in return for its efforts. The ES enabled it to become Y2K compliant and it can close the books better, faster and cheaper than before—but that may be about it in terms of benefits. Many companies think they are ES capable simply because they survived Y2K. Of course, they may have only installed some of the ES modules and may be limping along with mediocre results. The people are a bit bummed and a bit burned out; they spent endless hours sitting in meetings and in training sessions but they find that things haven't gotten any easier.

The good news is that having the software already installed certainly makes life easier in some important respects. First, the software selection step shown in Figure 4-1 can pretty much be dropped. The bulk of the software has already been selected, with the possible exception of one or several bolt-ons.

Second, the software installation and enhancement step on the Proven Path should be straightforward. Most of the work here will involve nothing more than re-setting some of the switches in the ES, to enable the core ERP functions to operate correctly. During this step, it's important to involve people with a good knowledge of the ES in order to help identify and facilitate this process of "tweaking" the system.

A caveat: This requires real expertise and great care. Remember that the linkages in ES are so extensive that even a minor change involving a few switches can have far-reaching effects. In Chapter 7, which deals with education, we'll discuss a process involving a series of business meetings; these can be an important forum for identifying necessary changes to the ES configuration.

One last point: Companies that have already installed an ES are strong candidates for a Quick-Slice ERP implementation. See Chapters 13 and 14.

Category 2: Installing ES Simultaneously with ERP

Frequently companies in this category do so because of an interest in ERP. They want to do ERP; they know they need software to do that, so they go out and buy an ES. Unfortunately, companies attempting this almost always get overwhelmed by the complexity and magnitude of the software. The result: The software gets installed but the ERP business processes are not implemented well or at all; the company is at a Class D level or maybe Class C if they got lucky.

The sad fact is that very few companies have successfully implemented both ERP and an ES at the same time. It's just too big a job. Therefore, we offer the following warning:

Before you attempt a combined ERP/ES implementation, evaluate your resources very carefully. Make certain that you are one of the few companies that have enough resources and organizational bandwidth to get the job done successfully. If you conclude otherwise, then your best route is probably to implement ERP first and then ES.

Figure 4-2 shows the high level of decision involved in this overall software issue.

If you decide that you can succeed with a combined ERP/ES implementation, then the section that follows applies to you. (It may also be of interest to companies that decide to install their ES prior to ERP.) An excellent source of information on installing ES software is the book we mentioned in the first chapter: *Mission Critical*[i] by Thomas H. Davenport. When installing an Enterprise System, you'll need all the good information you can get.

Let's be clear on the ERP/ES implementation concept. It is clearly the most efficient way to handle these two major changes. However, very few companies can provide the resources to pull it off. The resource drain is huge and hiring armies of outsiders to help is not the answer. Most who have tried to do both have stopped in mid-project and done one or the other. Typically, the nature of the ES installation requires that the company finish ES and then get back to ERP later. Danger lurks among the rewards!

Threatening? You bet. Chapter 5 will deal with the costs and benefits of the total ERP/ES implementation more completely but, for now, remember that the choice and installation of the software requires the same careful planning as any other project that costs millions of dollars and involves almost every person in the company.

CATEGORY 3: NO ES AND NO PLANS TO GET ONE

The typical company here has neither ERP nor an Enterprise Software system. It wants to implement ERP but is not interested in going through the blood, sweat, tears, and expense of an ES installation. Regarding software for its ERP implementation, it either has it or it doesn't. (Hard to argue with that, right?)

Figure 4-2
Implementing ERP

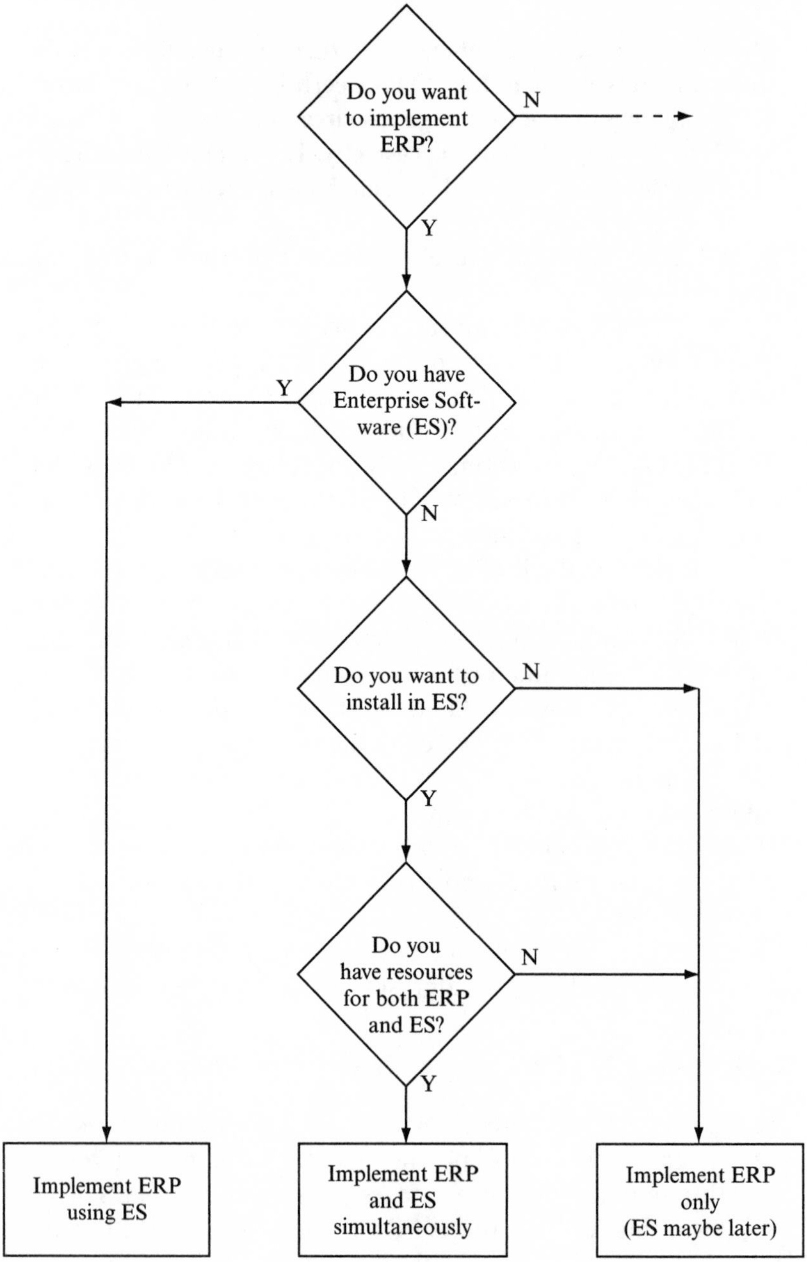

In the first case, "having it" usually means that it has an older, pre-ES set of software for MRP II. Perhaps the company took an earlier stab at implementing the resource planning processes—master scheduling, MRP, Plant and Supplier Scheduling, etc.—but didn't succeed. Or possibly it never attempted to do so. In either case, it has software. Now the people might not like it; they might be saying things like, "Our software stinks." But the odds are quite high that it'll be good enough to enable the basic ERP processes to work. The moral of this story: use what you have if it's workable. An excellent resource here is the MRP II Standard System, which details the features and functions that software must contain to support effective resource planning processes. As of this writing, this document is available via the Gray Research web site listed in Appendix D.

The second case states that the company doesn't have software to support ERP. Perhaps its legacy systems are home grown, and they contain logic that simply won't work in an ERP environment. In this case, we recommend you buy one of the many low-cost PC-based ERP/MRP II packages that are available today. You can probably get everything you need for less than $100,000. And most of it is quite good—fairly complete functionally and very user friendly. Since the price is relatively low, you can buy it and use it for a year or so, and then if need be, replace it with a full-blown set of ES software if you wish to head in that direction. Please keep in mind that this ERP/MRP II software is not an ES; it won't be truly stand-alone software; and it will in effect be "bolted-on" to your existing software.

ENTERPRISE SOFTWARE

Now that we have talked about the choices, it is time to discuss a bit more about Enterprise Software. We'll take you through our thoughts on ES in four steps: *Selection, Configuration and Enhancement, Installation,* and *Ongoing Support.*

The *Selection* step is the beginning of the project when the company must decide which software company will best handle the information transactions for its business.

Configuration and enhancement are handled by design teams. These are the internal teams that make sure that the right switches are thrown for each decision process and identify needed enhancements and extensions.

Installation is probably the most obvious step since whatever is chosen must be put in place. The opportunities and challenges are in maximizing learning during implementation and minimizing crashes.

Ongoing support refers to the maintenance and improvement of the system after start-up. Those who have looked at the ES initiative as a one-time project with no follow-up care and feeding have been very disappointed.

Software Selection

There are lots of software choices available. The key point here is that there is not a single right software choice. There are good choices and not so good choices for your business.

OK, how to proceed? First, understand your business and the opportunities for change. Yeah, this sounds insulting. Of course, you know your business. But do you know where the real weaknesses are in the business? Are you having trouble with delivery timeliness and accuracy for your customers? Are cost projections erratic and unreliable? Do customer orders "get lost" inside the system, requiring massive human intervention? Does the supplier interaction become so complex that the supply chain resembles a pretzel? Are human resource systems clogged with massive data that cannot be assessed to answer basic employee demographic questions?

Understanding these and other questions will tell you what areas are of most importance to you in choosing a software provider. Each of these questions impacts a different software module and each software provider offers different approaches to those areas. Without this knowledge of the company's strategic and tactical needs, you're subjected to sales presentations by the software vendors without knowing which areas of the pitch are most important. You need to know that the vendor you choose has solid offerings in the areas where you have the most need. A good question to ask is this: "If we have software from this provider, can we make a competitive breakthrough?" This question and its answer will typically point you to the ERP related modules that deal with demand management, master scheduling, MRP, plant and supplier scheduling, warehouse management, etc.

Also, you need to consider which vendor's approach best matches your present environment. Invite them to an extensive tour of your operations and provide a candid appraisal of your business needs. If the software provider seems to have software organized most like your current systems, then they win this part of the sweepstakes for your vote. This would include the possibility that one part of your company has already installed systems from a specific provider. If this unit has a good experience with the software, you are part way home in having a real live test in full operation.

A key deciding point for any software, particularly ES, is simplicity. Standardizing on one approach across the company is the big hitter here and not the sophistication of the software. Remember that people are going to use and maintain the software, so make sure that system is as simple as possible. Don't confuse features with functions and don't assume that more features means easier implementation. Actually it's usually the reverse: More features equal more complexity, and more complexity equals more chance for problems.

One of the advantages of installing an ES today versus ten years ago is that there are many companies in all parts of the world who have installed Enterprise Systems—some are actually using ERP at a Class A or B level. Each vendor should be able to arrange a meeting with some of their customers so you can learn from their experiences. If they can't provide references, drop them immediately.

Check the business press for articles about failed installations—these always make the press since the business impact is similar to a plane crash. A few calls can get you information about the provider from these troubled installations as well as those being bragged about. There are several excellent sources for information about ES software vendors. A list (current as of this writing) is available in Appendix D. You may have others, and certainly there are numerous consultants who can help you locate likely candidates.

Configuration and Enhancement

Following the selection of the software vendor, it is time to install the software. Right? Well, not exactly. The software will be excellent but it now must be adapted to your operations. Remember, Enterprise Software connects every facet of the company in such a way that every transaction becomes an available piece of data for the corporation. The software is not "one size fits all" but rather "one system adaptable to your business." Chris Gray says: "ES systems are flexible in the same way that concrete is flexible when it is poured. However once it hardens, it takes a jack hammer to change it."

Typically, for convenience in programming and use, the software will be in a number of modules that focus on particular parts of the company. Although there is variation among the providers, there will be seven to ten modules with titles like Finance and Accounting, Master Scheduling, Human Resources, Warehouse Management, and so on. Each of these must be tailored to your particular operations and business needs. Most of this tailoring will involve setting switches to control data flow and processing steps. However, in some cases, enhancements to the software package are necessary in order to support critical business functions. (We'll go into more detail on enhancements later in this chapter because what we have to say applies to both ES and to bolt-ons.)

Each module should have an assigned ES design team that reflects the company functions most involved in that area. These groups are different from the ERP project team and task forces. In a combined ERP/ES implementation, one of the challenges is keeping the ES design teams aligned with the ERP teams, and one of the best ways to accomplish this is with some degree of common membership. One or several members of a given ES design team are assigned to the related ERP organization and vice versa. The big difference between an ERP team and an ES team is that the *ERP team focuses primarily on people and data integrity while the ES team focuses primarily on the software and hardware.* However, both are involved in re-designing business processes, and thus it's critical that these processes be a joint effort.

So what do the ES design teams do? Well, think of the data flow in the company as hundreds or thousands of trains moving along a myriad of tracks toward one station—the central database. You must decide if those trains only go to the final station or if the data can be switched to a different track along the way, in order to serve a particular function. Also, once the train arrives at the station, the passengers or freight can be re-routed to other destinations. Deciding where all these switches should be located and where the data should go is the job of the design team, and it's a major task requiring knowledgeable people.

Choosing the design team is a delicate but essential task. For some individuals, their expertise will be critical to the design full time, for at least six to eighteen months. Others could be part timers called into meetings to provide their knowledge regarding specific questions. However, plan to err on the side of greater rather than lesser involvement, as this is very important work.

Most units inside the company will resist putting their top people on teams like this. It seems to be too far removed from "real work" and good people are always scarce. Also, they may have become accustomed to having their software custom-written for them, so they will assume that they can rewrite whatever comes from the team later. This obviously is an erroneous assumption, but they won't know that unless they're told. We recommend that the CEO/president/general manager take charge of this debate early in the process and let everyone know that the work will be done only once, via the ES design teams. Individual business units will no longer be able to develop software—except as part of the design teams.

A key requirement for membership on these teams is that all individuals must be able to make decisions for their organizations. They can't simply report back to their business units and ask, "Mother, may I?" on each decision that needs to be made. If you don't think that a unit is providing sufficiently senior and skillful people, one technique is simply to ask the business unit leader if this individual can speak for the organization on issues important to the leader's promotion. Obviously, team members must work out a way to keep in touch with their home units and get appropriate advice and counsel, but they must be able to represent that unit completely and make decisions on its behalf.

Of course, this raises the question about how big a team should be. Our response: It depends. The smaller the team the better, but teams have run successfully with up to 20 people. Obviously, the larger the team, the tougher the role for its leader. However, we have seen small teams struggle if the purpose and intent is not clear and leadership from the top is missing.

What about the leader? Teams for some of the software modules will have a leader from the IT area, as that is clearly the key business function for corporate software. In other cases, it can be effective to recruit the leader from the key function. For example, someone from sales could be very effective in leading the design team for the Demand Management module. The function in question—Sales, in our example—will have very clear ownership of the design result so it makes sense to put them in charge of the work.

At this point, some of you may have a growing concern about the number of people who will need to be committed to the design teams. This is very perceptive. This work is substantial, critical, and time consuming. In an ERP/ES implementation, if you find that your company can't staff all the design teams necessary, then you have two choices:

1. Combine ES design teams with ERP project groups, thus minimizing the head count required, or

2. Decide to go to an ES only project now, with ERP to follow.

Let's consider an ES installation without ERP, but with the inability to staff all the necessary design teams. Your best choice here is to decide how many teams you can staff and do a multi-phase project. Choose the most important two or three modules and set up teams for them alone. The rest of the modules will have to arrive later. It's far better to do a small number of modules well than a half-hearted job on all.

Software consultants can help with this process, but they simply can't replace your own knowledgeable people who understand the company so deeply. In fact, there is a danger that consultants can cause a bigger time demand on your people because they do interviews across the company to learn your business. A good middle-of-the-road option would be to have a few software consultants involved who can help facilitate the team decision process without having to be complete experts in your operation.

Installation

Now, let's consider the task of installing the software. Much of the really heavy-duty work is completed as the design phase has shaped the nature of data flow in the company. Now it's time to start to run the software, and this is normally a rather intense activity. So here are some hard and fast recommendations from your friendly authors about this installation process:

Be flexible. If the installation is a rigid process to install exactly what the design teams specified, then there may be considerable difficulty. It may not work, because the collective effort of the ES design teams may not be compatible. This incompatibility could exist among the ES design teams, or with the ERP project team. However, if you take the problems that arise as true learning opportunities, then the software configuration can be modified as you go, both to fit your business requirements and to work well. Thus, the seeds are sewn for continued growth and learning in the future.

Pilot the software before going live. An early step here should be to make pilot runs of the software using a typical business unit as a model. These computer and conference room pilots will go a long way to verify that the design teams' designs are working properly, and we'll cover them in more detail in Chapter 11. Although these pilot tests cannot confirm everything, don't even think of going forward without them. Every pilot like this that we've seen has turned up major adjustments that need to be made before going live. At this early stage, the software can be readily changed without business results at risk.

Make deliberate haste. Never, ever try to start up the ES across the entire company at one time. Even if the pilot gave everyone great enthusiasm and confidence, do not risk the entire business by cutting over all at once. This so-called "Big Bang" approach could describe the sound made by your business imploding. The best way to install the system is to choose a part of the business as the live pilot because this represents substantially lower risk than doing it all at once. You need an aggressive schedule to keep momentum on the project as a whole, but you need to protect your business at the same time. It is key to develop some early wins that build enthusiasm. But, in any case, get moving! More on this topic as well in Chapter 11.

Some companies attempt to minimize the risk by turning on only one or two modules across the entire company. We don't think this is the way to go, because the total risk can be very high if even just one module is installed across the entire corporation. For example, installing only the Warehouse or Distribution module for the corporation may seem like low risk. After all, it's just one module and the full design team can support it. The problem is that errors in the setting of the switches could stop the company from shipping—possibly for an extended time. It goes without saying that this could be devastating. The business press has reported on companies that did this, found themselves unable to ship the product, alienated many customers, and took a major earning hit for the quarter and possibly the fiscal year. Wow.

The pilot test risk is reduced by several important factors. One is that it is only a piece of the business, and the second is that you put all resources available against the test area. The people in the pilot area may like being guinea pigs, since they get a chance to shape the corporate software to their specifications. Also, there will be a lot more help available for the test installation than there will be later. The pilot test unit should have been involved in the conference room pilot and their people will be among the most knowledgeable in the company. Even a very risk-averse general manager should understand the value of leading the test.

After the pilot is up and running, the rest of the company rollout of the ES can proceed as with any other project. Some will want to move with consecutive business units, others may do a geographic region, and still others may install by function. There is no magic answer except to understand what was learned from the pilot and apply that learning to the rollout. As is true of any big project, it's always smart to avoid too big a rollout at the busiest time of the year.

What about the design teams? The design teams should stay intact during the entire process from conference room pilot to company rollout. They normally don't need to be deeply involved during this installation step, but they do need to be available for advice. There is no one who knows more about the functionality of the modules than the teams that designed them. In some cases, the questions or changes are routine enough that they can stay connected via email or conference calls. In others, they may need to meet to review the status. Regardless, design team members need to realize that they are critical to the success of the total project—not just the design phase. This is another place where a few words from the general manager can make a real difference.

On-Going Support

One big mistake made on major software installations is to consider the project finished once the software is up and running. Although project completion is certainly a time for champagne and parties, this software is now a living, breathing part of the company. As the company changes, so should the software that connects it. As we said earlier, the folks in the IT department have become information managers and not software writers. How do they do this?

The big change from old, fragmented systems to this new company-wide, transactional software is that it becomes the central nervous system for the company. As such, it's hard to think of this system as ever "finished." Besides the changes in business strategy that need to be reflected, there may be acquisitions, spin-offs, or consolidations that change the nature of data flow. Also, the software provider will routinely release new versions of their software, some of which may be quite worthwhile for your business.

This brings up a critical point about information technology resources. In the old days, many business units had control of their own IT people. This was essential to keep the localized systems alive and well. However, ESs have a central corporate database, and thus the need for high system reliability and clear networks. This certainly speaks to the need for very central direction of IT resources.

Let's not mince words. We strongly favor central control of IT resources to avoid fragmenting this critically important set of software. If local units have control of their own IT resources, the odds are very high that they will gradually start to chip away at the corporate-wide nature of the ES. Certainly the local units need IT resources to make sure that they're using the information system effectively and to deal with ever changing business requirements; however, these IT people should have the central IT group as their organizational home.

BOLT-ON SOFTWARE

This is the name given to software that's outside of the main ES suite or legacy system, typically coming from a third-party software supplier. Companies usually add bolt-ons to the main system to perform specific functions because the existing ES or legacy systems don't do them well or don't do them at all. Many bolt-on software packages are considered "best of breed" because they are seen as so superior to their counterpart modules within the Enterprise System suite.

Davenport, in his book on enterprise systems,[ii] identifies supply chain support tools for demand and supply planning, plant scheduling, and logistics systems as being primary candidates for bolt-ons: "Given the existence of best-of-breed packaged solutions in so many of these areas, the favored approach for most firms has been to go with a major vendor for core ES and then bolt on supply chain software developed by multiple other vendors."

Downsides to bolt-ons include a degradation in the ability of ES to integrate information and process, the need for additional files not linked to the central database, the effort required to integrate the bolt-on, and a maintenance task over time as changes occur to the enterprise system and/or to the bolt-on. These negatives are not insignificant, and we feel that bolt-ons should be used judiciously and only when clearly needed.

The good news is that bolt-ons typically do provide users with a superior tool. (If not, why use a bolt-on?) Sometimes these packages are brought forward from the legacy environment and get bolted onto the new ES, because it's so obviously the right thing to do for the users. More on this in a bit, when we talk about pockets of excellence.

Most bolt-ons we've seen in ERP environments come in three categories:

Resource planning enablers. This is the type of thing we've just been talking about: getting outside software (for Master Scheduling, MRP, etc.) and plugging it in to your existing system.

Front-end/back end. These are applications that focus on the front end of the resource planning process (sales forecasting, Sales & Operations Planning, vendor-managed inventories) or back end, such as finite scheduling packages for the plants. Bolt-ons generally cause the least difficulty when they're at the front or the back. For example, there are several excellent forecasting packages on the market, which do a far better job than most ES vendor's offerings. For companies where forecasting is a problem—and there are more than a few of these—a forecasting bolt-on might make a lot of sense.

Supply chain optimization/advanced planning systems. This category of packages attempts a better fine-tuning of the detailed demand–

supply relationships addressed by master scheduling, Material Requirements Planning, and so forth. When used properly, these packages typically can do a superior job. Through advanced logic and strong simulation capabilities, they can give superior recommendations to demand managers, planners, and schedulers regarding the best fit between customer demands and resource utilization.

In summary, bolt-ons can be quite valuable, but they come at a cost—not only in dollars of course, but in loss of integration and increase in maintenance. Using them indiscriminately will cause more trouble than they're worth. Using them on a very specific basis, to do a superior job in one or another given function, is frequently the way to go.

SELECTING BOLT-ON SOFTWARE

Here are some thoughts about selecting bolt-on software, whether it is a resource planning enabler, a front-end or back-end module, or a supply chain optimization package. (These may also have relevance in selecting an ES for those of you who'll be doing a combined ERP/ES project.) Here goes:

Don't be premature.

Some companies' first exposure to a given set of software is through the software salesman who sells them the package. Often, these people regret having made the purchase after they have gone to early education and learned about ERP and its better tools. The right way is to learn about ERP first, and get the software shortly after the company has made an informed decision and commitment to ERP.

Don't procrastinate.

This isn't as contradictory as it sounds. Don't make the mistake of trying to find the perfect software package. That's like searching for the Holy Grail or the perfect wave. There is no best software package. The correct approach, after learning about ERP and deciding to do it, is to decide which bolt-on packages, if any, you'll need for phase I. Go after those and get a good workable set of software. Then repeat the process for phase II. It's important to move through these selection phases with deliberate haste, so the company can get on with implementing ERP and getting paybacks.

Don't pioneer.

People who get too far out in front, pioneers, often get arrows in their backs. This certainly applies to software for ERP. Why buy untested, unproven software? You have enough change underway with people systems to worry about software glitches. Insist on seeing the package working in a company that operates at a Class A or high Class B level. If the prospective software supplier can't name a Class A or B user of their product, we recommend that you look elsewhere.

Save the pockets of excellence.

Many companies do some things very well. An example of this would be a company with an excellent shop floor or work unit control system, but little else. The computer part of this system may have been programmed in-house, and may contain some excellent features for the users. Let's assume that the supply chain software package selected by this company contains a shop floor control module that's workable, but not as good as the current system. This company should not blindly replace its superior system with the new, inferior one. Save the good stuff. Don't throw the baby out with the bath water.

Managing Requests for Changes

Whether you choose to go after ERP/ES or ERP only, you will have requests for changes to the software. In fact, making changes to software packages seems to have risen to the level of a national sport, sort of an X-Games of business. Over the years, billions and billions of dollars have been paid to consultants, software people, and contract programmers to modify packaged software. This has developed from a history of fragmented systems in companies with software systems designed for local applications. Now that we are moving to a common approach to business processes (ERP) and common software (either ES or supply chain support software) there is a real challenge to keep changes under control.

Requests for changes will be minimized if the company does a good job of ERP education. This will help the users solve their problems within the overall framework of ERP. Add to this a set of standard software, relatively complete in terms of functionality. Then the users will have learned why the software is configured to support the valid needs of ERP. However, even with excellent education and good software, requests for software modifications will still come rolling along. This is where effective management enters the picture.

Key people, particularly members of the steering committee and project team, need to:

• Principle 1—Resist isolated changes.

The mind-set of management must be to resist changes to the software that are isolated to a local need that is not essential for running the business and/or implementing ERP. They need to understand that too many changes during implementation will delay the project and changes after project initiation will confuse the users.

• Principle 2—Always follow a recognized change process.

What's this? Another contradiction? Nope—this is a clear and complementary principle. The way to avoid violating Principle 1 is to have a recognized process for change. Most attempts at any sort of standardization in a company fail because there is no recognized change process. This means that either too many changes are made or the system is stifling due to stagnation. Management needs to establish a clear change process focused on who can recommend change, what are the key points to be considered, and who approves the change. People can play the game—as long as they play by the rules. Even the X-Games have rules.

Those are the principles. Here's the procedure:

1. The IT department is geared up to provide modifications, changes, enhancements, and so on. This includes both those that are made internally and those that can be done by the software vendor. The necessary funds have been budgeted in the cost benefit analysis.

2. Requests for changes are submitted first to the IT department for an evaluation of the amount of work involved. There should be an understood dividing line between minor and major project

changes and the request should be classified accordingly. IT also adds any other comments about the technical nature of the change but does not comment on the business validity.

3. The request then goes to the project team. If the request is for a minor change, the project team decides whether to grant the request or defer it until phase III.

4. If the request is for a major change, the project team reviews it and makes a decision. The key issue here: Is this change necessary in order to run the business and/or for ERP to work properly? Does the function in question require the computer or can it be done manually? If the answers verify that the change is important for the business and requires the computer, then it must be done either now or very soon. If not, defer it to phase III.

5. At times, those proposing the change may have a very strong disagreement over rejection by the project team. In this case, there needs to be a process for the change idea to go to the steering committee. The steering committee needs to be prepared to hear both sides of the issue and then make the final decision.

Using a process such as this can keep the modifications down to the (important) few and not the (nuisance) many. There are no guarantees that will protect a management team under all circumstances. However, failure to establish a process like this is one of the most notable reasons for projects to get out of control.

New Releases

To continue the golf analogy that began this chapter, golf clubs are always changing. New shafts and club heads are developed and touted as "revolutionary." Software development has the same pattern. New releases are always coming from vendors promising major improvements in functionality. The difference is that you can probably play with the new golf clubs the day you buy them, and they may or may not make a difference in your game. With software, the new release can represent a major investment of resources and may not only *not* provide benefits to your business but may interfere with your operation. There is no sin in passing up the most recent "new release" unless you are absolutely confident that the enhancements are important to your business.

One last word about software changes. It is always easier to make changes on the output and the input than it is on the internal logic of the system. Any changes to the internal logic of either ES or supply chain software should be considered as major and thus, kept to a minimum. Many changes at the heart of the software are a good indication that you have the wrong software. This is usually more of a problem with supply chain add-on software than Enterprise Software. ESs are built to adjust the switches that control data flow so it is more common to find that there are "work arounds" built into an ES.

Q & A WITH THE AUTHORS

TOM: Mike, how did you and your colleagues deal with the ES/bolt-on issue? I understand that you standardized on one ES vendor. Did you use bolt-ons and, if so, how?

MIKE: Our initial position was to eliminate all bolt-ons to standardize on the ES system. I never received so much in-house hate mail in my life when this became known. It turns out that the battles we fought at the beginning were lost by our ES vendor who simply could not provide the functionality required. The CIO, along with the appropriate function head, then made the calls on which bolt-ons were really necessary.

NOTES

[i] *Mission Critical—Realizing the Promise of Enterprise Systems,* 2000, Harvard Business School Press, Boston, MA.

[ii] Ibid.

Chapter 5

Getting Ready

AUDIT/ASSESSMENT I

This step gets at questions like these:

It takes too long to respond to competitors' moves. How can we get better and faster internal coordination, so that we can be more responsive?

We really want to improve our ability to manufacture; what should we do first?

We have a real need to improve our financial reporting and want to do ES but can we do ERP too? Do we need to do ERP also?

We think we need ERP, but we also feel we should get started on reorganization. Can we do both at the same time?

We feel we're in big trouble. We hardly ever ship on time. As a result, customers are unhappy and we're losing market share; we have major cash-flow problems; and morale throughout the company is not good. What can we do to reduce the pain level, quickly?

We've just begun a major initiative with internet selling. However, we're still in order-launch-and-expedite mode, with backorders and material shortages like crazy. Some of us are convinced that we'll

79

Figure 5-1

ERP PROVEN PATH

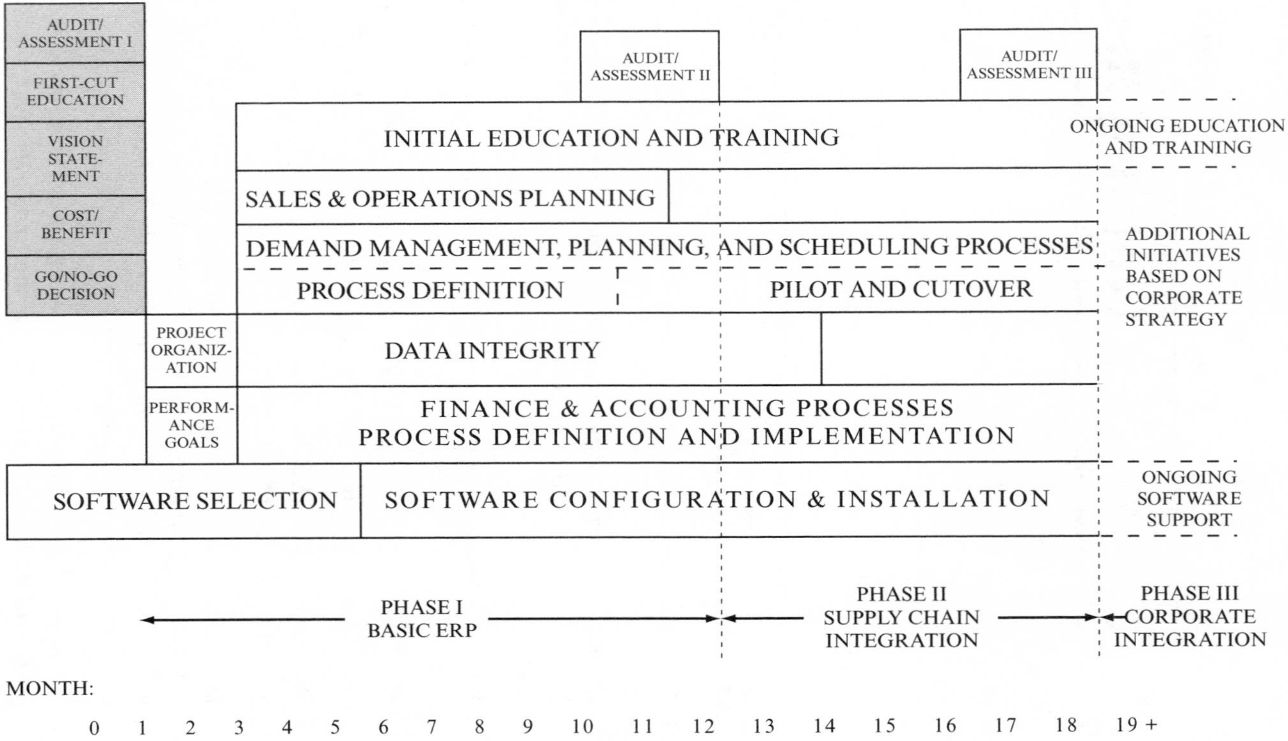

AUDIT/ASSESSMENT I

FIRST-CUT EDUCATION

VISION STATEMENT

COST/BENEFIT

GO/NO-GO DECISION

PROJECT ORGANIZATION

PERFORMANCE GOALS

SOFTWARE SELECTION

SOFTWARE CONFIGURATION & INSTALLATION

SOFTWARE CONFIGURATION & INSTALLATION

FINANCE & ACCOUNTING PROCESSES PROCESS DEFINITION AND IMPLEMENTATION

DATA INTEGRITY

DEMAND MANAGEMENT, PLANNING, AND SCHEDULING PROCESSES PROCESS DEFINITION

PILOT AND CUTOVER

SALES & OPERATIONS PLANNING

INITIAL EDUCATION AND TRAINING

ONGOING EDUCATION AND TRAINING

AUDIT/ASSESSMENT II

AUDIT/ASSESSMENT III

ADDITIONAL INITIATIVES BASED ON CORPORATE STRATEGY

ONGOING SOFTWARE SUPPORT

PHASE I BASIC ERP

PHASE II SUPPLY CHAIN INTEGRATION

PHASE III CORPORATE INTEGRATION

MONTH:

0   1   2   3   4   5   6   7   8   9   10   11   12   13   14   15   16   17   18   19 +

never get really good with internet sales if we can't learn to control or predict our basic business.

What to do, and how to get started—these are the kinds of issues addressed by audit/assessment I. Its purpose is to determine specifically which tools are needed, and in what manner they should be implemented—company wide or fast track. For example, a company may need Enterprise Resource Planning and Enterprise Software badly. It may want to implement ERP on a company-wide basis, mobilizing virtually all departments and people throughout the total organization.

However, this may not be possible. Other time-consuming activities may already be underway, such as introducing a new product line, building a new plant, entering a new market, and/or absorbing an acquired company. Everything about ERP may be perfect, except for the timing. Although the company may be willing to commit the necessary dollar resources to the project, the essential resource of people's time and attention simply might not be available. "Turning up the resource knob" is not an option.

In this case, the decision coming out of audit/assessment I might be to implement Quick-Slice ERP into one or several major product lines now. (A Quick-Slice ERP implementation involves far fewer people, and it's almost always possible to free up a handful of folks for a focused project like Quick Slice.) The early "slices," perhaps more than just one or two, would be followed by a company-wide implementation later, after completion of the other time-consuming high-priority project(s).

Audit/assessment I and its companion, audit/assessment II, are critically important to ensure that the improvement initiatives to be pursued by the company:

- match it's true needs.

- generate competitive advantages in the short run.

- are consistent with the company's long-term strategy.

Participants in this step include the executives, a wide range of operating managers, and, in virtually all cases, an outside consultant(s) with Class A credentials in ERP/MRP II who is knowledgeable regarding Enterprise Software. It's quite rare that a given business unit (company, group, division) possesses enough internal expertise and objectivity to put these important issues into focus.

The process is one of fact finding, identifying areas of consensus and disagreement, and matching the company's current status and strategies with the tools it has available for execution. The end result will be an action plan to move the company onto a path of improvement. Typically, the recommended action plan is presented in a business meeting with the executives and managers who've been involved to date. The purpose for this session is to have the action plan explained, questioned, challenged, modified as required, and adopted.

Another very important activity should take place in this meeting, and we call it consciousness raising. The presentation must establish the connection between the company's goals and the set of tools called ERP, and must outline how ERP can assist the company in reaching those goals and objectives (increased sales, reduced costs, better product quality, improved quality of life, enhanced ability to cope with change, etc.). The general manager and other key people can then see the real need to learn about ERP in order to make an informed decision about this potentially important issue. Learning about ERP is called first-cut education and we'll get into it in just a moment.

The time frame for audit/assessment I (elapsed time, not people-days) will range from several days to one month. Please note: This is not a prolonged, multi-month affair involving a detailed documentation of current systems. Rather, its focus and thrust is on what's not working well and what needs to be done now to become more competitive. (At this point, let's assume that the output from audit/assessment I has specified a company-wide implementation of ERP.)

First-Cut Education

Key people need to learn about ERP before they can do a proper job of creating the vision statement and estimating costs and benefits. They need to learn five crucial elements:

1. What is ERP?

2. Is it for us? Does it make sense for our business?

3. What will it cost?

4. What will it save? What are the benefits we'll get if we do it the right way and get to Class A?

and finally, if the company does not have Enterprise Software, but needs/wants it,

5. What are the linkages with ES and should we do both at the same time?

Some individuals may go through first-cut education prior to audit/assessment. Either they will not be aware of the value of the audit/assessment step or may want to become familiar with ERP prior to audit/assessment. The sequence is not important; the critical issue is to make sure that both steps are done. A management team should make a decision to proceed with ERP (or any other major initiative, for that matter) only after doing both audit/assessment I and first-cut education.

Some companies attempt to cost justify ERP before they understand what it's all about. Almost invariably, they'll underestimate the costs involved in implementation. They'll feel ERP is part of the computer system to order material. Therefore, most of the costs will be computer related and already funded with ES or other software projects. As a result, the project will not be properly funded.

Further, these companies almost always underestimate the benefits. If they think ERP is a computer system to order material, then most of the benefits will come from inventory reduction. It then becomes very difficult to peg the ERP implementation as a high priority in the company. The obvious moral of the story: First, learn about it; then do the cost/benefit analysis.

Who needs first-cut education? For a typical company, these people would be:

- *Top management.*

The CEO or general manager and the vice presidents of engineering, finance, manufacturing, and the marketing/sales departments. Basically, this should be the leadership team of the company or business unit.

- *Operating management.*

Managers from the sales department, customer service, logistics, production, information systems, engineering, accounting, materials, and supply chain management. Sales manager, customer service manager, production manager, logistics manager, systems manager, production control manager, purchasing manager, engineering manager, accounting manager. Obviously, the composition of this group can vary greatly from company to company. In smaller companies, top management and operating management are often one and the same. Larger companies may have senior vice presidents, directors, and others who would need early education on ERP. The guidelines to follow are:

1. Don't send many more people through first-cut education than necessary, since the final decision to implement hasn't yet been made.

2. On the other hand, be certain to include all key people—informal leaders as well as formal—who'll be held accountable for both costs and benefits. Their goal is to make an informed decision.

Sometimes companies have a difficult time convincing certain senior managers, possibly the general manager, to go through a first-cut education process. This can be a very serious problem, and Chapter 7 will address it in detail.

Vision Statement

In this step, the executives and operating managers who participated in first-cut education develop a written vision of the company's transformation: what will we look like and what new competitive capabilities will be in place following the implementation of ERP (and perhaps the ES/ERP combination). The statement must be written in a way that can be measured easily, so it'll be obvious when you get there.

This step is easy to skip. It's easy to feel that it takes more time and effort than it's worth. Not true. The reverse is actually the case: It's not much work, and it's *worth its weight in gold.* It's an essential part of laying the foundation for a successful project, along with the cost/benefit step. In fact, without a clear vision of the future, no sane person would embark on the journey to work through the major changes required.

The vision statement serves as a framework for consistent decision making over the life of the project, and can serve as a rallying point for the entire company. More immediately, the vision statement will serve as direct input to downstream steps on the Proven Path: cost/benefit analysis; establishment of performance goals; and development of the demand management, planning, and scheduling processes. Input to the preparation of the vision statement includes:

1. The executives' and managers' knowledge of:

   • The company and its problems. (Where are we today?)

   • Its strategic direction. (Where are we going?)

   • Its operating environment. (What does the marketplace require?)

   • Its competition. (What level of performance would gain us a competitive advantage in that marketplace?)

2. The recommendations made in audit/assessment I.

3. What was learned in first-cut education.

Brevity is good; less is more. Ideally, the vision statement will consist of one page. Some great vision statements are little more than one paragraph. It should be visceral, and it should drive action.

Since it's a relatively brief document, it shouldn't take a long time to prepare. One or several meetings should do the job, with heavy involvement by the general manager. However, if the vision is not clear and accepted by the leadership, or if it is not aligned with the company's strategy, don't go further. Remember, if the team doesn't know where they are going, everyone will work hard in different, and often conflicting directions.

One last point: Don't release the ERP vision statement quite yet. Remember, you haven't yet made a formal go/no-go decision. That'll come a bit later.

COST/BENEFIT ANALYSIS

Establishing the costs and benefits of an ERP project is essential. Here are some reasons why:

1. High priority.

Job 1 is to run the business. Very close to that in importance should be implementing ERP. It's very difficult to keep ERP pegged as a very high priority if the relevant costs and benefits have not been established and bought into. If ERP doesn't carry this high priority, the chances for success decrease.

2. A solid commitment.

Implementing ERP and ES means changing the way the business is run. Consequently, top management and operating management must be committed to making it happen. Without a solid projection of costs and benefits, the necessary degree of dedication may not be attained, and the chances for success will decrease sharply.

3. One allocation of funds.

By identifying costs thoroughly and completely before implementation, the company has to process only one spending authorization. This avoids repeated "trips to the well" (the board of directors, the corporate office, the executive committee) and their attendant delays during the life of the project. This factor leads some companies to combine ERP and ES into one project.

The people who attended first-cut education should now develop the cost/benefit study. Their objective is to develop a set of numbers to use in deciding for or against ERP. Do not, under any circumstances, allow yourselves to skip this step. Even though you may be convinced that you must do ERP and its benefits will be enormous, it's essential that you go through this process, for the reasons mentioned above. To do otherwise is like attempting to build a house on a foundation of sand.

Let's first focus on the likely areas of costs and benefits. After that, we'll work through several sample cost/benefit analyses.

Costs

A good way to group the costs is via our ABC categories: A = People, B = Data, C = Computer. Let's take them in reverse order.

C = Computer.

Include in this category the following costs:

1. New computer hardware necessary specifically for ERP or ES.

2. ES software for a combined ERP/ES project, and possibly supply chain bolt-ons for either ERP/ES or ERP only.

3. Systems people and others to:

   • Configure and enhance the ES software.

   • Install the software, test it, and debug it.

   • Interface the purchased software with existing systems that will remain in place after ERP and ES are implemented.

   • Assist in user training.

   • Develop documentation.

   • Provide system maintenance.

These people may already be on staff, may have to be hired, and/or may be temporary contract personnel. Please note: These costs can be very large. Software industry sources report cost ratios of up to 1:8 or more. In other words, for every dollar that a company spends on the purchased software, it may spend *eight dollars* for these installation activities.

4. Forms, supplies, miscellaneous.

5. Software maintenance costs. Be sure to include the any expected upgrades of the new software here.

6. Other anticipated charges from the software supplier (plus perhaps some contingency money for unanticipated charges).

B = Data.

Include here the costs involved to get and maintain the necessary data:

1. Inventory record accuracy, which could involve:

    • New fences, gates, scales, shelves, bins, lift trucks, and other types of new equipment.

    • Mobile scanners on lift trucks to read bar codes on stock.

    • Costs associated with plant re-design, sometimes necessary to create and/or consolidate stockrooms.

    • Cycle counting costs.

    • Other increases in staffing necessary to achieve and maintain inventory accuracy.

2. Bill of material accuracy, structure, and completeness.

3. Routing accuracy.

4. Other elements of data such as forecasts, customer orders, item data, work center data, and so forth.

A = People.

Include here costs for:

1. The project team, typically full-time project leader and also the many other people identified with individual segments of the business.

2. Education, including travel and lodging.

3. Professional guidance.

4. Increases in the indirect payroll, either temporary or ongoing, not included elsewhere. Examples include a new demand manager or master scheduler, additional material planning people, or another dispatcher. For most companies, this number is not large at all. For a few, usually with no planning function prior to ERP, it might be much higher.

These are the major categories of cost. Which of them can be eliminated? None; they're all essential. Which one is most important? The A item, of course, because it involves the people. If, for whatever reason, it's absolutely necessary to shave some money out of the project budget, from where should it come? Certainly not the A item. How about cutting back on the C item, the computer? Well, if you absolutely have to cut somewhere, that's the best place to do it. But why on earth would we say to cut out computer costs with the strong ES linkage with ERP?

The answer goes back to Chapter 1—installing ES without the proper ERP demand management, planning and scheduling tools will gain little. Many companies have had decent success without major computer or information system changes by working hard on their ERP capability. Obviously, we recommend that you do both. But, if there is a serious shortage of resources, do the planning systems first and automate the information systems later. Later in this chapter, we'll show you an example of the costs of the full ERP/ES combination and also ERP alone.

Companies are reporting costs for the total ERP/ES installation over $500 million for a large multinational corporation. In our ERP/ES example, the company is an average-sized business unit with $500 million in sales and about 1000 people, and the projected costs are over $8 million to do the full job. This number is not based on conjecture but rather on the direct experience of many companies. Our sample company doing ERP alone (no ES, a much less intensive software effort) shows considerably lower costs, but still a big swallow at $3.9 million. These are big numbers; it's a big project.

Benefits

Now let's look at the good news, the benefits.

1. Increased sales, as a direct result of improved customer service. For some companies, the goal may be to retain sales lost to aggressive competition. In any case, the improved reliability of the total system means that sales are no longer lost due to internal clumsiness. ERP has enabled many companies to:

- Ship on time virtually all the time.

- Ship in less time than the competition.

- Have their sales force spend their time selling, rather than expediting shipments and making excuses to customers over missed shipments.

In short, ERP can represent a significant competitive weapon. Surveys of ERP-using companies[i] have verified improved customer service gains of 15 percent for all respondents; 26 percent for the companies who identified themselves as Class A. For most companies, better customer service means more sales.

   2. Increased direct labor productivity, resulting from the valid, attainable schedules which ERP can enable companies to have. Productivity is increased via:

- Providing matched sets of components to the assembly areas, thereby eliminating much of the inefficiency and idle time often present.

- Reducing sharply the amount of expediting, lot splitting, emergency changeovers, short runs, and so forth in the fabrication areas.

- Requiring much less unplanned overtime, because the forward visibility is so much better.

Survey results show respondents reporting an average productivity gain of 11 percent; the Class A users got 20 percent. Think of the value to the bottom line of that kind of productivity gain!

   3. Reduced purchase cost. ERP provides the tools to give suppliers valid schedules and better forward visibility. Once the customer company gets out of the order-launch-and-expedite mode, its suppliers can produce the customer's items more efficiently, at lower cost. A portion of these savings can be passed back to the buying company to be used either for increased profits or reduced product pricing which can mean increased sales and profits.

   Further, valid schedules can free the buyers from a life of expediting and paper shuffling, so that they can do the important parts of their jobs (sourcing, negotiation, contracting, value analysis, cost reduction, etc.). Therefore, these savings don't come solely from lower prices but rather from reducing *total purchase costs.* Survey results: Companies report an average reduction in total purchased costs of 7 percent; the Class A companies got 13 percent. In many companies, the single largest financial benefit from ERP comes from purchase cost reduction.

4. Reduced inventories. Effective demand management, planning, and scheduling result in valid schedules. Valid schedules mean matched sets of components, which means making the products on schedule and shipping them on time. This typically results in lower inventories at all, or at least most, levels—raw material, work-in-process, finished goods.

For most companies, the four benefit areas identified above are the big ones. However, there are other benefits that are potentially very significant and should not be overlooked. They include:

5. Reduced obsolescence, from an enhanced ability to manage engineering changes, better forward visibility, and an overall smaller risk of obsolescence due to lower inventories in general. This is often a hidden cost at most companies and no one likes to focus on the stuff that is sold at discount or thrown away. However, it can be very large and certainly requires attention.

6. Reduced quality costs. Valid schedules can result in a more stable environment, which can mean less scrap. Eliminating the end-of-the month lump, where perhaps 75 percent of the shipments go out in the last 25 percent of the month, can lead to reduced warranty costs.

7. Reduced premium freight, both inbound, by having a better handle on what's needed, and outbound, by being able to ship on time. Many companies are delighted when they can air express a shipment to fulfill a customer order without thinking about the money that they could have saved with an on-time land shipment.

8. Elimination of the annual physical inventory. If the inventory numbers are accurate enough for ERP, they'll be more than good enough for the balance sheet. Many Class A and B companies don't take annual physical inventories. This can be a substantial savings in some companies. It can include not only the costs of taking the inventory itself but also the costs of disrupting production, since many companies can't produce while they count.

9. *Reduced floor space.* As raw material, work-in-process, and finished inventories drop sharply, space is freed up. As a result, you may not need to expand the plant or build the new warehouse or rent more office space for some time to come. Do a mental connection between ERP and your building plans. You may not need as much—or any— new brick and mortar once you get really good at manufacturing. Don't build a white elephant.

10. *Improved cash flow.* Lower inventories mean quicker conversion of purchased material and labor costs into cash.

11. *Increased productivity of the indirect workforce.* ERP will help not only the direct production associates to be more productive but also the indirect folks. An obvious example is the large expediting group maintained by some companies. Under ERP, this group should no longer be needed, and its members could be absorbed into other, more productive jobs.

Another aspect of this, more subtle and perhaps difficult to quantify, is the increased productivity of the supervisors and managers. That includes engineers, quality control people, production supervisors and managers, vice presidents of marketing, and let's not forget about the guy or gal in the corner office—the general manager. They should all be able to do their jobs better when the company is operating with a valid game plan and an effective set of tools to help them execute it.

They'll have more fun, also. More satisfaction from a job well done. More of a feeling of accomplishment. That's called quality of life and, while it's almost impossible to quantify that benefit, it may be the most important one of all.

Responsibility

A question often asked is: "Who should do the cost/benefit analysis? Who should put the numbers together?" First of all, it should not be a one-person process—it's much too important for that. Second, the process should not be confined to a single group. Let's look at several ways to do a cost/benefit analysis:

Method 1: Middle management sells up.

Operating managers put together the cost/benefit analysis and then attempt to sell the project to their bosses. If top management has been to first-cut education, there should be no need for them to be sold. Rather, they and their key managers should be evaluating specifically how ERP will benefit their company and what it'll cost to get to Class A.

This method is not recommended.

Method 2: Top management decree.

The executive group does the cost/benefit analysis and then decrees that the company will implement ERP. This doesn't allow for building the kind of consensus and teamwork that's so important.

This method is not recommended.

Method 3: Joint venture.

This is the recommended approach. The cost/benefit analysis should be done by those executives and managers who'll be held accountable for achieving the projected benefits within the framework of the identified costs. Here's how to do it:

1. A given department head, let's say the manager of sales administration and customer service, attends first-cut education.

2. The vice president of the sales and marketing department attends first-cut education.

3. Upon returning to the company, both persons do some homework, focusing on what benefits the sales side of the business would get from a Class A ERP system, plus what costs might be involved.

4. In one or several sessions, they develop their numbers. In this example, the most likely benefit would be increased sales resulting from improved customer service, and the biggest cost elements might be in education and training.

5. This process is also done in the other key functional areas of the business. Then the numbers are consolidated into a single state-

ment of costs and benefits in all of the key areas of the business (finance, manufacturing, logistics, product development, etc.).

Please note the participatory nature of the joint venture approach. Since both top management and operating management are involved, it promotes consensus up and down the organization, as well as cross functionally. We've found it to be far better than the other approaches identified above.

A word of caution: Be fiscally conservative. When in doubt, estimate the costs to the high side and the benefits low. If you're not sure whether certain costs may be necessary in a given area, include them. Tag them as contingency if you like, but get 'em in there. There's little risk that this approach will make your cost/benefit numbers unattractive because ERP is such a high payback project. Therefore, be conservative. Don't promise more than you can deliver.

We'll give you an example of the costs and benefits to illustrate the potential. You know that your company will have different numbers, but we want to show that a conservative approach still gives big savings. Note that the dramatic savings that are shown are still **VERY** conservative.

Examples of Cost/Benefit Analysis

To illustrate the process, let's create a hypothetical company with the following characteristics:

Annual sales: $500 million

Employees: 1000

Number of plants: 2

Distribution centers: 3

Manufacturing process: Fabrication and assembly

Product: A complex assembled make-to-order product, with many options

Pretax net profit: 10 percent of sales

Annual direct labor cost: $25 million

Annual purchase volume (production materials): $150 million

Annual cost of goods sold: $300 million

Current inventories: $50 million

Combined ERP/ES

Let's take a look at its projected costs and benefits both for a combined ERP/ES implementation and then for an ERP only project. First, a warning:

> *Beware! The numbers that follow are* not *your company's numbers. They are sample numbers only. Do not use them. They may be too high or too low for your specific situation. Using them could be hazardous to the health of your company and your career.*

With that caution, let's examine the numbers. Figure 5-2 contains our estimates for the sample company. Costs are divided into one-time (acquisition) costs and recurring (annual operating) costs . . . and are in our three categories: C = Computer, B = Data, A = People. Note that we have not tried to adjust the payout period or the rate of return for the obvious tax consequences of expenses versus capital. This is for simplicity (but also recognizes that the great majority of the costs are current expenses, and that expenses considered as capital investment represent a relatively small number). You may want to make the more accurate, tax-sensitive calculation for your operation.

These numbers are interesting, for several reasons. First, they indicate the total ERP/ES project will pay for itself in seven to eight months after full implementation.

Second, the lost opportunity cost of a one-month delay is $1,049,250. This very powerful number should be made highly visible during the entire project, for several reasons:

1. It imparts a sense of urgency. ("We really do need to get ERP and ES implemented as soon as we can.")

2. It helps to establish priorities. ("This project really is the number two priority in the company.")

3. It brings the resource allocation issue into clearer focus.

Regarding this last point, think back to the concept of the three knobs from Chapter 2—*work* to be done, *time* available in which to

Figure 5-2
Sample Cost/Benefit Analysis: Full ERP/ES

COSTS			
Item	*One Time*	*Recurring*	*Comments*
C- Computer			
Hardware	$400,000		Costs primarily for workstations.
Software	500,000	$75,000	Can vary widely, based on package.
Systems and programming	2,500,000	200,000	Adapting the software to your company, and training in its use. These costs are pegged here at 5 times the software purchase cost.
B - Data			
Inventory record accuracy	700,000	100,000	Includes new equipment and added cycle counters.
Bill of material accuracy and structure	200,000		Bills will need to be restructured into the modular format. Experienced engineers will be needed for this step.
Routing accuracy	100,000		
Forecasting	200,000	100,000	Full time person for Sales forecasting. Needs to come on board early.
A- People			
Project Team	1,200,000		Six full-time equivalent people for two years.
Education	800,000	100,000	Includes costs for education time and teaching the new ES interactions to the organization.

Figure 5-2
Continued

COSTS Item	One Time	Recurring	Comments
Professional guidance	400,000	50,000	4 days per month during installation.
SUB-TOTAL	$7,000,000	$725,000	
Contingency 15%	$8,050,000 1,050,000	$834,000 109,000	A conservative precaution against surprises.
TOTAL	$9,100,000	$943,000	

BENEFITS Item	Current	% Improvement	Annual Benefits	Comments
Sales	$500,000,00	7% @ 10%	$3,500,000	Modest improvement due to improved product availability at the profit margin of 10%.
Direct labor productivity	25,000,000	10%	2,500,000	Reductions in idle time, overtime, layoffs, and other items caused by the lack of planning and information flow.
Purchase cost	150,000,000	5%	7,500,000	Better planning and information will reduce total purchase costs.

Inventories				One time cash flow:
Raw Material and WIP	25,000,000	10% @ 15%	380,000	2,500,000

continued

Figure 5-2
Continued

Inventories				One time cash flow:
Finished goods	25,000,000	30% @ 15%	1,130,000	7,500,000
Obsolescence	500,000	30%	150,000	Conservative savings.
Premium freight	1,000,000	50%	500,000	Produce and ship on time reduces emergencies.
SUB-TOTAL			$15,660,000	$10,000,000 One time cash flow.

Less costs for:				
Contingency		15%	–2,349,000	1,500,000
Recurring			–720,000	
NET ANNUAL BENEFITS			$12,591,000	$8,500,000 One time cash flow.

Cost of a one month delay (Total /12)	$1,049,250
Payback time (One Time Cost/monthly benefits)	7.7 months
Return on investment (Annual benefits/ One Time Costs)	193%

do it, and *resources* that can be applied. Recall that any two of these elements can be held constant by varying the third.

Too often in the past, companies have assumed their only option is to increase the time. They assumed (often incorrectly) that both the work load and resources are fixed. The result of this assumption: A stretched-out implementation, with its attendant decrease in the odds for success.

Making everyone aware of the cost of a one-month delay can help companies avoid that trap. But the key people really must believe the numbers. For example, let's assume the company's in a bind on the project schedule. They're short of people in a key function. The choices are:

Figure 5-3
Projected Cash Flow from ERP/ES

Year	Annual	Cumulative	Comments
1	– $6,440,000	– $6,440,000	80% of onetime costs
2	– 1,610,000		Remainder (20%) of one-time cost
	– 417,000		6 months of recurring cost
	+ 5,036,400		40% of annual benefit
	+ 2,125,000		25% of inventory reduction
	+ $5,134,000	– $1,306,000	
3	– 834,000		Annual recurring cost
	+ 12,591,000		Gross annual benefits
	+ 6,475,000		
	+ 18,233,000	+ $16,926,000	Balance 75% of inventory reduction
			Total cash flow at end of year 3

1. Delay the implementation for three months. Cost: $3,147,750 ($1,049K x 3).

2. Stay on schedule by getting temporary help from outside the company (to free up the company's people to work on ERP and ES, not to work on these projects themselves). Cost: $300,000.

Few will deny $300,000 is a lot of money. But, it's a whole lot less than $3,147,750. Yes, we know this is obvious, but you would be amazed at how many companies forget the real cost of delayed benefits.

So far in this example, we've been talking about costs (expenses) and benefits (income). Cash flow is another important financial consideration, and there's good news and bad news here. First, the bad news.

A company must spend virtually all of the $8 million (one-time costs) before getting anything back. The good news: Enormous amounts of cash are freed up, largely as a result of the inventory decrease. The cost/benefit analysis for the total effort projects an inventory reduction of $10 million (10 percent of $25 million raw material and work in progress and 30 percent of $25 million in finished product). This represents incoming cash flow. (See Figure 5-3 for details.) The company does have negative cash flow in year 1 since most costs occur (as with virtually every project) before savings materialize. However, while the cumulative cash position is still negative at the end of year 2, the project will have generated over $5 million of cash for that year. By year 3, you are generating cash in a big way.

How many large projects has your company undertaken that have no cash impact in the second year with full savings in the third? We bet not many. For our example company, ERP and ES appear to be very attractive: An excellent return on investment (193 percent) and substantial amounts of cash delivered to the bank.

ERP Only

Now, what about a company that separates doing ERP only? Figure 5-4 shows a possible cost and benefits analysis for ERP by itself. Although each situation is wildly different, you can make a rough assumption that the ERP only numbers are additive to an ES project that has come before or will come after ERP.

What's exciting about this ERP only analysis is the payout and cash flow are as attractive as the ERP/ES total effort. Certainly, the numbers on both sides of the cost/benefit ledger are smaller but equally attractive. The project pays out in 7 months with a 170 percent rate of return. If you can find a better investment, go for it. But remember that this one will continue to return $553,000 each year in savings along with the one-time inventory cash savings of $4,500,000.

Please note that the benefit numbers are larger for ERP/ES than for ERP alone. The major difference between doing ERP and ES together or doing just ERP is the enhanced speed and accuracy of information flow when using an ES. Every decision from forecasting to sales to production will be more accurate and faster and will thus generate added benefits.

However, you can still have an impressive change in your business with ERP even with a non-integrated information system. We have assumed that the ERP project would fund one of several attractive supply chain software packages available but this would be a standalone assist to the forecasting/planning effort. There may be some

Figure 5-4
Sample Cost/Benefit Analysis: ERP Only

COSTS Item	One Time	Recurring	Comments
C- Computer			
Hardware	$200,000		Additional workstations or system upgrade.
Software	200,000	$50,000	Supply chain support software.
Systems and programming	200,000	100,000	Fitting the SC software to your system.
B - Data			
Inventory record accuracy	700,000	100,000	Includes new equipment and added cycle counters.
Bill of material accuracy and structure	200,000		Bills will need to be restructured into the modular format. Experienced engineers will be needed for this step.
Routing accuracy	100,000		
Forecasting	200,000	100,000	Full-time person for Sales forecasting. Needs to come on board early.
A- People			
Project Team	600,000		One FT person per plant and one corporate leader for two years.
Education	800,000	150,000	Key leaders and teams to learn ERP principles and techniques, and their application within the company.
Professional guidance	200,000	50,000	Two days per month during installation.

continued

Figure 5-4
Continued

COSTS Item	One Time	Recurring	Comments
SUB-TOTAL	$3,400,000	$550,000	
Contingency 15%	510,000	82,500	A conservative precaution against surprises.
TOTAL	$3,910,000	$632,000	

BENEFITS Item	Current	% Improvement	Annual Benefits	Comments
Sales	$500,000,000	3% @ 10%	$1,500,000	Modest improvement due to improved product availability at the profit margin. You could assume this as no improvement to be more conservative
Direct labor	25,000,000	5%	1,250,00	Reductions in productivity idle time, overtime, layoffs, and other items caused by the lack of planning and information flow This is very conservative.
Purchase cost	150,000,000	3%	4,500,000	Better planning and information will reduce supplier costs. Not as much as with complete ES connections and speed.
Inventories				One time cash flow:
Raw Material and WIP	25,000,000	6% @ 15%	230,000	1,500,000

continued

Figure 5-4
Continued

BENEFITS Item	Current	% Improve- ment	Annual Benefits	Comments
Finished Product	25,000,000	18% @ 15%	680,000	4,500,000 These are very low numbers for a Class A company.
Obsolescence	500,000	20%	100,000	Conservative savings
Premium freight	1,000,000	30%	300,000	Produce and ship on time reduces emergencies—but not as good as with thecomplete information system.
SUB-TOTAL			$8,560,000	$6,000,000 One time cash flow.
Contingency		15%	– 1,284,000	– 1,500,000
Recurring			– 632,000	
TOTAL			$6,644,000	$4,500,000 One time cash flow

Cost of one-month delay	$553,000
Payback months period	7 months
Return on investment	170%

added costs if ES comes after ERP due to the need to connect the ERP wiring to ES. However, this cost should be relatively small compared to the rest of the project.

Here's a familiar question: Does size matter? In terms of the payout, not as much as you might think. For a very small company, the challenge usually is resources. There are simply too few people to add a major effort such as this without risk to the basic business. Too often, small companies (and, to be fair, large ones also) will hire consultants to install ES and will ignore the ERP potential. These companies are usually very disappointed when they realize the costs have not brought along the benefits.

Large, multinational companies should be able to allocate resources and should find that the benefits are even more strategic. The problem with larger companies is trying to get all parts of the company, worldwide, to adhere to a common set of principles and practices. If pulling together all aspects of the company is difficult (like herding cats), we recommend that the project be attacked one business unit at a time. The impact for the total company will be delayed but the more enlightened business units that do install the total project will see rapid results.

Here are a few final thoughts on cost/benefit analysis.

1. What we've been trying to illustrate here is primarily the process of cost/benefit analysis, not how to format the numbers. Use whatever format the corporate office requires. For internal use within the business unit, however, keep it simple—two or three pages should do just fine. Many companies have used the format shown here and found it to be very helpful for operational and project management purposes.

2. We've dealt mostly with out-of-pocket costs. For example, the opportunity costs of the managers' time have not been applied to the project; these people are on the exempt payroll and have a job to do, regardless of how many hours will be involved. Some companies don't do it that way. They include the estimated costs of management's time in order to decide on the relative merits of competing projects. This is also a valid approach and can certainly be followed.

3. Get widespread participation in the cost/benefit process. Have all of the key departments involved. Avoid the trap of cost justifying the entire project on the basis of inventory reduction alone. It's probably possible to do it that way and come up with the necessary payback and return on investment numbers. Unfortunately, it sends exactly the wrong message to the rest of the company. It says: "This is an inventory reduction project," and that's wrong. We are talking about a whole lot more than that.

4. We did include a contingency to increase costs and decrease savings. Many companies do this as a normal way to justify any project. If yours does not, then you can choose to delete this piece of conservatism. However, we do encourage the use of contingency

to avoid distractions during the project if surprises happen. Nothing is more discouraging than being forced to explain a change in costs or benefits even if the total project has not changed in financial benefit. Contingency is an easily understood way to provide the protection needed to keep working as various costs and benefits ebb and flow.

GO/NO-GO DECISION

Getting commitment via the go/no-go decision is the first moment of truth in an implementation project. This is when the company turns thumbs-up or thumbs-down on ERP.

Key people within the company have gone through audit/assessment and first-cut education, and have done the vision statement and cost/benefit analysis. They should now know: What is ERP; is it right for our company; what will it cost; what will it save; how long will it take; and who are the likely candidates for project leader and for torchbearer?

How do the numbers in the cost/benefit analysis look? Are they good enough to peg the implementation as a very high—hopefully number two—priority in the company?

Jerry Clement, a senior member of the Oliver Wight organization, has an interesting approach involving four categories of questions:

- Are we financially ready? Do we believe the numbers in the cost/benefit analysis? Am I prepared to commit to my financial piece of the costs?

- Are we resource ready? Have we picked the right people for the team? Have we adequately back-filled, reassigned work or eliminated work so the chosen resources can be successful? Am I prepared to commit myself and my people to the task ahead?

- Are we priority ready? Can we really make this work with everything else going on? Have we eliminated non-essential priorities? Can we keep this as a high number two priority for the next year and a half?

- Are we emotionally ready? Do I feel a little fire in the belly? Do I believe the vision? Am I ready to play my role as one of the champions of this initiative along with the torchbearer?

If the answer to any of these is no, don't go ahead. Fix what's not right. When the answers are all yes, put it in *writing.*

The Written Project Charter

Do a formal sign-off on the cost/benefit analysis. The people who developed and accepted the numbers should sign their names on the cost/benefit study. This and the vision statement will form the written project charter. They will spell out what the company will look like following implementation, levels of performance to be achieved, costs and benefits, and time frame.

Why make this process so formal? First, it will stress the importance of the project. Second, the written charter can serve as a beacon, a rallying point during the next year or so of implementation when the tough times come. *And they will come.* Business may get really good, or really bad. Or the government may get on the company's back. Or, perhaps most frightening of all, the ERP-knowledgeable and enthusiastic general manager will be transferred to another division. Her successor may not share the enthusiasm.

A written charter won't make these problems disappear. But it will make it easier to address them, and to stay the course.

Don't be bashful with this document. Consider doing what some companies have done: Get three or four high-quality copies of this document; get 'em framed; hang one on the wall in the executive conference room, one in the conference room where the project team will be meeting, one in the education and training room, one in the cafeteria, and maybe elsewhere. Drive a stake in the ground. Make a statement that this implementation is not just another "flavor-of-the-month," we're serious about it and we're going to do it right.

We've just completed the first four steps on the Proven Path: audit/assessment I, first-cut education, vision statement, and cost/benefit analysis. A company at this point has accomplished a number of things. First of all, its key people, typically with help from outside experts, have done a focused assessment of the company's current problems and opportunities, which has pointed them to Enterprise Resource Planning. Next, these key people received some initial education on ERP. They've created a vision of the future, estimated costs and benefits, and have made a commitment to implement, via the Proven Path so that the company can get to Class A quickly.

THE IMPLEMENTERS' CHECKLISTS

At this point, it's time to introduce the concept of Implementers' Checklists. These are documents that detail the major tasks necessary to ensure total compliance with the Proven Path approach.

A company that is able to check yes for each task on each list can be virtually guaranteed of a successful implementation. As such, these checklists can be important tools for key implementers—people like project leaders, torchbearers, general managers, and other members of the steering committee and project team.

Beginning here, an Implementers' Checklist will appear at the end of most of the following chapters. The reader may be able to expand his utility by adding tasks, as appropriate. However, we recommend against the deletion of tasks from any of the checklists. To do so would weaken their ability to help monitor compliance with the Proven Path.

Q & A WITH THE AUTHORS

TOM: Probably the biggest threat during an ERP implementation is when the general manager of a business changes. You've lived through a number of those, and I'm curious as to how you folks handled it.

MIKE: First, try to get commitment that the torchbearer will be with the project for two years. If the general manager is likely to be moved out in less than that time, it might be best to select one of his or her staff members who'll be around for the long haul. Second, if the general manager leaves, the executive steering committee has to earn its pay and set the join-up process for the replacement. This means the new general manager must get ERP education and become thoroughly versed with the project's vision, cost/benefit structure, organization, timetable, and—most important—his or her role vis-à-vis ERP.

In big companies, change in management leadership is often a constant and I have seen several business units flounder when change happens without a "full court press" on engaging the new leader.

Note

[i] The Oliver Wight Companies' Survey of Implementation Results.

IMPLEMENTERS' CHECKLIST

Functions: Audit/Assessment I, First-cut Education, Vision Statement, Cost/Benefit Analysis, and Commitment

Task	Complete Yes	No
1. Audit/assessment I conducted with participation by top management, operating management, and outside consultants with Class A experience in ERP.	___	___
2. The general manager and key staff members have attended first-cut education.	___	___
3. All key operating managers (department heads) have attended first-cut education.	___	___
4. Vision statement prepared and accepted by top management and operating management from all involved functions.	___	___
5. Cost/benefit analysis prepared on a joint venture basis, with both top management and operating management from all involved functions participating.	___	___
6. Cost/benefit analysis approved by general manager and all other necessary individuals.	___	___
7. Enterprise Resource Planning established as a very high priority within the entire organization.	___	___
8. Written project charter created and formally signed off by all participating executives and managers.	___	___

Chapter 6

Project Launch

PROJECT ORGANIZATION

Once a commitment to implement ERP is made, it's time to get organized for the project. New groups will need to be created, as well as one or more temporary positions.

Project Leader

The project leader will head up the ERP project team, and spearhead the implementation at the operational level. Let's examine some of the requirements of this position.

Requirement 1: The project leader should be full-time. Having a full-time project leader is one way to break through the catch-22 (as discussed in Chapter 2) and get to Class A within two years.

Except in very small organizations (those with about 100 or fewer employees), it's essential to free a key person from all operational responsibilities. If this doesn't happen, that part-time project leader/part-time operating person will often have to spend time on priority number one (running the business) at the expense of priority number two (making progress on ERP). The result: delays, a stretched-out implementation, and sharply reduced odds for success.

Requirement 2: The project leader should be someone from within

Figure 6-1
ERP PROVEN PATH

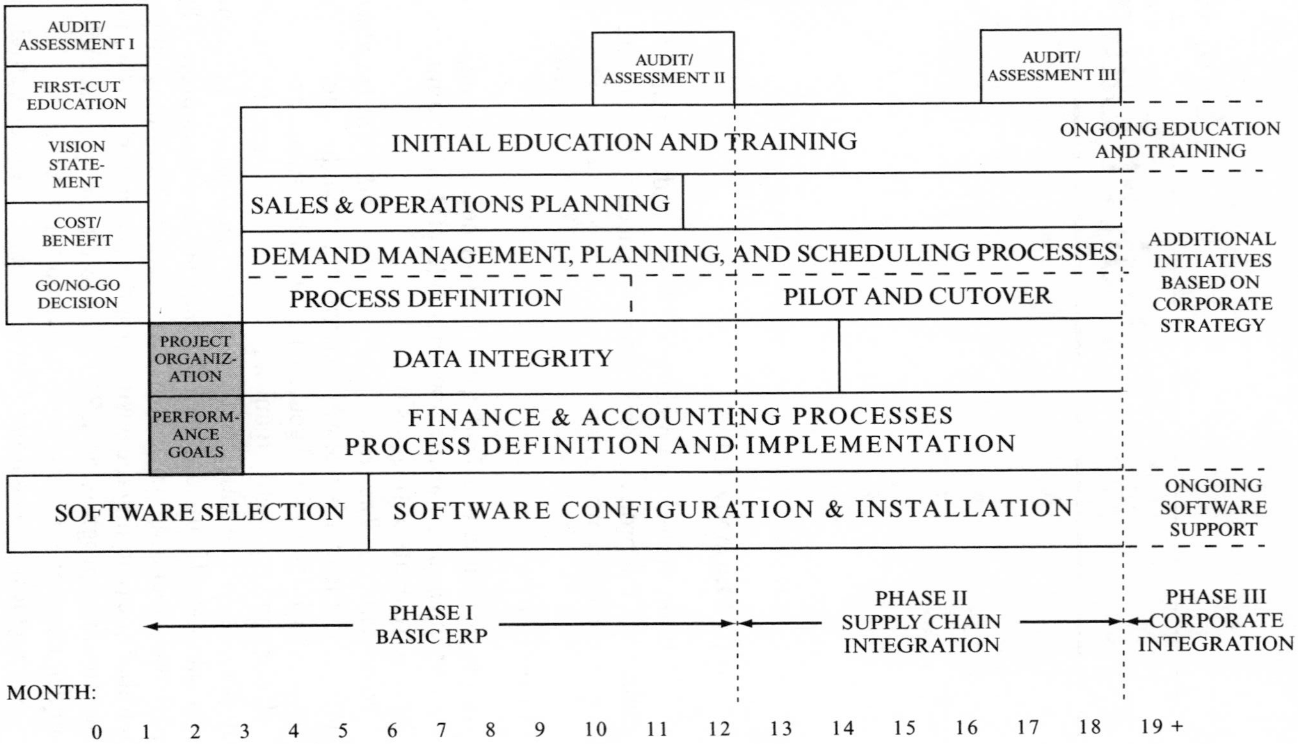

the company. Resist the temptation to hire an expert from outside to be the project leader. There are several important reasons:

1. ERP itself isn't complicated, so it won't take long for the insider to learn all that is needed to know about ERP, even though that person may have no background in logistics, supply chain management, systems, or the like.

2. It will take the outsider (a project leader from outside the company who knows ERP) far longer to learn about the company: Its products, its processes, and its people. The project leader must know these things, because implementing ERP successfully means changing the way the business will be run. This requires knowing how the business is being run today.

3. It will take a long time for the outsider to learn the products, the processes, and the people—and it will take even longer for the people to learn the outsider. The outside expert brings little credibility, little trust, and probably little rapport. This individual may be a terrific person, but he or she is fundamentally an unknown quantity to the people inside the company.

This approach can often result in the insiders sitting back, reluctant to get involved, and prepared to watch the new guy "do a wheelie." Their attitude: "ERP? Oh, that's Charlie's job. He's that new guy the company hired to install something. He's taking care of that." This results in ERP no longer being an operational effort to change the way the business is run. Rather, it becomes another systems project headed up by an outsider, and the odds for success drop sharply.

Requirement 3: The project leader should have an operational background. He or she should come from an operating department within the company—a department involved in a key function regarding the products: Design, sales, production, purchasing, planning. We recommend against selecting the project leader from the systems department unless that person also has recent operating experience within the company. One reason is that, typically, a systems person hasn't been directly involved in the challenging business of getting product shipped, week after week, month after month. This outsider hasn't "been there," even though this manager may have been working longer hours than the operational folks.

Another problem with selecting a systems person to head up the entire project is that it sends the wrong signal throughout the company. It says: "This is a computer project." Obviously, it's not. It's a line management activity, involving virtually all areas of the business. As we said in Chapter 2, the ES portion of an ERP/ES project will probably require a leader with a systems background. But, the leader for the whole project should have an operational background.

Requirement 4: The project leader should be the best available person for the job from within the ranks of the operating managers of the business—the department heads. (Or maybe even higher in the organization. We've seen some companies appoint a vice president as the full time project leader.) Bite the bullet, and relieve one of your very best managers from all operating responsibilities, and appoint that manager as project leader. It's that important.

In any given company, there's a wide variety of candidates:

- Sales administration manager.

- Logistics manager.

- Customer service manager.

- Production manager.

- Product engineering manager.

- Purchasing manager.

- Supply chain manager.

- Manufacturing engineering manager.

- Materials manager.

- Distribution manager.

One of the best background project leaders we've ever seen was in a machine tool company. The project leader had been the assembly superintendent. Of all the people in a typical machine tool company, perhaps the assembly superintendent understands the problems best. The key is that someone like the assembly manager has credibility inside the organization since everyone has heard that manager say things like: "We don't have the parts. Give us the parts and we'll make the product." If that person becomes project leader, the organization will say: "If Charley (or Sue) says this will work—it must be true."

Often, senior executives are reluctant to assign that excellent operating manager totally to ERP. While they realize the critical importance of ERP and the need for a heavyweight to manage it, they're hesitant. Perhaps they're concerned, understandably, about the impact on priority number one (running the business).

Imagine the following conversation between a general manager and Tom and Mike:

GENERAL MANAGER (GM): We can't afford to free up any of our operating managers to be the full-time project leader. We just don' t have enough management depth. We'll have to hire the project leader from outside.

TOM & MIKE (T&M): Oh, really? Suppose one of your key managers was to get run over by a train tomorrow. Are you telling me that your company would be in big trouble?

GM: Oh, no, not at all.

T&M: What would you do in that case?

GM: We'd have to hire the replacement from outside the company. As I said, we don't have much bench strength.

T&M: Great. Make believe your best manager just got run over by a train. Make him or her the full-time project leader. And then, if absolutely necessary, use an outside hire to fill the operating job that was just vacated.

Bottom line: If it doesn't hurt to free up the person who'll be your project leader, you probably have the wrong person. Further, if you select the person you can least afford to free up, then you can be sure you've got the right person. This is an early and important test of true management commitment.

Requirement 5: The project leader should be a veteran—someone who's been with the company for a good while, and has the scar tissue to prove it. People who are quite new to the company are still

Figure 6-2
Project Leader Characteristics

- Full time on the project.

- Assigned from within the company, not hired from outside.

- An operating person—someone who has been deeply involved in getting customer orders, making shipments and/or other fundamental aspects of running the business.

- A heavyweight, not a lightweight.

- A veteran with the company, not a rookie.

- A good manager and a respected person within the company.

---

technically outsiders. They don't know the business or the people. The people don't know them; trust hasn't had time to develop. Companies, other than very young ones, should try to get as their project leader someone who's been on board for about five years or more.

Requirement 6: The project leader should have good people skills, good communication skills, the respect and trust of his or her peers, and a good track record. In short, someone who's a good person and a good manager. It's important, because the project leader's job is almost entirely involved with people. The important elements are trust, mutual respect, frequent and open communications, and enthusiasm. (See Figure 6-2 for a summary of the characteristics of the project leader.)

What does the project leader do? Quite a bit, and we'll discuss some of the details later, after examining the other elements of organization for ERP. For the time being, however, refer to Figure 6-3 for an outline of the job.

One last question about the project leader: What does the project leader do after ERP is successfully implemented? After all, his or her previous job has probably been filled by someone else.

In some cases, they become deeply involved with other initiatives in their company—Lean Manufacturing, Six Sigma Quality Management, or others. Sometimes they return to their prior jobs, perhaps moving to a bigger one. It stands to reason because these people are really valuable; they've demonstrated excellent people and orga-

Figure 6-3
Project Leader Job Outline

- Chairs the ERP project team.

- Is a member of the ERP executive steering committee.

- Oversees the educational process—both outside and inside.

- Coordinates the preparation of the ERP project schedule, obtaining concurrence and commitment from all involved parties.

- Updates the project schedule each week and highlights jobs behind schedule.

- Counsels with departments and individuals who are behind schedule, and attempts to help them get back on schedule.

- Reports serious behind-schedule situations to the executive steering committee and makes recommendations for their solution.

- Reschedules the project as necessary, and only when directed by the executive steering committee.

- Works closely with the outside consultant, routinely keeping that person advised of progress and problems.

- Reports to the torchbearer on all project-related matters.

The essence of the project leader's job is to remove obstacles and to support the people doing the work of implementing ERP:

Production Managers	Systems People
Buyers	Marketing People
Engineers	Warehouse People
Planners	Executives
Accountants	Etc.

nizational skills as project leader, and they certainly know the set of tools being used to manage the day-to-day business.

In some cases, they become deeply involved with other improvement initiatives in their company. In other cases, they return to their prior jobs, because their jobs have been filled with a temporary for that one- to two-year period.

The use of temporaries offers several interesting possibilities. First there's a wealth of talented, vigorous ex-managers in North America who've retired from their long-term employers. Many of them are delighted to get back into the saddle for a year or two. Win-win.

Secondly, some organizations with bench strength have moved people up temporarily for the duration of the project. For example, the number two person in the customer service department may become the acting manager, filling the job vacated by the newly appointed project leader. When the project's over, everyone returns to their original jobs. The junior people get good experience and a chance to prove themselves; the project leader has a job to return to. Here also, win-win.

In a company with multiple divisions, it's not unusual for the ex-project leader at division A to move to division B as that division begins implementation. But a word of caution: This person should not be the project leader at division B because *this manager is an outsider.* Rather, the ex-project manager should fill an operating job there, perhaps the one vacated by the person tapped to be the project leader.

When offering the project leader's job to your first choice, make it a real offer. Make it clear that he or she can accept it or turn it down, and that their career won't be impacted negatively if it's the latter. Furthermore, one would like to see some career planning going on at that point, spelling out plans for after the project is completed.

One of the best ways to offer the job to the chosen project manager is to have the offer come directly from the general manager (president, CEO). After all, this is one of the biggest projects that the company will see for the next two years and the general manager has a big stake in its success. In our experience, it is rare for a manager to refuse an assignment like this after the general manager has pointed out the importance of the project, his or her personal interest in it, and likely career opportunities for the project manager.

Project Team

The next step in getting organized is to establish the ERP project team. This is the group responsible for implementing the system at the operational level. Its jobs include:

- Establishing the ERP project schedule.

- Reporting actual performance against the schedule.

- Identifying problems and obstacles to successful implementation.

- Activating ad hoc groups called spin-off task forces (discussed later in this chapter) to solve these problems.

- Making decisions, as appropriate, regarding priorities, resource reallocation, and so forth.

- Making recommendations, when necessary, to the executive steering committee (discussed later in this chapter).

- Doing whatever is required to permit a smooth, rapid, and successful implementation of ERP at the operational level of the business.

- Linking to the ES team if concurrent projects.

The project team consists of relatively few full-time members. Typically, they are the project leader, perhaps one or several assistant project leaders (to support the project leader, coordinate education, write procedures, provide support to other departments, etc.), and often one or several systems people. Most of the members of the project team can be part-time members.

These part-time people are the department heads—the operating managers of the business. Below is an example of a project team from our sample company (as described in Chapter 5: 1000 people, two plant locations, fabrication and assembly, make-to-order product, etc.). This group totals 15 people, which is big enough to handle the job but not too large to execute responsibilities effectively. Some of you may question how effective a group of 15 people can be. Well, actual experience has shown that an ERP project team of 15, or even 20, can function very well—provided that the meetings are well structured and well managed. Stay tuned.

Full-time Members	*Part-time Members*
Project leader	Cost accounting manager
Assistant project leader	Customer service manager

Systems analyst   Demand manager

ES Project Leader[1]   Distribution manager

General accounting manager

Human resources manager

Information systems manager

Manufacturing engineering manager

Materials manager

Production superintendent

Product engineering manager

Production control manager

Purchasing manager

Quality control manager

Sales administration manager

Supply chain manager

Do you have a structured Total Quality project (or other major improvement initiative) underway at the same time as ERP? If so, be careful. These projects should not be viewed as competing, but rather complementary; they support, reinforce, and benefit each other. Ideally, the Total Quality project leader would be a member of the ERP project team and vice versa.

The project team meets once or twice a week for about an hour. When done properly, meetings are crisp and to the point. A typical meeting would consist of:

1. Feedback on the status of the project schedule—what tasks have been completed in the past week, what tasks have been started in the past week, what's behind schedule.

---

[1] In an ERP/ES implementation. If an enterprise system has already been installed, the person representing the ES would probably be a part-time member of this team.

2. A review of an interim report from a task force that has been addressing a specific problem.

3. A decision on the priority of a requested enhancement to the software.

4. A decision on questions of required functionality to meet the specific business need.

5. Identification of a potential or real problem. Perhaps the creation of another task force to address the problem.

6. Initiation of necessary actions to maintain schedule attainment.

Please note: No education is being done here, not a lot of consensus building, not much getting into the nitty-gritty. These things are all essential but should be minimized in a project management meeting such as this. Rather, they should be addressed in a series of business meetings, and we'll cover those in the next chapter. The message regarding project team meetings: Keep 'em brief. Remember, the managers still have a business to run, plus other things to do to get ERP implemented.

Upward Delegation

Brevity is one important characteristic of the project team meetings. Another is that they be mandatory. The members of the project team need to attend each meeting.

Except . . . what about priority number one? What about running the business? Situations just might arise when it's more important for a manager to be somewhere else. For example, the plant manager may be needed on the plant floor to solve a critical production problem; the customer service manager may need to meet with an important new customer who's come in to see the plant; the purchasing manager may have to visit a problem supplier who's providing some critical items.

Some companies have used a technique called upward delegation very effectively. If, at any time, a given project team member has a higher priority than attending a project team meeting, that's fine. No problem. Appoint a designated alternate to be there instead.

Who's the designated alternate? It's that person's boss . . . the vice president of manufacturing or marketing or materials, as per the above examples. The boss covers for the department head. In this way, priority number one is taken care of by keeping the project team meetings populated by people who can make decisions. This is a critical design point. There should be no "spectators" at these meetings. If you can't speak for your business area, you shouldn't be there.

Executive Steering Committee

The executive steering committee consists primarily of the top management group in the company. It's mission is to ensure a successful implementation. The project leader cannot do this; the project team can't do it: only the top management group can ensure success.

To do this, the executive steering committee meets once or twice a month for about an hour. Its members include the general manager and the vice presidents, all of whom understand that leading this implementation effort is an important part of their jobs. There's one additional person on the executive steering committee—the full-time project leader. The project leader acts as the link between the executive steering committee and the project team.

The main order of business at the steering committee meetings is a review of the project's status. It's the project leader's responsibility to report progress relative to the schedule, specifically where they're behind. The seriousness of schedule delays are explained, the critical path is reviewed, plans to get the project back on schedule are outlined, additional resources required are identified, and so on. In a combined ERP/ES project, a single steering committee is appropriate to insure full coordination and linkage between the two projects.

The steering committee's job is to review these situations and make the tough decisions. In the case of a serious schedule slippage on the critical path, the steering committee needs to consider the following questions (not necessarily in the sequence listed):

Can resources already existing within the company be re-allocated and applied to the project? (Remember the three knobs principle discussed in Chapter 2? This represents turning up the resource knob.)

Is it possible to acquire additional resources from outside the company? (The resource knob.) If so, how much will that cost versus the cost of a number of months of delay?

Is all the work called for by the project schedule really necessary? Would it be possible to reduce somewhat the amount of work without harming the chances for success with ERP? (The work knob.)

Will it be necessary to reschedule a portion of the project or, worst case, the entire project? (The time knob.)

Only the executive steering committee can authorize a delay in the project. These are the only people with the visibility, the control, and the leverage to make such a decision. They are the ones ultimately accountable. This is like any other major project or product launch. Top management must set the tone and maintain the organization's focus on this key change for the company.

In addition to schedule slippage, the executive steering committee may have to address other difficult issues (unforeseen obstacles, problem individuals in key positions, difficulties with the software supplier, etc.).

The Torchbearer

The term torchbearer refers very specifically to that executive with assigned top-level responsibility for ERP. The role of the torchbearer[2] is to be the top-management focal point for the entire project. Typically, this individual chairs the meetings of the executive steering committee.

Who should be the torchbearer? Ideally, the general manager, and that's very common today. Sometimes that's not possible because of time pressures, travel, or whatever. If so, take your pick from any of the vice presidents. Most often, it's the VP of finance or the VP of operations. The key ingredients are enthusiasm for the project and a willingness to devote some additional time to it.

Often, the project leader will be assigned to report directly to the

---

[2] Often called champion or sponsor. Take your pick.

Figure 6-4

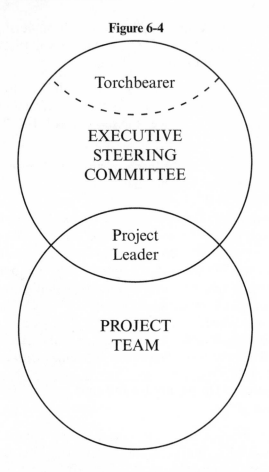

torchbearer. This could happen despite a different reporting relationship prior to the ERP project. For example, the project leader
may have been purchasing manager and, as such, had reported to the
VP of manufacturing. Now, as project leader, the reporting is to the
torchbearer, who may be the general manager or perhaps the vice
president of marketing.

What else does the torchbearer do? Shows the top management
flag, serves as an executive sounding board for the project team, and
perhaps provides some top-level muscle in dealings with suppliers.
He or she rallies support from other executives as required. He or she
is the top management conscience for the project, and needs to have
high enthusiasm for the project.

Being a torchbearer isn't a terribly time-consuming function, but it can be very, very important. The best person for the job, in most cases, is the general manager.

Special Situations

What we've described here—one steering committee and one project team—is the standard organizational arrangement for an average-sized company, say from about 200 to 1,200 people—that is implementing ERP only. It's a two-group structure. (See Figure 6-4.)

This arrangement doesn't always apply. Take a smaller company, less than 200 people. In many companies of this size, the department heads report directly to the general manager. Thus, there is no need for separate groups; the steering committee and the ERP project team can be merged into one.

In larger companies, for example multiplant organizations, there's yet another approach. The first thing to ask is: "Do we need a project team at each plant?" This is best answered with another question: "Well, who's going to make it work at, for example, Plant 3?"

Answer: "The guys and gals who work at Plant 3." Therefore, you'd better have a project team at Plant 3. And also at Plants 1 and 2.

Next question: "Do we need a full-time project leader at each plant?" Answer: "Yes, if they're large plants and/or if they have a fairly full range of functions: sales, accounting, product engineering, purchasing, as well as the traditional manufacturing activities. In other cases, the project leader might be a part-timer, devoting about halftime to the project." See Figure 6-5 for how this arrangement ties together.

You can see that the steering committee is in place, as is the project team at the general office. This project team would include people from all the key general office departments: marketing and sales, purchasing, finance and accounting, human resources, R&D/product engineering, and others. It would also include plant people, if there were a plant located at or near the general office. The remote plants, in this example all three of them, each have their own team and project leader. The project leader is also a member of the project team at the general office, although typically he or she will not attend each meeting there, but rather a meeting once or twice per month.

Figure 6-5

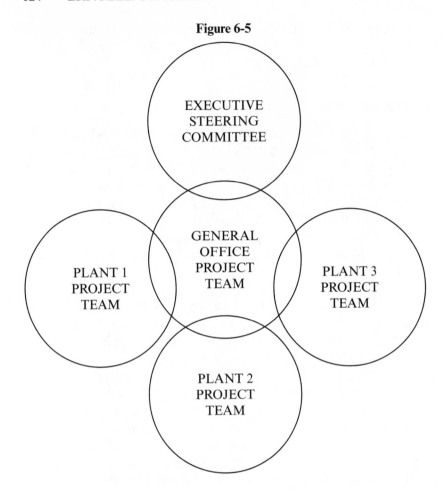

Now let's double back on the two-group arrangement shown in Figure 6-4. We need to ask the question: What would this look like in a combined ERP/ES implementation? And the answer is shown in Figure 6-6, which shows two parallel organizations at the project team level but with only one overall executive steering committee.

The reason for the two project teams: The team installing the enterprise system has so many technical tasks to accomplish that the nature of the work is quite different. Also, the ES will affect some areas of the company that are outside the scope of ERP, human resources being one example.

Here again, in a smaller company there may be an opportunity to

Figure 6-6

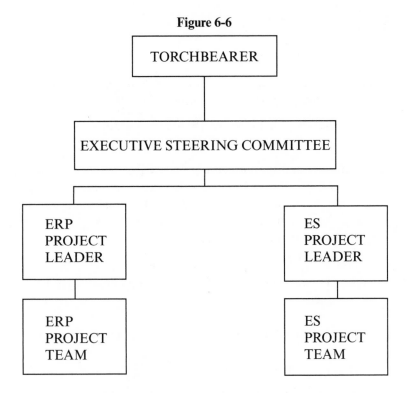

avoid the two-team approach shown here, but we do recommend it for all companies other than quite small ones.

Spin-Off Task Forces

Spin-off task forces are the ad hoc groups we referred to earlier. They represent a key tool to keep the project team from getting bogged down in a lot of detail.

A spin-off task force is typically created to address a specific issue. The issue could be relatively major (e.g., selecting a piece of bolt-on software, structuring modular bills of material, deciding how to master schedule satellite plants) or less critical (floor-stock inventory control, engineering change procedures, etc.). The spin-off task force is given a specific amount of time—a week or so for a lesser issue, perhaps a bit longer for those more significant. Its job is to research the issue, formulate alternative solutions, and report back to the project team with recommendations.

Spin-off task forces:

- Are created by the project team.[3]

- Are temporary—lasting for only several days, several weeks or, at most, several months.

- Normally involve no more than one member of the project team.

- Are cross-functional, involving people from more than one department. (If all task force members are from one department, then the problem must exist totally within that department. In that case, why have a task force? It should simply be the responsibility of the department manager and his people to get the problem fixed.)

- Make their recommendations to the project team, then go out of existence.

Upon receiving a spin-off task force's report, the project team may:

- Accept the task force's recommended solutions.

- Adopt one of the different alternatives identified by the task force.

- Forward the matter to the executive steering committee, with a recommendation, if it requires their approval (e.g., the software decision).

- Disagree with the task force's report, and re-activate the task force with additional instructions.

A disclaimer: Let's not lose sight of the fact that, in many cases, the ideal task force is a single person. If Joan has all the necessary background, experience, problem-solving skills, and communication skills, she could well serve as a "one person task force"—an individ-

---

[3] Or maybe none. More and more companies are pushing decision making and accountability farther down in the organization. Further, if there is to be a project team member on the spin-off task force, he or she needn't be the task force leader but could mainly serve as the contact point with the project team.

ual with a special assignment. Other people's time could be spent elsewhere.

Once the decision is made as to what to do, then people must be assigned to do it. This may include one or more members of the spin-off task force, or it may not. The task force's job is to *develop* the solution. The steps to implement the solution should be integrated into the project schedule and carried out by people as a part of their departmental activities.

Back in Chapter 3, we discussed time wasters such as documenting the current system or designing the new system. The organizational format that we're recommending here—executive steering committee, project team, and spin-off task forces—is part of what's needed to ensure that the details of how ERP is to be used will fit the business. The other part is education, and that's coming up in the next chapter.

Spin-off task forces are win-win. They reduce time pressures on the busy department heads, involve other people within the organization, and, most of the time, the task force sees its recommendations being put into practice. One torchbearer at a Class A company said it well: "Spin-off task forces work so well, they must be illegal, immoral, or fattening."

Professional Guidance

ERP is not an extension of past experience. For those who've never done it before, it's a whole new ball game. And most companies don't have anyone on board who has ever done it before—successfully.

Companies implementing ERP need some help from an *experienced, qualified* professional in the field. They're sailing into uncharted (for them) waters; they need some navigation help to avoid the rocks and shoals. They need access to *someone who's been there.*

Note the use of the words *experienced* and *qualified* and *someone who's been there.* This refers to *meaningful Class A* experience. The key question is: Where has this person made it work? Was this person involved, in a significant way, in at least one Class A implementation? In other words, has this person truly been there?

Some companies recognize the need for professional guidance but make the mistake of retaining someone without Class A credentials.

They're no better off than before, because they're receiving advice on how to do it from a person who has not yet done it successfully.

Before deciding on a specific consultant, find out where that person got his or her Class A experience. Then contact the company or companies given as references and establish:

1. Are they Class A?

2. Did the prospective consultant serve in a key role in the implementation?

If the answer to either question is no, then run, don't walk, the other way! Find someone who has Class A ERP/MRP II credentials. Happily, there are many more consultants today with Class A experience than 20 years ago. Use one of them. To do otherwise means that the company will be paying for the inexperienced outsider's on-the-job training and, at the same time, won't be getting the expert advice it needs so badly.

The consultant supports the general manager, the torchbearer (if other than the GM), the project leader, and other members of the executive steering committee and the project team. In addition to giving advice on specific issues, the outside professional also:

- Serves as a conscience to top management. This is perhaps the most important job for the consultant. In all the many implementations we've been involved in over the years, we can't remember even one where we didn't have to have a heart-to-heart talk with the general manager. Frequently the conversation goes like this: "Beth, your vice president of manufacturing is becoming a problem on this implementation. Let's talk about how we might help him to get on board." Or, even more critical, "Harry, what you're doing is sending some very mixed messages. Here's what I recommend you do instead." These kinds of things are often difficult or impossible for people within the company to do.

- Helps people focus on the right priorities and, hence, keep the project on the right track. Example: "I'm concerned about the sequence of some of the tasks on your project schedule. It seems to me that the cart may be ahead of the horse in some of these steps. Let's take a look."

- Serves as a sounding board, perhaps helping to resolve issues of disagreement among several people or groups.

- Coaches the top management group through its early Sales & Operations Planning meetings.

- Asks questions that force people to address the tough issues. Example: "Are your inventories really 95-percent accurate overall? What about the floor stock? How about your work-in-process counts? How good are your production-order close-out procedures? What about your open purchase orders?" In other words, he or she "shoots bullets" at the project; it's the job of the project team and the steering committee to do the bulletproofing.

How much consulting is the right amount? How often should you see your consultant?

Answer: Key issues here are results and ownership. The right amount of consulting, of the right kind, can often make the difference between success and failure. Too much consulting, of whatever quality, is almost always counterproductive to a successful implementation.

Why? Because frequently the consultants take over to one degree or another. They can become deeply involved in the implementation process, including the decision-making aspects of it. And that's exactly the wrong way to do it. It inhibits the development of essential ingredients for success: ownership of the system and line accountability for results. The company's goal, regarding the consultant, must be one of self-sufficiency; the consultant is a temporary resource, to be used sparingly and whose knowledge must be transferred to the company's people. The consultant's goal should be the same.

In summary, the consultant should be an adviser, not a doer. For an average-sized business unit (200 to 1,200 people) about one to three days every month or two should be fine, once the project gets rolling following initial education and project start-up.

What happens during these consulting visits?

Answer: A typical consulting day could take this format:

8:00   Preliminary meeting with general manager, torch-bearer, and project leader. Purpose: Identify special problems, firm up the agenda for 9:30 to 3:30.

8:30–9:30	Project team meeting. Purpose: Get updated, probe for problems.
9:30–3:30	Meetings with individuals and smaller groups to focus on specific issues and problems.
3:30–4:00	Solitary time for consultant to review notes, collect thoughts, and formulate recommendations.
4:00–5:00	Wrap-up meeting with executive steering committee and project team. Purpose: Consultant updates members on his or her findings, makes recommendations, and so forth.

In between visits, the consultant must be easily reachable by telephone. The consultant needs to be a *routinely available* resource for information and recommendations . . . but visits the plant in person only one or two or three times each month or two.

Performance Goals

This step flows directly from the work done in the audit/assessment, vision statement and cost/benefit analysis. It is more detailed than those prior steps. It defines specific and detailed performance targets that the company is committing itself to reach, and that it will begin to measure soon to ensure that it's getting the bang for the buck. These targets are usually expressed in operational, not financial, terms and should link directly back to the financial benefits specified in the cost/benefit analysis. Examples:

For our make-to-stock product lines, we will ship 99 percent of our customers' orders complete, within twenty four hours of order receipt. Benefit: SALES INCREASE.

For our make-to-order products, we will ship 98 percent of our customers' orders on time, per our original promise to them. Benefit: SALES INCREASE.

For all our products, we will reduce the combined cycle time to purchase and manufacture by a 50-percent minimum. Benefit: SALES INCREASE.

We will reduce material and component shortages by at least 90 percent. Benefit: DIRECT LABOR PRODUCTIVITY.

We will reduce unplanned overtime (less than one-week advance notice) by 75 percent. Benefit: DIRECT LABOR PRODUCTIVITY.

We will establish supplier partnerships, long-term supplier contracts, and supplier scheduling covering 80 percent or more of our purchased volume within the next 18 months. Benefit: PURCHASE COST REDUCTION.

We could go on and on, but by now you have the idea. A quantified set of performance goals can serve as benchmarks down the road. After implementation, actual results can be compared to those projected here. Is the company getting the benefits? If not, why not? The people can then find out what's wrong, fix it, and start getting the benefits they targeted.

Please note: *Each financial benefit in the cost/benefit analysis should be backed by one or more operational performance measures,* such as the ones above.

The key players in developing performance measurements are essentially the same folks who've been involved in the prior steps: top management and operating management, perhaps with a little help from their friends elsewhere in the company.

This chapter and the previous one have covered four key steps on the Proven Path following first-cut education. They are the vision statement, cost/benefit analysis, project organization, and performance goals. Here's an important point, which can work in your favor: It's often possible for these four steps to be accomplished by the same people in the same several meetings. This is good, since there is urgency to get started and time is of the essence.

Q & A with the Authors

Mike: Of all the project leaders you've seen over the years, which one had the best background for the job?

Tom: The person with the best background had significant experience in both sales & marketing and operations. He really knew the products, the processes, the people—and the customers. He had been a field sales guy, and actually came into the project leaders' job from a sales management position. Earlier he'd been an area supervisor in one of the plants and also had spent time in the production control function. He was a good (not great) communicator, had adequate computer knowledge, and had just completed a night school M.B.A.

I've saved the best for last: he had great people skills. People—up, down, and sideways in the organization—really liked him. He was non-political and he didn't play games. People trusted him.

IMPLEMENTERS' CHECKLIST

Function: Project Organization and Responsibilities, Performance Goals

Task	Complete Yes	No
1. Full-time project leader selected from a key management role in an operating department within the company.	___	___
2. Torchbearer identified and formally appointed.	___	___
3. Project team formed, consisting mainly of operating managers of all involved departments.	___	___

Task	Complete	
	Yes	No
4. Executive steering committee formed, consisting of the general manager, all staff members, and the project leader	⎯	⎯
5. Project team meeting at least once per week.	⎯	⎯
6. Executive steering committee meeting at least once per month.	⎯	⎯
7. Outside consultant, with Class A experience, retained and on-site as required.	⎯	⎯
8. Detailed performance goals established, linking directly back to each of the benefits specified in the cost/benefit analysis.	⎯	⎯

Chapter 7

Initial Education

It's fascinating to look at how education for MRP, MRP II, and ERP has been viewed since the beginning. Quite an evolution has taken place.

At the beginning, in what could be called the Dark Ages, education was perceived as unnecessary. The implication was that the folks would figure it out on the fly. The relatively few early successes were, not surprisingly, in companies whose people were deeply involved in the design of the new tools and, hence, became educated as part of that process.

The Dark Ages were followed by the How Not Why era. Attention was focused on telling people *how* to do things but not *why* certain things needed to be done. This approach may work in certain parts of the world, but its track record in North America has proved to be poor indeed.

Next came the age of Give 'Em the Facts. With it came the recognition that people needed to see the big picture, that they needed to understand the principles and concepts, as well as the mechanics.

Was this new awareness a step forward? Yes. Did it help to improve the success rate? You bet. Was it the total answer? Not by a long shot.

Figure 7-1

ERP PROVEN PATH

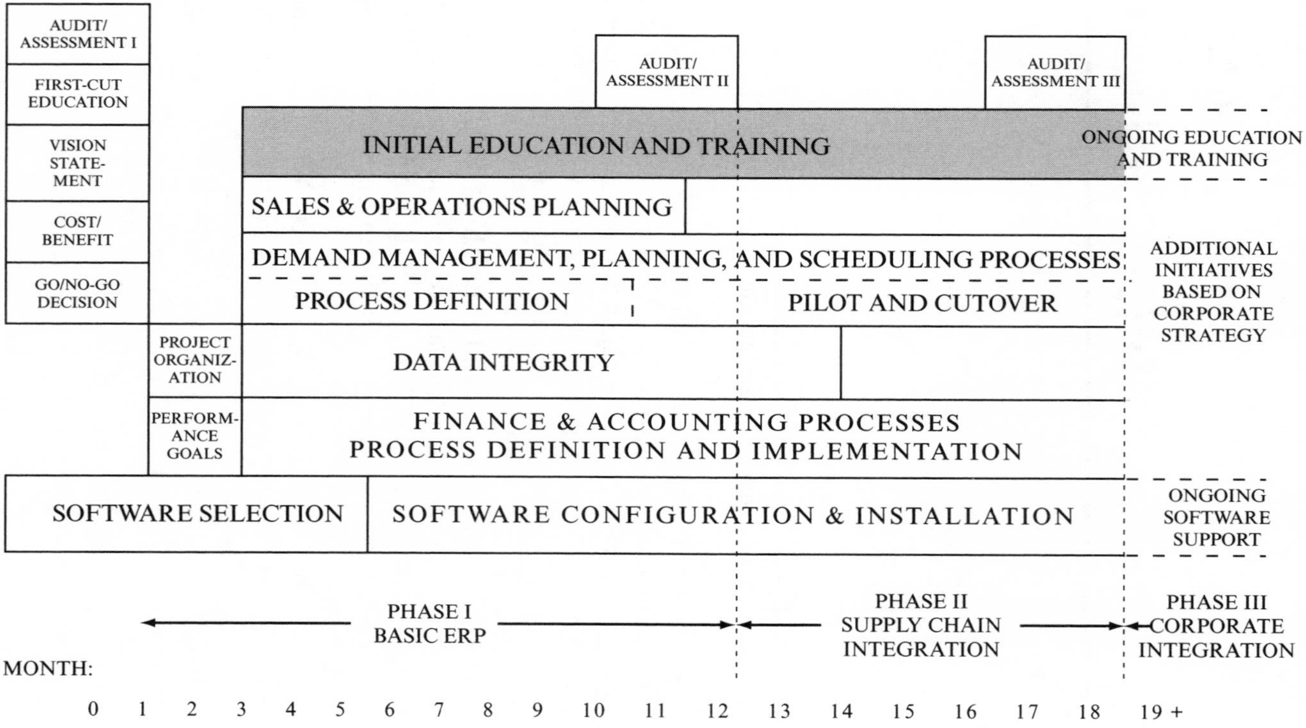

OBJECTIVES OF EDUCATION FOR ERP

Today, education for ERP is seen as having a far broader mission. It's recognized as having not one but two critically important objectives:

1. *Fact Transfer.* This takes place when people learn the *whats, whys,* and *hows.* It's essential but, by itself, not nearly enough.

2. *Behavior Change.* This occurs when people who have lived in the world of the informal system—missed shipments, angry customers, funny numbers, lack of accountability—become convinced of the need to do their jobs differently. It's when they truly understand why and how they should use a formal system as a team to run the business more professionally and how it will benefit them. Here are some examples:

Fact transfer occurs when the people in the marketing and sales departments learn how demand management and master scheduling operate, how the master schedule should be used as the source of customer order promising, and how to calculate the available-to-promise quantity.

Behavior change takes place when the folks in marketing and sales participate willingly in the Demand Management process because they recognize it as the way to give better and faster service to their customers, increase sales volume, and make the company more competitive.

Fact transfer happens when the production manager learns about how the plant floor schedules can be used by area supervisors and group leaders to manage their departments more efficiently. *Behavior change* is when the production manager banishes hot lists from the plant floor because he or she is convinced that the formal system can and will work.

Fact transfer is the engineers learning about the engineering-change control capabilities within Material Requirements Planning.

Behavior change is the engineers communicating early and often with material planners about new products and pending engineering changes because they understand how this will help drastically to reduce obsolescence, disruptions to production, and late shipments to customers.

Fact transfer is when the cost accounting manager learns about ERP's extremely high requirements for inventory record accuracy. *Behavior change* occurs when that manager leads the charge to eliminate the annual physical inventory, because he or she knows that inventory records sufficiently accurate for successful ERP are more than accurate enough for balance sheet verification—and that physical inventories cost time and money but often degrade inventory accuracy.

Behavior change is central to a successful implementation of Enterprise Resource Planning. It's also an awesome task—to enable hundreds, perhaps thousands, of people to change the way they do their jobs.

The mission of the ERP education program is thus of enormous importance. It involves not only fact transfer, by itself not a small task, but far more important, behavior change. One can speculate about the odds for success at a company using an off-the-wall, half-baked approach to education.

Therefore, a key element in the Proven Path, perhaps the most important of all, is effective education. This is synonymous with managing the process of change. Behavior change is a process that leads people to believe in this new set of tools, this new set of values, this new way of managing a manufacturing enterprise.

People acquire ownership of it. It becomes theirs; it becomes "the way we're going to run the business." Executing the process of behavior change, (i.e., education for ERP) is a management issue, not a technical one. The results of this process are teams of people who believe in this new way to run the business and who are prepared to change the way they do their jobs to make it happen.

CRITERIA FOR A PROGRAM TO ACCOMPLISH BEHAVIOR CHANGE

Following are the criteria for this process of ERP education that will achieve the primary objective of behavior change widely throughout the company. (See Figure 7-2 for a summary of these criteria.)

1. *Active, visible and informed top management leadership and participation.*

The need to involve top management deeply in this change process is absolute. This group is the most important of all, and within this

Figure 7-2
Criteria for a Program to Accomplish Behavior Change

1. Active top management leadership and participation.

2. Line accountability for change.

3. Total immersion for key people.

4. Total coverage throughout the company.

5. Continuing reinforcement.

6. Instructor credibility.

7. Peer confirmation.

8. Enthusiasm.

group, the general manager is the most important person. Failure to educate top management, and most specifically the general manager, is probably the single most significant cause why companies do not get beyond Class C. Why? For several reasons, one being the law of organizational gravity. Change must cascade *down* the organization chart; it rarely flows uphill. Leadership, by informed and knowledgeable senior management people including the general manager, is essential.

Another reason: The risk factor. How could a company possibly succeed in acquiring a superior set of tools to manage the business when the senior managers of the business don't understand the tools and how to use them? One well-intentioned decision by an uninformed general manager can kill an otherwise solid ERP process. An example: The general manager says, "Business is great! Put all those new orders into the master schedule. So what if it gets overloaded? That'll motivate the troops." There goes the integrity of the master schedule; customer order promises become meaningless; schedules for the plants and the suppliers are no longer valid.

Another example: "Business is lousy! We have to cut indirect payroll expense. Lay off the cycle counter." There goes the integrity of the inventory records; shortages abound; shipments are missed.

Okay so far? Now the next question to address is how to convince top management, specifically the general manager (GM), to get educated. In many companies, this is no problem. The GM is open-minded, and more than willing to take time out of a busy schedule to learn about the ERP set of decision-making processes.

This is particularly true when audit/assessment I is done at the first step in the entire process. Even where there may have been initial reluctance towards education on the part of the GM and others, it tends to evaporate during the wrap-up phase of audit/assessment I. (See Chapter 5.)

In some companies, unfortunately, this is not so. The general manager is totally disinterested in ERP, and won't even authorize an audit/assessment. Further, he or she refuses to take the time to learn about ERP. Common objections:

I don't need to know that. That's for the guys and gals in the back room.

I know it all already. I went to a seminar by our computer hardware supplier three years ago.

I'll support the project. I'm committed. I'll sign the appropriations requests. I don't need to do any more than that. [Authors' note: Support isn't good enough. Neither is commitment. What's absolutely necessary is *informed leadership* by the general manager. Note the use of word "informed"; this comes about through education.]

I'm too busy.

And on and on. The reluctance by GMs to get educated often falls into one of two categories:

- Lack of understanding (they either think they know all about it, or they don't think they need to know about it at all).

- Lack of comfort with the notion of needing education.

The first category—lack of understanding—can usually be addressed by logic. Articles, books, videotapes, and oral presentations have been used with success. Perhaps the most effective approach, besides audit/assessment, is what's called an Executive Briefing. This is a presentation by a qualified ERP professional, lasting for several hours, to the general manager and his or her staff. This is not education but rather an introduction to ERP. Its mission: Consciousness raising, once again. It enables the GM and others to see that important connection between their problems/opportunities on the one hand and ERP as the solution on the other.

The second category—discomfort with the idea of education—is often not amenable to logic. It's emotional, and can run deep. Here are three approaches that have been successful in dealing with this problem:

Peer input. Put the reluctant general manager in touch with other GMs who have been through both ERP education and a successful implementation. Their input can be sufficiently reassuring to defuse the issue.

The trusted lieutenant. Expose one or several of the reluctant GMs most trusted vice presidents to ERP education. Their subsequent recommendation, hopefully, will be something like this: "Boss, you have to get some education on ERP if we're going to make this thing work. Take our word for it—we can't do it without you."

The safety glasses approach. Imagine this dialogue between the reluctant GM and another person, perhaps the torchbearer for ERP.

TORCHBEARER (TB): Boss, when you go out on the plant floor, do you wear safety glasses?

GENERAL MANAGER (GM): Of course.

TB: Why? Are you afraid of getting metal in your eye?

GM (CHUCKLING): No, of course not. I don't get my head that close to the machinery. The reason I wear safety glasses on the plant floor is that to do otherwise would send out the wrong signal. It would say that wearing safety glasses wasn't important. It would make it difficult for the managers and supervisors to enforce the rule that everyone must wear safety glasses.

TB: Well, boss, what kind of signal are you going to send out if you refuse to go through the ERP education? We'll be asking that many of our people devote many hours to getting educated on ERP. Without you setting the example, that'll be a whole lot harder.

If a general manager won't get educated on ERP, then the company *should not* go ahead with a company-wide implementation. It will probably not succeed. Far better not to attempt it, than to attempt it in the face of such long odds. What should you do in this case? Well, your best bet may be to do a Quick-Slice ERP implementation, and we'll cover that in detail in Chapters 13 and 14.

2. Line accountability for change.

Remember the ABCs of ERP? The A item, the most important element, is the people. It's people who'll make it work.

Education is fundamental to making it happen. It's teaching the people how to use the tools, and getting them to believe they can work with the tools as a team. Therefore, an education program must be structured so that a specific group of key managers can be held *accountable* for properly educating the people. The process of changing how the business is run must not be delegated to the training department, the HR department, a few full-time people on the project team, or, worst of all, outsiders. To attempt to do so seriously weakens accountability for effective education and, hence, sharply reduces the odds for success.

In order to enable ownership and behavior change, the process of change must be managed and led by a key group of people with the following characteristics:

- They must be held accountable for the success of the change process, hence, the success of ERP at the operational level of the business.

- They must know, as a group, how the business is being run today.

- They must have the authority to make changes in how the business is run.

Who are these people? They're the department heads, the operating managers of the business. Who else could they be? Only these operating managers can legitimately be held accountable for success in their areas, be intimately knowledgeable with how the business is being run today in their departments, and have the authority to make changes.

3. Total immersion for key people.

These managers, these key people who'll facilitate and manage this process of change, first need to go through the change process themselves. They'll need more help with this, since they're the first group in the company to go through the process. What they need is total immersion—an intensive, in-depth educational experience to equip them to be change agents. Obviously, it's essential that top management understand this need, and enable it to happen.

4. Total coverage throughout the company.

The question arises: "Who in a typical company needs ERP education?" Answer: Darn near everybody. Education has to be widespread because of the need for behavior change so widely throughout the company.

What's needed is to educate the critical mass to achieve a high level of ERP awareness and enthusiasm throughout the entire organization. When that occurs, the result is not unlike a chemical reaction. ERP becomes the way we do it around here—the way we run the business.

The critical mass in most companies means 80 percent—*minimum*—of all the people in the company prior to going live with ERP, with the balance being educated shortly thereafter. That's *all* the people, from the folks in mahogany row to the people on the plant floor. It also includes the people in the middle (the managers, the supervisors, the buyers, the salespeople, etc.). An excellent way of focusing on the need for widespread education is depicted graphically in Figure 7-3.

There's a small group of people who believe in ERP, who are en-

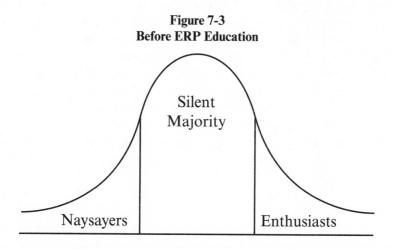

Figure 7-3
Before ERP Education

thusiastic, and who want to get going. There's also a small percentage of naysayers, people who don't believe ERP will work and who are vocally against it. Most folks are in the middle—arms folded, sitting back, not saying much and not expecting much. They're thinking, "Here we go again—another management fad that'll blow over before long."

Figure 7-4 shows what needs to happen:

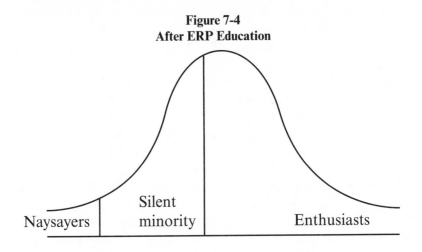

Figure 7-4
After ERP Education

Naysayers | Silent minority | Enthusiasts

That's the mission: Get a majority of the people enthusiastically on board, reduce the folded-arm set into a minority, and minimize the ranks of the prophets of doom and gloom.

Yes, but (you may be saying to yourself) . . . is it really necessary to educate folks such as production associates, group leaders, maintenance people? You bet it is. Here's one example why:

Hank, an excellent machine operator and a hard worker, has been with the company for 18 years. There's been a large queue of work-in-process jobs at Hank's machine during all of those years, except for a time during the early 1990s when business was really bad. Hank got laid off for a while.

Hank's come to associate, rightly, large queues with job security and shrinking queues with reduced business and the possibility of a layoff.

QUESTION: As ERP is implemented, what should happen to the queues?

ANSWER: Go down.

QUESTION: When Hank sees the queues dropping, what might he tend to do?

ANSWER: Slow down.

QUESTION: What will Hank's coworkers tend to do?

ANSWER: Slow down.

QUESTION: What happens then?

ANSWER: Output drops, queues don't get smaller, plant schedules are missed, and so on.

QUESTION: What's the solution?

ANSWER: Simple. Tell 'em about ERP. Tell 'em what's coming and why. Tell 'em how it will affect them and their jobs. Make sure that Hank knows that we no longer need to have large queues of work physically on the floor; rather we can queue the work inside the computer and Hank can look in there whenever he wants and see what jobs will be coming to his work center.

"Telling 'em about it" is called education, and it's essential. If you don't tell them what's going to happen and why, they'll hear about it anyway and will probably assume the worst. Even if you do tell them what and why, they may not believe it all. Our experience, however, has been that most folks in most companies will at least keep an open mind and give it the benefit of the doubt.

The best advice I've ever heard about which people should be educated comes from Walter Goddard, formerly head of the Oliver Wight organization. Walt said, "The question is not 'who to include' in this change process. Rather, it's 'who to exclude.'" Indeed! Companies should start with the assumption that they'll involve everyone, and then ask themselves whom to leave out. One might say, "Well, we really don't need to educate the folks who cut the grass and shovel the snow. And I guess we could exclude those who answer the phones and open the mail. But do we really want to do that? It could be interpreted that we don't feel these people are important, but that's not true. Everyone who works here is important."

Total coverage means *mandatory*. Education for ERP can be optional under only one condition—if success with ERP is considered as optional. On the other hand, if the company's committed to making it work, then it can't be left up to individuals to decide whether or not they'll get educated on ERP. Education is a process with the objectives of behavior change, teamwork, ownership. The process can't succeed with spotty, sporadic, random participation.

5. Continuing reinforcement.

Ollie Wight said it well: "Grease-gun education doesn't work." He was referring to the one-shot, quick-hit educational approaches tried so often without lasting results. Retention of the facts is poor, and that's the least of it. It's difficult to get down to the details of how ERP will work within the company; ownership and, hence, behavior change is almost impossible to get in this environment. What's needed is a process that occurs over an extended period of time. People can learn some things about ERP, go back and do their jobs, think about what they've learned, let it sink in, evaluate it in the light of how they do their jobs, formulate questions, and then ask those questions at the next session.

Repetition is important. When our kids were in grade school, in addition to readin' and 'rithmetic, they also took 'ritin'. Writing in this context means grammar, spelling, punctuation, composition. When they got to high school, they took freshman English, which dealt with grammar, spelling, and so forth. Upon arriving at college, believe it or not, one of the first courses they took was English 101: Grammar and Composition. They took the same subject matter over and over again. Why? Because the ability to speak and write well is so important. Likewise, ERP is important; people will need to change the way they do their jobs and run the business. Before that can happen, they'll need to acquire ownership of it. To do that, in most cases, means that they'll have to learn about it more than once. In short, reinforcement facilitates ownership; ownership leads directly to behavior change.

In this process of facilitating behavior change, two-way communication is essential. Putting 200 people in a hall and talking at them about ERP may constitute exposure, but not education. The essence of ERP education is dialogue—where people discuss, ask questions, and get answers, focus on issues, get specific. It must be involving ("This stuff is interesting") and reassuring ("I'm beginning to see how we can make this work for us").

People asking questions means people getting believable answers, and this leads us to the next criterion.

6. Instructor credibility.

Education sessions for ERP can be lead by outsiders or insiders. Both are necessary. It's essential that some key people go through classes lead by outside experts, so that they can start to become the company's experts on ERP. These sessions are most frequently conducted inside the company, but public classes are available. (See Appendix D.) It's essential that the instructors of these sessions already be experts, that they've been deeply involved in successful implementations, that they can speak from firsthand experience. If not, credibility will suffer, and behavior change for their key people may never get started. The credentials required of an outside instructor are the same as the requirements for an ERP consultant: Class A experience. In practice, in almost all cases, these two roles are filled by the same person. Therefore, as you're selecting a consultant for your project, keep in mind that he or she will be providing instruction to many of your key people. The consultant will need good teaching skills and experience.

Since it's usually impractical to send large numbers of people to lots of outsider-led classes, education led by insiders is also necessary. The leaders of these sessions must not only know about ERP; they must be experts on the company—its products, its processes, its people, its customers, its suppliers, and so on. If not, credibility will suffer and behavior change by the critical mass may never happen.

7. Peer confirmation.

It's likely that the president in a given company feels that he or she has no peer within that company. Not only is no one on an equal level, perhaps he or she feels that no one really understands the problems, the challenges, the requirements of the job.

Interestingly, the vice president of marketing (or finance or engineering or whatever) may feel exactly the same way—that they have no peer within the company when it comes to their jobs. And so might the purchasing manager feel that way, and the plant superintendent, and others.

Peer confirmation is essential to build confidence in success, so that the process of acquiring ownership can take place. Outsider-led sessions can help with this in two ways. First, during the sessions themselves, the outside expert can cite experiences of executives in other companies who became successful in using the ERP business processes; secondly, when appropriate, the outsider should arrange visits between executives in the implementing company and their counterparts in a company that has successfully implemented ERP. This should be easy for outside experts to do if they are truly experts, with a string of A and B implementations under their belt.

Insider-led sessions are often grouped departmentally.[1] When a number of people in similar jobs are in the same class, peer confirmation, hence ownership, hence behavior change are facilitated. The area buyers can talk to other buyers, hear them ask questions, hear the answers coming back from their boss (who's been to one or more outsider-led classes). This process is reassuring. It lowers the level of uncertainty and anxiety; it raises the level of confidence in success; it builds ownership. It enables people to see the need to change the way they do their jobs.

Let's go back to outsider-led classes for a moment. They make another major contribution, in that they get at the uniqueness syndrome. One of the things heard from time to time is: "We're unique. We're different. ERP won't work for us." Almost invariably, this comes from people who've not yet received proper ERP education.

One of the key missions of outsider-led education is to help people work through the uniqueness syndrome, to begin to see ERP as a generalized set of tools that has virtually universal application potential. Outsider-led sessions require high-quality instructors, with Class A credentials of course. Further, they require homework to be done up front, in terms of customizing and tailoring the sessions.

8. Enthusiasm.

Remember the catch-22 of ERP? It's a lot of work; we have to do it ourselves; it's not the number one priority. Widespread enthusiasm is one of the key elements needed to break through the catch-22.

---

[1] But not all of them. Some of the earlier, less-detailed sessions should include people from a variety of departments. This encourages communication across departments and helps to break down barriers.

Enthusiasm comes about when people begin mentally matching their problems (missed shipments, massive expediting, excessive overtime, material shortages, finger pointing, funny numbers, and on and on) with ERP as the solution. The kind of enthusiasm we're talking about here doesn't necessarily mean the flag-waving, rah-rah variety. More important is a solid conviction that might go like this:

ERP makes sense. It's valid for our business. If we do it right, we can solve many of the problems that have been nagging us for years. We, as a company, can become more competitive, more secure, more prosperous—and we can have more fun in the process.

Enthusiasm is contagious.[2] Most successful ERP implementations happen without hiring lots of extra people. It's the people already on board who fix the inventory records, the bills of material, and the routings; do the education; solve the problems and knock down the roadblocks—and all the while they're making shipments and running the business as well or better than before. Here's Ollie again: "Those who've been through a Class A . . . [ERP] installation repeatedly use the phrase 'a sense of mission.' To those who haven't, that may sound like an overstatement. It isn't."

Enthusiasm is also enhanced by early wins. One early win is implementing Sales & Operations Planning and thereby being better able to balance demand and supply—which leads to better customer service and lower inventories and lead times.

Another is achieving high levels of inventory record accuracy, which can sharply improve the company's ability to make valid delivery promises to customers. Remember, the General Manager gets enthused with success in growing the business—and his or her enthusiasm is the most important of all.

THE CHANGE PROCESS

Thus far we've looked at the *objectives* of ERP education, the most important by far being behavior change, and also the necessary *cri-*

---

[2] A warning: the ho-hum syndrome is also contagious. If you don't go through this change process correctly, you'll probably get the opposite of enthusiasm.

teria for such a program. Now let's look at the *process,* one that will meet the above criteria and enable behavior change to happen. In other words, this process has to bring people to see the need and benefits of running the business differently and, hence, of the need and benefits of doing their jobs differently.

There are two major aspects to this change process. First, create the team of experts, and second, reach the critical mass of people within the company

Create the Team of Experts

The future team of experts has already been identified—the department heads, the operating managers of the business. The good news here is that these folks are already halfway to the goal of becoming the team of experts. They're already experts in how the business is being run today. What remains is for them to become experts in how the business will be run in the future, using the new set of tools called ERP.

Let's take a look at how that happens—at how the operating management group within a company becomes a team of experts to facilitate and manage the change process.

Very simply, the people themselves go through the change process via the following steps:

1. Outsider-led classes.

It's important for this future team of experts to go through an in-depth educational experience on ERP. (See criterion 3.) In an outsider-led class, there should be a variety of job functions represented—sales folks, engineers, marketers, production managers, accountants, materials people (see criterion 7).

Of course, these outsider-led classes must be taught by ERP professionals, people who have a solid track record of participating in successful Class A implementations of ERP. These instructors not only need to be able to communicate the principles, techniques, and mechanics of ERP but also to illustrate the results, the benefits that companies have realized from ERP.

Here's some good news. Virtually all the members of the future team of experts have already been to an outsider-led class, as a part of first-cut education (see Chapter 5). A number of them will need to attend one or several specialty classes, and perhaps a few haven't been to class at all yet and will need to go. (Similarly, most of the top management group has already received most of its outsider-led education, again via the first-cut process.)

2. A series of business meetings.

Next on the agenda for the team of experts is to go through a series of business meetings. The objectives here are:

• To accelerate and strengthen the change process begun in the outsider-led classes.

• To equip these operating managers with the tools to reach the critical mass.

• To develop detailed definitions of how the company's demand management, planning, and scheduling processes will look after ERP has been implemented.

Important: Please note that these are decision-making meetings. They are not show-and-tell; they're not Saturday-night-at-the-movies. More on this in a moment.

Doing this properly requires a substantial amount of time, probably between 20 to 40 business meetings of about two hours each, spread over several months. Not nearly as much time would be required here if the only objective were fact transfer. However, because the main objective is behavior change, project team members—the team of experts—should be prepared for a substantial time commitment. (See criteria 3 and 5.)

Because we refer to these sessions as a series of business meetings, the question arises: "Does any education take place at these meetings?" Yes, indeed. Education is essential, as a means to the goal of making behavior change happen. It needs to occur at three levels:

• Principles, concepts, and techniques.

• Application.

• Training.

Figure 7-5
ERP Training and Education

	Training	*Education*
Focus	Details and specific aspects of the software	Principles, concepts, and techniques, and their application to the business
Emphasis	Technical	Managerial
Will determine	How you operate your system	How well you manage the business

Principles, concepts, and techniques relate to the defined body of knowledge that we call Enterprise Resource Planning—the various functions, how they tie together, the need for feedback, the details of how planned orders are created, how the available-to-promise quantity is calculated, the mechanics of the dispatch list, and so forth.

The next level involves the application of those principles, concepts, and techniques into the individual company. It gets at the details of how we're going to make this set of tools work for us.

Training is not synonymous with education. Rather, it's a subset of education. Training is heavily software dependent, involving things like how to interpret the master schedule screens, what keys to hit to release a production order, how to record an inventory transaction, and so on. (See Figure 7-5.) Training focuses on how to run the software; education is about how to run the business.

A key point: Don't train before you educate. People need to know *what* and *why* before they're taught *how*. Education should occur either prior to, or simultaneously with the training.

The series of business meetings should function at all three levels. However, it may not be possible to do all of the training at this point. This would be so if, for example, new software were required but not yet selected. In such a case, the software aspects of training must be done later, after the new software package had been chosen. (For you folks who have already installed an ES, these business meetings can also help to identify changes in the ES configuration—switch settings—required to support the ERP processes.) In any case, don't delay education while waiting for all the training materials to become available. See Figure 7-6 for an outline of a typical session.

Figure 7-6
Typical Agenda for a Business Meeting

1. Fact transfer

2. Summary of key points

3. Discussion of application

4. Reach consensus

5. Identify assignments

6. Document decisions

Figure 7-7
Business Meeting Time Allocation

Activity	Purpose	Ratio of Total Time Spent
Presentation of educational materials	Fact transfer	¼
Discussion	Behavior change	¾

The overall agenda for these business meetings needs to be provided by the educational materials themselves. A variety of media are possible candidates. Very large companies tend to develop their own video and printed matter, drawn from what they learned in the outsider-led classes. Most other companies will acquire commercially available educational material.

Some of the educational material presented to the future (and rapidly developing) team of experts will contain specific topics, which are new to them. However, much of it should be material to which they've already been exposed. These are key people, and they'll need to hear a number of things more than once. (See criterion 5.)

The heart of these business meetings is that approximately three-fourths of the time is devoted to discussion. This is where the key people focus on application, on how the tools of ERP will be used within the company to run the business. (See Figure 7-7.)

Let's get our minds completely out of implementing ERP for a moment, and talk about a business meeting to explore a specific problem. Let's say our company is experiencing a 10 percent sales decrease in the western region. What's the first thing we'd cover in the meeting? Probably, the person leading the meeting would present the background data, in some degree of detail (fact transfer). Then, he or she would condense the detail into the one or several most important points (summary of key points). Next, the group would explore alternative solutions to the problem, and identify which of the company's resources could be applied to solve the problem of the sales decline (discussion on application). The group would strive for agreement, ideally but not necessarily unanimous, as to the best course of action (reach consensus). Then they'd lay out the game plan and decide who's going to do what (identify assignments). One of the assignments would be for one or more of the attendees to write up the decisions and action plan developed at the meeting (document decisions).

The business meetings for ERP implementation are much the same. The educational materials cover the fact transfer, enabling the meeting leaders to function effectively without having to become proficient classroom instructors. The meeting leader, who is not expected to know everything, does summarize the key points, and helps to focus the group toward the important areas to be discussed: How are we going to apply these specific tools to run the business better? Consensus is an important goal in these sessions, the outcome of which is often uncertain going in. Frequently, specific assignments are made to work on an issue that surfaced in the meeting. To us, all of this sounds a lot more like the business meeting to solve the sales problem than it does a training session.

It's in these business meetings where, for example, Bill, the operations manager, might say: "Okay, I understand about plant scheduling." [Author's note: He understands the principles, concepts and techniques.] "But how are we going to make it work back in department 15? Man, that's a whole different world back there."

The operations manager in this case, and the company in a larger sense, need an answer. How are we going to schedule department 15 using the tools contained within ERP? Perhaps the answer can be obtained right in the same session, following some discussion. Perhaps it needs some research, and the answer might not be forthcoming until the following week. Perhaps it's a very sticky issue. Input from the consultant may be sought, either at his next visit or via telephone. Alternatively, a spin-off task force may be required, perhaps with the production manager as the leader. This is the right way to "design the system."

It can be thought of as bulletproofing ERP. People need to have opportunities to "take potshots" at ERP, to try to shoot holes in it. That's what the production manager just did. Giving people answers that make sense helps to bulletproof ERP. Making necessary changes to how the system will be used is further bulletproofing. Bulletproofing isn't instantaneous. It's not like turning on a light switch. It's a gradual process, the result of responding to people's questions and being sensitive to their concerns.

Bulletproofing doesn't happen if answers to questions aren't valid or if essential changes are not recognized. In that case, ERP has just had a hole shot in it. Holes in ERP mean that ownership won't take place, and, therefore, behavior change won't happen. Most people need to:

- Understand it.

- Think about it.

- Talk to each other about it.

- Ask questions about it (take potshots) and get answers.

- Hear their peers ask questions about it (take potshots), and get answers.

- See how it will help them and help the company before they'll willingly and enthusiastically change the way they do their jobs.

A word about enthusiasm (see criterion 8). During this series of business meetings, enthusiasm should noticeably start to build. Enthusiasm is the visual signal that the change process is happening. If that signal isn't forthcoming, then the change process is probably not happening. Stop right there. Fix what's not being done properly before moving forward.

Who's the best person to run these business meetings for the team of experts? Probably the project leader, at the outset. He or she has more time to devote to getting ready to lead each meeting and subsequently getting answers to questions. Some companies have varied this approach somewhat, with fine results. What they've done is to have the project leader initially run the meetings, lead the discussions, and so on. However, after several weeks, as enthusiasm noticeably starts to build, the meetings can start to be run by others in the group. This gets the managers accustomed to running these kinds of meetings before they start leading the sessions for their own departments.

The important step of documenting decisions is often handled by the project leader, and we'll discuss that more in Chapter 9 when we cover the defining of the demand management, planning, and scheduling processes.

(For a recap of what we've covered for the team of experts, see Figure 7-8.)

Reach the Critical Mass

Here's where the company begins to leverage on the time invested in creating the team of experts. The next step is for the experts to reach the critical mass, the majority of people within the company who become knowledgeable and enthusiastic about ERP and who see the need and benefits from changing the way they do their jobs.

How is this accomplished? Very simply, by a series of business meetings. These meetings are conducted by the members of the team of experts (see criterion 6) for all the people within their respective departments (see criteria 2 and 4). (Figure 7-9 depicts this process graphically.)

All the other people in the company? Yes. Including top management? Definitely. Even though they went to an outsider-led class on ERP? Yes, indeed, for a number of reasons, but primarily because for ERP to succeed, they will need to change the way they do their jobs in some important ways. They will need to manage the business differently than they have in the past. Attending a one or two-day outsider-led class on ERP is rarely sufficient to make possible that kind of behavior change on a permanent basis.

Top management people, like everyone else, need repetition and reinforcement. They need to hear some things more than once (criterion 5). They need to get deeper into application than they were able to in the outsider-led classes, particularly in the areas of Sales &

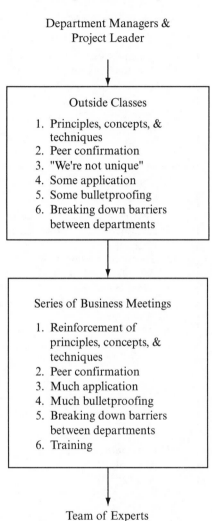

Figure 7-8

Creating the Team of Experts

Department Managers &
Project Leader

Outside Classes

1. Principles, concepts, &
   techniques
2. Peer confirmation
3. "We're not unique"
4. Some application
5. Some bulletproofing
6. Breaking down barriers
   between departments

Series of Business Meetings

1. Reinforcement of
   principles, concepts, &
   techniques
2. Peer confirmation
3. Much application
4. Much bulletproofing
5. Breaking down barriers
   between departments
6. Training

Team of Experts

Operations Planning, Rough-Cut Capacity Planning, and master scheduling. It's essential that they see how these tools will work within the company (criterion 8). Additionally, they need to lead by example (criterion 1).

This series of business meetings, for the top management group

Figure 7-9

Creating the Critical Mass

Department Managers &
Project Leader

↓

Outside Classes

1. Principles, concepts, & techniques
2. Peer confirmation
3. "We're not unique"
4. Some application
5. Some bulletproofing
6. Breaking down barriers between
   departments

↓

Series of Business Meetings

1. Reinforcement of principles, concepts,
   & techniques
2. Peer confirmation
3. Much application
4. Much bulletproofing
5. Breaking down barriers between
   departments
6. Training

Team of Experts

↓

Series of Business Meetings

**All
the People
in the
Company** →

1. Principles, concepts, & techniques
2. Peer confirmation
3. Application
4. Bulletproofing
5. Breaking down barriers between
   departments
6. Training

↓

**Critical Mass of enthusiastic
and MRP II knowledgeable people,
ready and willing to change the way
they do their jobs**

and others, is very similar to those for the team of experts. The same format is employed (about one-quarter fact transfer, three-quarters discussion and decisions); and the duration of these meetings generally should be about one and a half to two hours. These also are decision-making meetings, and those decisions need to be documented and communicated. Some may trigger revisions to the sales, logistics, and manufacturing process definitions created in the business meetings for the team of experts.

A key difference is with frequency. The meetings for the team of experts are normally held every day because there's urgency to get these folks up to speed. Only then can they nail down the details of how ERP will be used within the company and begin to spread the word. An accelerated schedule like this isn't necessary or desirable for the rest of the people. It's better for them to meet about once per week, learn some new things, discuss them with their coworkers (criterion 7), shoot some bullets at ERP, get some answers, and so forth. Then they go back to their jobs, think about what they learned, and match it up to what they're currently doing. As they're doing their jobs during the rest of the week, they can shoot some more bullets (mental, not verbal) at ERP. In some cases, they can do their own bulletproofing, internally, as they mentally formulate the solution to the problem that just occurred to them. In other cases, not so. They think of the problem but not the solution.

Hence, the first agenda item for each business meeting should be Questions and Answers from the Last Meeting. This includes answers to questions raised but unanswered at the last week's session and also questions that occurred to people during the week. Here, also, they must be given an answer, either right away or at a subsequent session or as the result of a larger effort involving a spin-off task force.

Certain groups don't need to meet nearly as often as once per week. One good example is the direct production associates. A few sessions of about one hour each, spread over some months, has been shown to work very well (criterion 4). These people need to know about ERP and how it'll affect them and the way they do their jobs. However, in most companies, they simply don't need to know as much about ERP as others.

When should these sessions take place? We favor a "just-in-time" kind of approach here. For a given group, do the education (conduct the business meetings) shortly before that particular function will be implemented. For example, top management's turn will come early, since they'll be involved in implementing Sales & Operations Planning. Ditto for Sales & Marketing. Purchasing will come just a bit later. Production associates will get involved later still, since the plant scheduling piece of ERP gets implemented later rather than sooner.

The principle of need-to-know is a key element in developing an internal education program to support this series of business meetings. Need-to-know operates at two levels: company characteristics and job functions.

Company characteristics involve such things as having make-to-stock products, make-to-order products with many options, custom engineered products, or a distribution network for finished goods, all of which are addressed by the defined body of knowledge called ERP. The inside education program needs to be sensitive to these characteristics. There are few things worse than forcing people to learn a solution to a problem they don't have. What is worse is not giving them the solution to a problem they do have.

The second element of need-to-know reflects the different functions within a company, which call for different depths of education and discussion. This gets us back to reinforcement—the concept that people need to hear the important things more than once. Well, what's very important to people in one department may be less so to those in another department.

For example, the vice president of marketing does not need to know a great deal about the mechanics of generating the supplier schedule. She does need to know that this tool exists, that it's valid, and that it's derived via a rack-and-pinion relationship from Material Requirements Planning, the master schedule, and the Sales & Operations Plan.

However, the plant supervisors and plant schedulers need to know more about the supplier schedules than the VP of marketing. This is because they're dependent on availability of purchased material to support their plant schedules, and they need the confidence to know that the tool being used is valid. Conversely, the VP of marketing and other executives will need to know more about Sales & Operations Planning than the people on the plant floor. Sales & Operations Planning is their responsibility; it's their part of the ship (we'll cover this important tool in the next chapter).

The supplier schedulers and buyers need to know more about the supplier schedule than the plant supervisors. It's their tool; they'll be living with it every day. They'll need more education, more discussion, more bulletproofing on this topic than anyone else.

One last point regarding the principle of need-to-know: The educational materials must lend themselves to need-to-know. They must be comprehensive and detailed. Providing only overview material can frustrate the people; their reaction will most likely be: "Where's the beef?" The materials should be tailored to reflect company characteristics and to support the differing levels of depth required by the various departments and job functions.

How does one know if it's working, this process of change? The test to apply as the sessions proceed is *enthusiasm* (criterion 8). If enthusiasm, teamwork, a sense of mission, and a sense of ownership are not visibly increasing during this process, then stop the process and fix it. Ask: "What's missing? What's not being done properly? Which of the eight criteria are being violated? Is bulletproofing working, or are people *not* getting answers?" (That means holes in ERP, and not many people want to get aboard a leaking ship.)

A MINI CASE STUDY

Company CS (the name has been disguised to protect the successful) sent about a dozen of its senior executives through an outsider-led top management class on ERP. All but one became convinced that ERP was essential for the continued growth and prosperity of the business because it would enable them to solve many of their problems with customer service, productivity, and high inventory levels.

The one exception was the CEO. His response after attending was less than completely enthusiastic. He was not anti-ERP, but rather he was lukewarm. This caused great concern to Sam, the project leader, who said the following to one of your friendly authors.

SAM: "I'm really concerned about our CEO. He's very neutral toward ERP. With that mind-set, I don't think we can succeed."

FRIENDLY AUTHOR (FA): "I think you're right. What do you plan to do about it?"

SAM: "We're going to start the ERP business meetings for top management next month. If that doesn't turn our CEO around, I'm going to recommend that we pull the plug on the entire project."

FA: "Sam, I don't think it'll come to that. But if it does, I'll back you up 100 percent."

Company CS started the series of ERP business meetings for its top management, with the CEO in attendance. After a half dozen or so sessions, the lukewarm CEO got the fire lit. He was able to see that ERP, implemented properly, could enable him and his people to solve many of their nagging problems. He did, among other things, the following:

1. Sent a memo to each one of the nine plant managers, directing them to send him a report each week listing any unauthorized absences from the ERP business meetings.

2. He then sent a personal letter to each person so identified. He expressed his concern over their unauthorized absence, asked them to attend the makeup session as soon as possible, and to do everything they could to avoid missing future sessions.

Needless to say, people receiving such a letter would be very unlikely to miss future sessions. So would their fellow buyers and salespeople and schedulers, because the word quickly got around.

Within a few years, all nine of company CS's divisions were operating at a Class A level. The key to their success—education. They did it right.

- They educated virtually everyone in the company.

- They educated from top to bottom, from the CEO to the production associates on the plant floors.

- They educated using both outsider-led and insider-led sessions. (Note: It wasn't until *insider-led* education that the CEO really got on board. Why? We're not sure. One cause could be the need for reinforcement, the need to hear some things more than once. Or perhaps it was getting down to specifics. Some folks really can't get the fire lit until they can see in specific terms how ERP's going to be used in the company.)

- Education became mandatory, thanks to the CEO and the repeated education he received. Consequently, success became mandatory. And succeed they did.

Q & A WITH THE AUTHORS

TOM: Mike, if you had it to do all over again, would you do more or less education on ERP during your implementation?

MIKE: More! More! And then some more! I would have developed more internal materials and teachers early on, and then made the business units throw me out when they had enough. The particular focus would have been on corporate and business unit leaders. We spent too much time struggling to keep various leaders involved and dedicated to the project. With more education, we wouldn't have had to do nearly as much of that.

IMPLEMENTERS' CHECKLIST

Function: Initial Education

Task	Complete Yes	No
1. All members of executive steering committee, including general manager, attend outsider-led ERP class.	____	____
2. All members of project team attend outsider-led ERP class.	____	____
3. Series of insider-led business meetings conducted for operating managers, completing the total immersion process and resulting in the team of experts.	____	____
4. Series of business meetings conducted by the team of experts for all persons within the company, including the general manager and staff.	____	____
5. Enthusiasm, teamwork, and a sense of ownership becoming visible throughout the company.	____	____

Chapter 8

Sales & Operations Planning

Sales & Operations Planning—called "top management's handle on the business" as we saw in Chapter 2—is an essential part of ERP. In fact, it may be *the most important element* of all. ERP simply won't work well without it.

One of the major reasons for ERP's poor success rate is that many companies don't include Sales & Operations Planning (S&OP) in their ERP implementation. ERP efforts that exclude S&OP are preordained to less than total success. As we said earlier, ERP is often viewed as a software project; the software is the center of the implementation universe. Well, if the chosen software vendor's offerings do not include support for S&OP (which is the norm), it never gets mentioned. Thus, it doesn't get implemented. Thus, the implementation is not highly successful.

The moral of this story: Neglect Sales & Operations Planning at your peril.

Because you probably won't read about S&OP in your software vendor's literature, we need to take a moment now and describe the process before we talk about how to implement it. A recent book on Sales & Operations Planning[i] points out that one of S&OP's main missions "is to balance demand and supply—at the *volume* level." Volume refers to rates—overall rates of sales, rates of production, aggregate inventories, and order backlogs. Companies have found that when they do a good job of planning and replanning volume—rates and levels—then problems with *mix*—individual products and

165

Figure 8-1

ERP PROVEN PATH

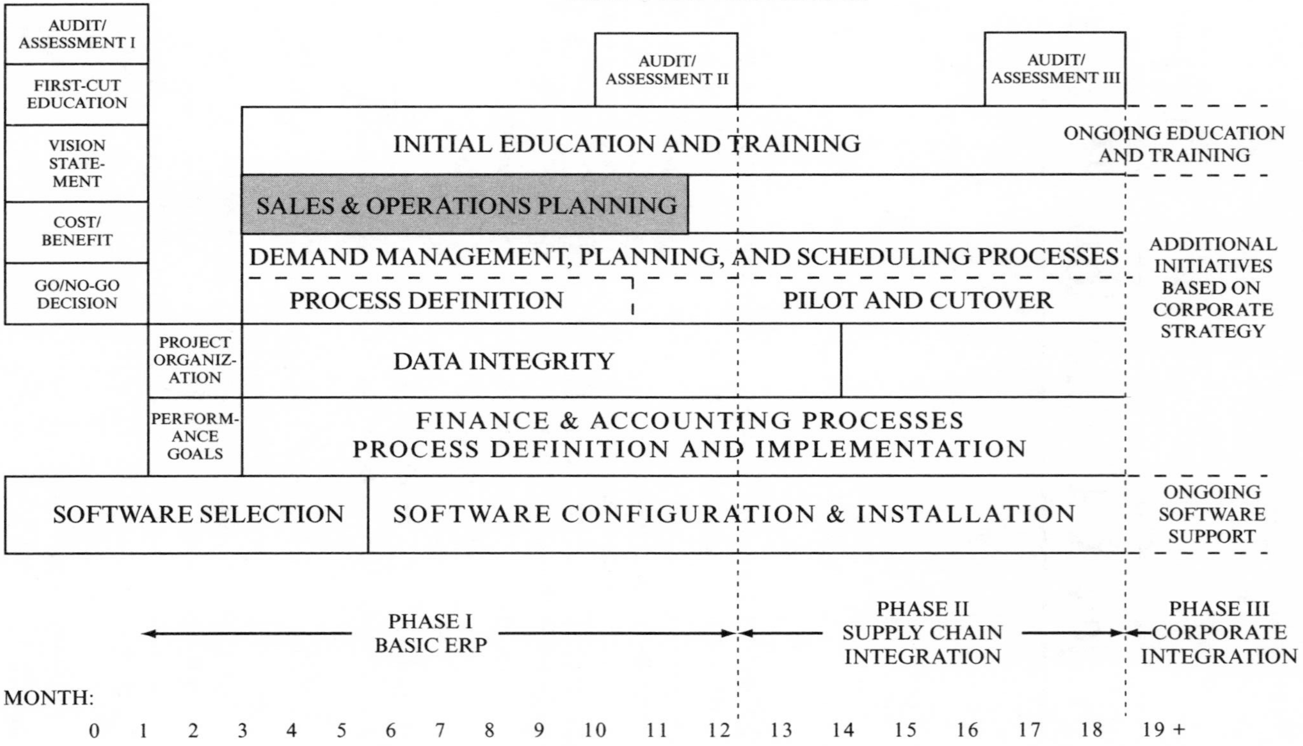

| | AUDIT/ ASSESSMENT I | | | | | | | | | | | | | | | | | | | |
| FIRST-CUT EDUCATION | | | | | | | | | | | | | | | | | | | | |

AUDIT/ASSESSMENT II

AUDIT/ASSESSMENT III

INITIAL EDUCATION AND TRAINING

ONGOING EDUCATION AND TRAINING

VISION STATE-MENT

COST/ BENEFIT

GO/NO-GO DECISION

SALES & OPERATIONS PLANNING

DEMAND MANAGEMENT, PLANNING, AND SCHEDULING PROCESSES

ADDITIONAL INITIATIVES BASED ON CORPORATE STRATEGY

PROCESS DEFINITION

PILOT AND CUTOVER

PROJECT ORGANIZ-ATION

DATA INTEGRITY

PERFORM-ANCE GOALS

FINANCE & ACCOUNTING PROCESSES

PROCESS DEFINITION AND IMPLEMENTATION

SOFTWARE SELECTION

SOFTWARE CONFIGURATION & INSTALLATION

ONGOING SOFTWARE SUPPORT

PHASE I
BASIC ERP

PHASE II
SUPPLY CHAIN INTEGRATION

PHASE III
CORPORATE INTEGRATION

MONTH:

0   1   2   3   4   5   6   7   8   9   10   11   12   13   14   15   16   17   18   19 +

orders—become less difficult. Companies have found they can ship better, ship more quickly, and do it with less inventory.

Sales & Operations Planning does the following:

It helps to keep demand and supply in balance—at the aggregate, volume level.

It occurs on a monthly cycle.

It operates in both units and dollars.

It is cross-functional—involving general management, sales, operations, finance, and product development.

It occurs at multiple levels within the company, up to and including the executive in charge of the business unit—the person we're calling the general manager.

It links the company's strategic plans and business plan to its detailed processes—the order entry, master scheduling, plant scheduling, and purchasing tools it uses to run the business on a week-to-week, day-to-day, and hour-to-hour basis.

Used properly, S&OP enables the company's managers to view the business holistically and gives them a window into the future.

WHERE DOES IT FIT?

At this point, it may be helpful to look at Figure 8-2, which depicts the structure of the resource planning process. Several points are worthy of our attention:

The horizontal dotted line indicates that Strategic Planning and Business Planning are not integral parts of the overall resource planning process. Rather, they are important drivers into the process.

Sales & Operations Planning forms an essential *linkage,* tying the Strategic and Business Plans together with the Master Scheduling function. It's the Master Schedule that serves as the source of customer order promising and drives all of the "downstream" schedules for the plants and the suppliers.

Figure 8-2
ENTERPRISE RESOURCE PLANNING

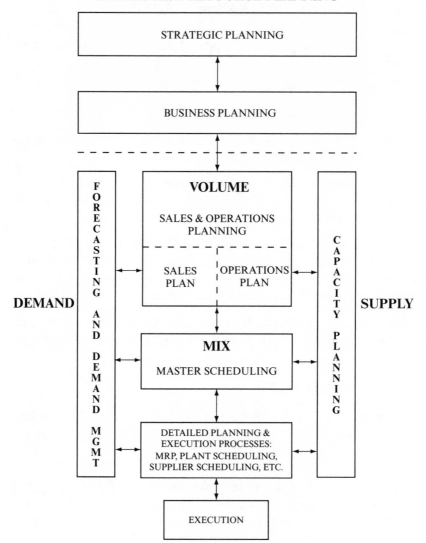

Thus another important mission for S&OP is to integrate the planning process. In companies without S&OP, there is frequently a disconnect between the Business Plan and the Master Schedule. In other words, the plans that top management has authorized are not connected to the plans and schedules that drive day-to-day activities on the plant floor, the receiving dock, and most important, the shipping dock. That is why some companies frequently get unpleasant "surprises" late in the fiscal year.

WHY IS TOP MANAGEMENT NECESSARY?

Saying it another way, does the boss really need to be involved with S&OP and, if so, why? Well, we believe that active, involved leadership and participation by the head of the business unit is essential for S&OP to work anywhere near its full potential. The two most important reasons are stewardship and leadership.

Many of the decisions made in S&OP affect the Business Plan—the financial plan for the current year, and top management "owns" that Business Plan. They have a stewardship responsibility for it, and only they can make decisions to change it. When the Business Plan is not changed to reflect the new Sales & Operations Plan, there's a disconnect between the financial numbers top management is expecting and the forecasts and production plans being used to operate the business. "Best in class" performance in this area means that the business is managed—at all levels—using one and only one set of numbers.

Regarding leadership, participation by the head of the business makes a strong statement that S&OP is the process being used to manage these highly important activities: integrating operational and financial planning, balancing demand and supply, and enhancing customer service. This encourages other people throughout the organization to do their part in supporting the process. Without such leadership by senior management, participation in the S&OP process is often viewed as optional, with the result that over time, the process erodes down to nothing.

Executive participation shouldn't be a problem, because so relatively little of the executive's time is required. We're talking about one meeting per month, lasting for two hours or less. This event, called the Executive Sales & Operations Planning meeting, can often replace several other meetings, thus resulting in a net reduction in meeting time. For general managers, preparation time is zero. For members of their staff, some preparation may be helpful—mainly in the form of briefings by their people—to enable the necessary sign-offs to take place.

So how can something so productive require so little time? Well, most of the heavy lifting is done in earlier steps in the process: Middle-management people update the forecast, aggregate the data into product family groupings, identify capacity constraints and raw material problems, and formulate the recommendations to be presented in the top management meeting.

One last caveat: If your S&OP process does not include the general manager and most of his or her staff, then *you're really not doing Sales & Operations Planning.* You may think you're doing S&OP; you may call it S&OP; you may have a nice process that yields some positive results through inter-departmental communication. But you will not be realizing anything close to the benefits that come from effective S&OP.

THE MONTHLY S&OP PROCESS

The essence of S&OP is decision-making. For each product family, a decision is made on the basis of recent history, recommendations from middle management, and the executive team's knowledge of business conditions. The decision can be:

change the Sales Plan,

change the Operations Plan,

change the inventory/backlog plan, or

none of the above: the current plans are okay.

The decisions form the agreed-upon, authorized plans by the general manager, other executives in charge of various parts of the business, and other members of the executive S&OP team. These are documented and disseminated throughout the organization. They form the overall game plan for Sales, Operations, Finance, and Product Development. (New product plans are reviewed within S&OP in terms of

Figure 8-3

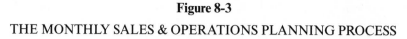

THE MONTHLY SALES & OPERATIONS PLANNING PROCESS

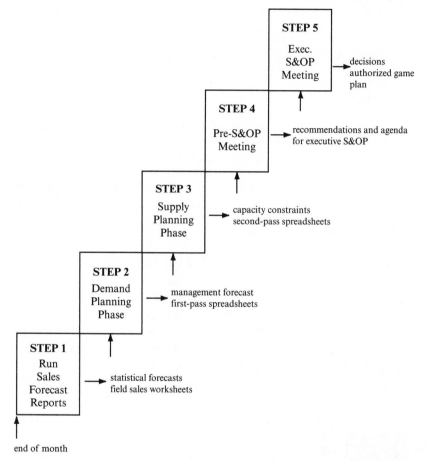

their impact on the demand and supply picture.) These groups break down the aggregate plans from S&OP into the necessary level of detail: individual products, customers, regions, plants, and materials.

Sales & Operations Planning, however, is not a single event that occurs in a two-hour executive S&OP meeting each month. Rather, preliminary work begins shortly after month's end and continues for some days. The steps involve middle management and some others throughout the company (see Figure 8-3). They include:

- updating the Sales Forecast;

- reviewing the impact of changes on the Operations Plan, and determining whether adequate capacity and material will be available to support them;

- identifying alternatives where problems exist;

- identifying variances to the Business Plan (budget) and potential solutions;

- formulating agreed-upon recommendations for top management regarding overall changes to the plans, and identifying areas of disagreement where consensus is not possible; and

- communicating this information to top management with sufficient time for them to review it prior to the executive S&OP meeting.

Thanks to the work that's gone before, the executive S&OP meeting should not take a long time—two hours or less is the norm with companies that do this well. The net result of S&OP for the top management group should be less time in meetings, more productivity in their decision-making processes, and a higher quality of work life. And most of the middle-management people involved in the earlier S&OP steps will experience the same benefits.

THE S&OP IMPLEMENTATION STEPS

The S&OP process itself, and the steps in involved in implementing it, are straightforward. But there's a paradox here: It is *difficult* to implement S&OP successfully. This is because it's a new process for the company; new processes mean change; and change, in this context, means people changing some aspects of how they do their jobs.

Top management people are typically very busy and thus have a low tolerance for spending time on unproductive activities. Progress must be made quickly and consistently. When that happens, the implementation project can proceed to a successful conclusion.

Here's another paradox. Why does something that involves relatively few people take six or eight months to implement? It's because of the nature of the S&OP process. It occurs on a monthly cycle. During implementation, incremental experience and expertise are gained only once each month.

The good news: For almost all of the companies we've observed implementing S&OP, benefits come sooner than six months. The reason lies in S&OP's ability to provide that window into the future we mentioned earlier. Almost invariably, by about month two or three, people are able to see things that they wouldn't have without S&OP. It's common to hear comments like, "Golly. If we weren't doing this, we'd have had a big problem four months from now on Medium Widgets." Being able to get a better focus on the future means that problems can be avoided by taking early corrective action.

Here are the main steps involved in implementing S&OP as part of an ERP implementation:

1. Confirm/modify sales forecasting processes. The company's processes for forecasting future demand need to be reviewed and, if necessary, modified to support S&OP. One important requirement here: "single-number forecasts." This means that one and only one forecast is recognized as official, and that's the one authorized by senior sales and marketing department management. No longer is it okay to have one forecast coming from the Sales Department, one from Marketing, and—oh yeah—there's a third one that Finance uses. That won't work in S&OP. What will work is a single-number forecast.

2. Establish product families and subfamilies. Families should be chosen based on what works best for the sales and marketing functions, to make their forecasting job as easy as possible. The operations view may require an entirely different arrangement, typically called "resources" as opposed to families. The process of rough-cut capacity planning "translates" the information from product families to resources, so that operations people can identify bottlenecks, future overload and under load conditions.

A good number of families, for the monthly top management review, is around a half dozen to a dozen. Many companies make effective use of subfamilies in their pre-S&OP steps, and then aggregate up to the family level for the executive S&OP meeting.

3. Develop S&OP spreadsheet. S&OP is all about decision-making, and the spreadsheets contain the facts upon which the decisions are made. So you'll have to have S&OP spreadsheets and that'll probably be a do-it-yourself project.

There are two chances that your ERP software vendor will provide you with the capability to generate S&OP spreadsheets: slim and none. As we write these words, we're not aware of any really effective S&OP modules within Enterprise Software packages. Figure on doing this yourselves, most probably using spreadsheet software. And be prepared to modify your early layouts frequently as you go through the first six months of operating S&OP.

4. Develop S&OP policy. Here and elsewhere in this book, we'll recommend the creation of a few bedrock policies, necessary for running the business with these new processes. The S&OP policy needs to spell out the objectives of the company's S&OP process, the steps in the process, the participants in each step, and the actions to be taken at each step. We recommend that this document be signed by the general manager and other individuals as appropriate. The S&OP policy should address issues such as who's accountable, who attends the S&OP meetings, who develops the data, frequency of the meetings, meeting content, guidelines for making changes to the S&OP, product families, and so forth.

5. Pilot one or two families. We'll talk more about the need for pilot runs later. For now, suffice it to say that we're big believers in them and recommend them strongly for the non-finance and accounting aspects of implementation. For S&OP, the main reason to do a pilot is, quite simply, that trying to do all families right out of the gate is overwhelming.

Which family should you pick, the hardest one or the easiest? Here we opt for the middle of the road. Don't pick the most complicated or trickiest product family, because you might have a really tough time getting it off the ground. Keep in mind that the main mission in this early stage is not to get operational results but rather to implement a process and get it working. On the other hand, we'd be reluctant to pick a family that represents, say, less than two percent of the total business. It just doesn't have enough impact to get people excited.

A note regarding timing: Try to get the S&OP pilot up and running within 90 days after getting started. Doing so can be significant; it's an early win. It shows that visible progress is being made; often operational benefits are realized from the S&OP pilot; top management is active and engaged in the most important part of S&OP; and all of this whets people's appetites for more effort and more progress across the entire ERP implementation.

6. *Develop capacity reports.* Most often, a company's resources (plants, departments, etc.) don't line up exactly with its product families. In these cases, it's necessary to collate all of the production loads from the various families into resource displays. These show overloads and underloads, from which the operations people can make adjustments to supply plans in order to achieve a reasonable, effective plan.

7. *Bring all families onto S&OP.* After the pilot is completed successfully, most companies will add three or four families per month for the next several months until all families are on the process. Ideally this will happen within 90 days after bringing up the pilot. Another early win.

8. *Add supply planning, financial planning, and new product introduction to the S&OP process.* These functions typically can't operate well until all of the product families are on S&OP. For example, if a given production department produces for all nine product families, then it won't be possible to get a full picture of that department's workload until all families have been added.

Here are several things to keep in mind regarding S&OP implementation. First, even though the logic of S&OP is simple, implementing it is not. Implementing it requires people to make changes—to do some aspects of their jobs differently—up to and including the senior executive in charge of the business.

Second, because of the monthly cycle, it will take about eight months to fully implement basic S&OP. Benefits, however, will start to come much sooner.

Third, in most companies people should be prepared to operate with a higher degree of accountability than before. One of the important elements of S&OP is the clarity of its metrics: It focuses on actual performance to the plan. Thus, given a single-number forecast, it's easy to see how the commercial side of the business (Sales & Marketing) did in hitting their agreed-upon plan. It's the same for Operations, given one single plan for the supply of product: What was the actual production versus the committed-to production plan? Metrics, and the resultant accountability, are a very important benefit of S&OP.

S&OP ACROSS THE BOARD

Two key points apply here:

Implementing S&OP involves relatively few people, relatively little money, and not much time.

S&OP can be operated on a "stand-alone" basis. It doesn't need all of the other ERP pieces in place to function well. (It will function even better when they're all there.)

Therefore, S&OP can readily be implemented across the entire business unit—even though *ERP is not being implemented across the board.* This would be the case in a phased multiplant implementation as we saw in Chapter 3, or in a Quick-Slice implementation (Chapters 13 and 14).

Well, what about a company that's installing its Enterprise Software (ES) first and deferring ERP until later, because of resource constraints? This company is certainly a candidate to implement S&OP during its ES installation. Here's why: It has probably deferred the implementation of ERP business processes because of resource constraints. The workload to do both ES and ERP simultaneously is, as we said, daunting. But . . . S&OP doesn't use lots of resources and it can function stand-alone. Thus the "ES-now-ERP-later" company may be well served by implementing S&OP early, gaining benefits and experience that will stand it in good stead when it gets into the ERP implementation.

Jerry Clement, of the Oliver Wight organization: "You should do Sales & Operations Planning in a full ERP/ES implementation, in an ERP only implementation, and in an ES only installation. S&OP has low dependence on software and it pays big returns. The Nike® approach applies here: Just do it."

Q & A WITH THE AUTHORS

MIKE: Did you ever have a general manager or CEO tell you that they were already "doing S&OP" when in fact they were doing only some of the pieces?

TOM: Yeah, more than once. My response has been: "I'll get back to you." Then I check with key people to find out what's really going on. What I've invariably found is that there really isn't an agreed-upon forecast; that Sales and Marketing haven't had the opportunity to review, and thus buy into, the production plan; Finance hasn't seen the resulting inventory plan, much less okayed it. Then I go back to the general manager and talk about harmonizing demand and supply, cross-functional decision-making, one set of numbers to run the business, and enhanced teamwork and cooperation within upper and middle management. That almost always does the job.

NOTE

[i] *Sales & Operations Planning: The How-to Handbook,* 1999, Thomas F. Wallace, T. F. Wallace & Company, Cincinnati, Ohio.

IMPLEMENTERS' CHECKLIST

Function: Sales & Operations Planning

	Complete	
Task	Yes	No
1. Sales forecasting processes reviewed and modified as necessary.	———	———
2. Product families and subfamilies identified.	———	———
3. Develop S&OP policy and report formats.	———	———
4. Pilot family(s) selected.	———	———
5. Pilot successfully completed.	———	———
6. Supply (capacity) planning initiated.	———	———
7. S&OP processes expanded to include all families, resources, financial integration, and new products.	———	———

Chapter 9

Process Definition

This step ensures that the implementation will be consistent with the vision statement. It spells out the new processes by which the company will be managed. It adds essential detail to the vision statement and creates the detailed schedule necessary for effective project management. As shown in Figure 9-1, this step consists of two elements: one is to define processes for demand management, planning, and scheduling while the other element addresses the finance and accounting side. Their implementation is quite different, so we need to look at them separately. Let's start with the operational processes.

DEFINING DEMAND MANAGEMENT, PLANNING, AND SCHEDULING PROCESSES

This is where people spell out the details of how the business will be run. It answers questions such as:

Where do we meet the customer today and should we be doing it differently? Should we be design-to-order, make-to-order, finish-to-order, or make-to-stock? Would a change here make us more competitive in the marketplace?

How are we going to promise customer orders? Will the people in inside sales have direct access to the available-to-promise information, and if not, how will they assign promised ship dates?

179

Figure 9-1

ERP PROVEN PATH

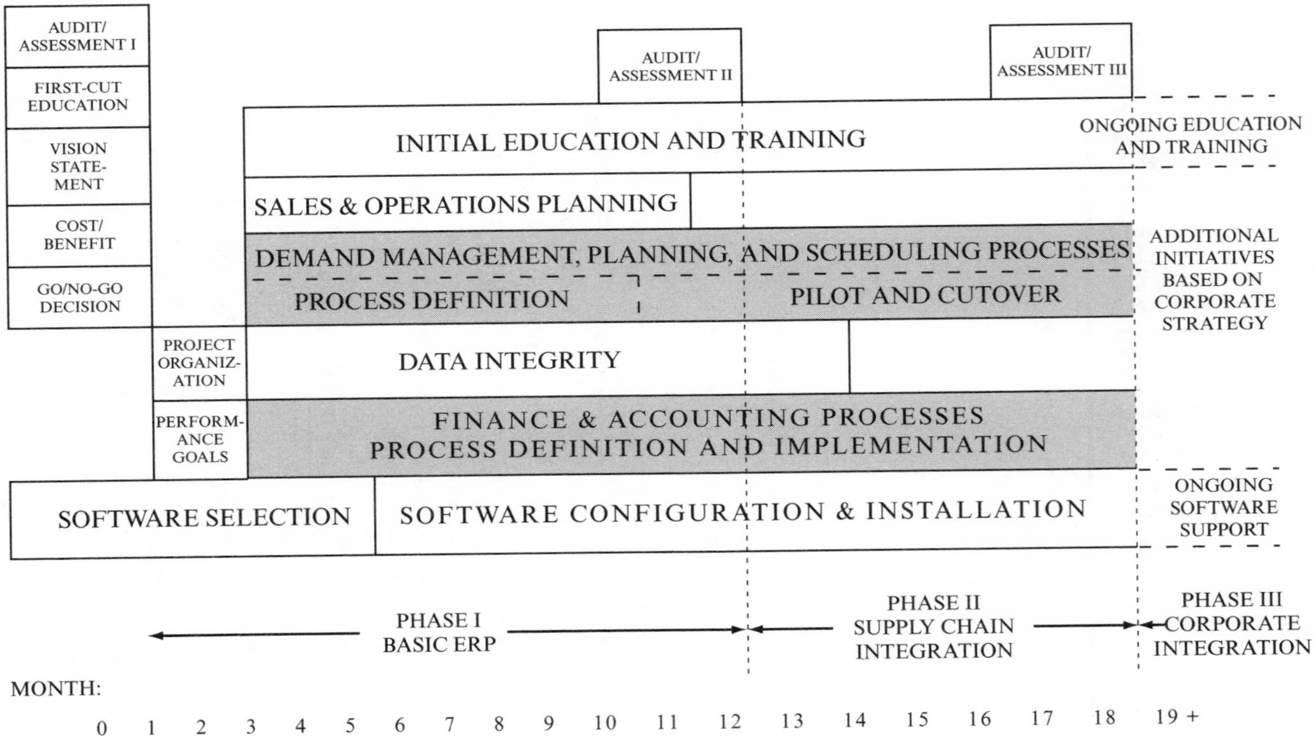

AUDIT/ASSESSMENT I

FIRST-CUT EDUCATION

VISION STATEMENT

COST/BENEFIT

GO/NO-GO DECISION

PROJECT ORGANIZATION

PERFORMANCE GOALS

SOFTWARE SELECTION

SOFTWARE CONFIGURATION & INSTALLATION

SALES & OPERATIONS PLANNING

INITIAL EDUCATION AND TRAINING

DEMAND MANAGEMENT, PLANNING, AND SCHEDULING PROCESSES
PROCESS DEFINITION

DATA INTEGRITY

PILOT AND CUTOVER

FINANCE & ACCOUNTING PROCESSES
PROCESS DEFINITION AND IMPLEMENTATION

AUDIT/ASSESSMENT II

AUDIT/ASSESSMENT III

ONGOING EDUCATION AND TRAINING

ADDITIONAL INITIATIVES BASED ON CORPORATE STRATEGY

ONGOING SOFTWARE SUPPORT

PHASE I
BASIC ERP

PHASE II
SUPPLY CHAIN INTEGRATION

PHASE III
CORPORATE INTEGRATION

MONTH:

0   1   2   3   4   5   6   7   8   9   10   11   12   13   14   15   16   17   18   19 +

Specifically, how will we communicate and collaborate with our supply chain partners—our customers, suppliers, and sister divisions—regarding their and our needs for product and material? What media will we use to send and receive schedules—the Internet, EDI, fax, phone, and/or U.S. mail?

We don't have branch warehouses, but we do have consignment inventories at our stocking reps. Will we need to do a form of Distribution Resource Planning (DRP) on those inventories? If so, who will be responsible for operating the DRP system: the Sales Department, Logistics, or someone else?

We understand supplier scheduling and how it works. But specifically, how will we do it with our overseas suppliers? And what about our sister divisions within the corporation from whom we buy material; will we provide them with supplier schedules or with something else?

Less than half of our manufacturing processes are job shop, and they're not very complex. Will we need to implement job plant oriented tools such as capacity requirements planning and plant floor control? Could we avoid having to implement those tools by creating cells and moving even closer to 100 percent flow?

This is an early task for project team people, with a little help from their friends on the steering committee. We've already discussed the forum for this step: the series of business meetings for the department heads covered in Chapter 7. On the Proven Path diagram, we break out this definition step separately to emphasize its importance. However, these detailed definitions are largely the output from the series of business meetings, perhaps with some additional refinement and improvements by the manager(s) involved. As a final step, the executive steering committee as a whole should review and authorize these definitions.

This step provides an important linkage function: It flows logically from audit/assessment I, from the vision statement, and from education, and it serves as a major input into the project schedule. It verifies that the details of the schedule—what actually will be done—are consistent with the vision statement. Figure 9-2, developed by Pete Skurla of the Oliver Wight organization, depicts this process.

Figure 9-2

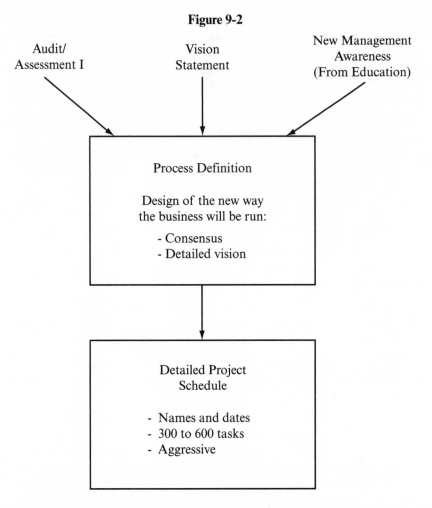

CREATING THE PROJECT SCHEDULE

The ERP project schedule is the basic control tool used to manage the project to a timely and successful conclusion. For a company-wide implementation, it needs to be:

- Aggressive but attainable (the approximately18-month schedule we've seen).

- Expressed in days or weeks, for at least the short-to-medium term. Months are too large a time frame for effective scheduling.

- Complete, covering all the tasks through the end of phase II (supply chain integration).

- In sufficient detail to manage the project effectively, but not so weighty it overwhelms the people using it. For an average-sized company or business unit, a project schedule with between 300 and 600 tasks could serve as an effective project management tool.

- Specific in assigning accountability. It should name names, not merely job titles and/or departments.

Creating the project schedule. There needs to be widespread buy-in to the project schedule, or it'll be just another piece of paper. It follows, then, that the people who develop the project schedule need to be the same people who'll be held accountable for sticking to it. They're primarily the department managers, and they're on the project team.

The project leader can help the department heads and other project team members develop the project schedule. He or she cannot, however, do it for them or dictate to them what will be done and when.

Here's one good way to approach it:

1. The project leader creates a first-cut schedule, containing some of those 300 to 600 tasks we just mentioned, plus major milestones. More on this in a moment.

2. This first-cut schedule is given to the project team members for their review and adjustment, as needed. During this process, they may wish to consult with their bosses, most of whom are on the executive steering committee.

3. The project team finalizes the project schedule.

4. The project leader presents the schedule to the executive steering committee for approval.

A process such as this helps to generate consensus, commitment, and willingness to work hard to hit the schedule. For a brief example of how a detailed project might look, please see Appendix C.

Maintaining the Project Schedule

Chris Gray has what we feel is an excellent approach to this task: "The potential problem is that with a 12–18 month project, you can't anticipate all the things that have to be done to hit the major milestones. What I tell my clients is that they should lay out the initial project schedule at the beginning of the project focusing on major milestones and the 'typical' 300 to 600 activities to support them. In the near term—90 days—they need to have lots of detail, while beyond that it may be more sketchy. As part of project management, it's essential that the 'near term' project plan be continually reviewed as time moves forward. The project team shouldn't see the project plan as cast in concrete (except the major milestones)—tasks should be added and changed as more information is available and as designs are fleshed out in other processes (initial education, task teamwork, etc.). The 90-day detailed schedule should be regenerated every 60 days or so."

Managing the Schedule—A Scenario

Consider the following case. This is a typical example of what could occur in practically any company implementing ERP using the Proven Path. The project leader (PL) is talking to the manufacturing engineering manager (ME), possibly in a project team meeting.

PL: "Mort, we've got a problem. Your department is three weeks late on the ERP project schedule, specifically routing accuracy."

ME: "I know we are, Pat, and I really don't know what to do about it. We've got all that new equipment back in department 15, and all of my people are tied up on that project."

[Authors' comment: This is possibly a case of conflict between priority number two—implement ERP, and priority number one—run the business.]

PL: "Can I help?"

ME: "Thanks, Pat, but I don't think so. I'll have to talk to my boss. What's the impact of us being behind?"

PL: "With this one, we're on the critical path for plant scheduling.

Each week late means a one-week delay in the overall implementation of ERP."

ME: "Ouch, that smarts. When's the next steering committee meeting?"

[Author's comment: Mort knows that Pat and the other members of the executive steering committee will be meeting shortly to review performance to the project schedule.]

PL: "Next Tuesday."

ME: "Okay. I'll get back to you."

PL: "Fine. Remember, if I can help in any way . . ."

At this point, from the project leader's point of view, the matter is well on the way to resolution. Here's why:

Mort, the manufacturing engineering manager, knows his department's schedule slippage will be reported at the executive steering committee meeting. (Pat, the project leader, has no choice but to report it; that's part of her job.)

Mort knows that his boss, the VP of manufacturing, will be in that meeting along with his boss's boss, the general manager.

Mort knows his boss doesn't like surprises of this type (who does?).

Unless Mort likes to play Russian roulette with his career, he'll get together with his boss prior to the steering committee meeting.

When they meet, they'll discuss how to get back on schedule, identifying alternatives, costs, and so on. They may be able to solve the problem themselves. On the other hand, the only possible solution may be expensive and thus, may require higher-level approval. In that case, the executive steering committee would be the appropriate forum.

Or, worst case, there may be no feasible solution at all. That's when it becomes bullet-biting time for the steering committee. That group, and only that group, can authorize a rescheduling of the ERP project.

One last point before leaving Pat and Mort. Note the project leader's approach: *"We* have a problem," "Can *I* help?", *"We're* on the critical path." One of Robert Townsend's comments on managers in general certainly applies to ERP project leaders—a large part of their job is to facilitate, to carry the water bucket[i] for the folks doing the work.

POLICIES

A few key policy statements are required for the successful operation of Enterprise Resource Planning. Five bedrock policies are the ones that address Sales & Operations Planning (discussed in Chapter 8), demand management, master scheduling, material planning, and engineering change.

The demand management policy focuses on the role of the demand manager and other key sales and marketing department people, their communications requirements to and from the master scheduler, ground rules for forecasting and promising customer orders, and performance measurements.

The master scheduling policy needs to define the roles of the master scheduler, time fences, who's authorized to change the schedule in time zones, allowable safety stock and/or hedges, feedback requirements, performance measurements, the fact that the master schedule must match the production plan and must fit within capacity constraints, and others as appropriate.

The material planning policy focuses on guidelines for allowable order quantities, use of safety stock and safety time, where to use scrap and shrinkage factors, ground rules for lead time compression, feedback required from purchasing and plant, feedback to master scheduler, performance measurements, and so on.

The engineering change policy should define the various categories of engineering change. Further, for each category, it needs to spell out who's responsible for initiating changes, for establishing effectivity dates, and for implementing and monitoring the changes. Also included here should be guidelines on new product introduction, communications between engineering and planning, performance measurements, and the like.

These four, along with the Sales & Operations Planning policy, are the basic policies that most companies need to operate ERP effectively, but others may be required for specific situations. Developing these policies is essential in the implementation process. The Oliver Wight ABCD Checklist is an excellent source for points to be included in these policies. This is another case where both the project team and executive steering committee need to be involved. The project team should:

1. Identify the required policies.

2. Create spin-off task forces to develop them.

3. Revise/approve the draft policies.

4. Forward the approved drafts to the executive steering committee.

The steering committee revises/approves the draft policy and the general manager signs it, to go into effect on a given date.

A warning! Make certain the policy does go into effect and is used to run the business. Don't make the mistake of generating pieces of paper with signatures on them (policy statements), claim they're in effect, but continue to run the business the same old way.[1]

Also, as you create these policies and use them, don't feel they're carved in granite. Be prepared to fine-tune the policies as you gain experience. You'll be getting better and better, and your policies will need to reflect this.

DEFINING AND IMPLEMENTING FINANCE AND ACCOUNTING PROCESSES

Mike Landrigan is the CFO at Innotek Inc. in Ft. Wayne, Indiana. Mike has Class A experience in with a prior employer, so he knows what this ERP stuff is all about. Here's Mike: "Accounting and Fi-

---

[1] Sometimes it's not possible to put all elements of the new policy into effect before the related new planning tool has been implemented. (Example: Perhaps master scheduling has not been implemented yet on all the products. Therefore the demand management and master scheduling policies can't be applied 100 percent to those products until they're added into master scheduling.) In these cases, the policies should spell out which pieces of it are effective at what times. As the new planning tools are implemented, the policy can be modified to remove these interim timing references.

nance personnel should be some of the biggest supporters of the ERP/ES implementation. This process makes their jobs easier. Using the S&OP process, you can tie financial implications to the forecasts and determine where the organization should be headed financially for the period, year, or even longer. . . . This information can be used to insure that you meet bank forecasts, growth forecasts, and increase the value of the organization. For most firms, if you can hit the estimate for sales, the departmental budgets generally fall in line so that profit goals are met. Use this process to plan for profits, growth, or to manage through difficult periods."

In the heading at the start of this section, please note the words *and Implementing*. For many companies, it's easier to implement the accounting applications than those for resource planning. This is because less time is typically required for process definition and also because the implementation path is more straightforward. (Note: the section that follows applies primarily to companies doing a combined ERP/ES implementation. Most companies that have already installed an ES have already upgraded their finance and accounting processes.)

The reasons for this are based on the relative immaturity of effective formal resource planning and scheduling processes versus the high degree of maturity on the finance and accounting side. Now we're not saying that accounting people act like grown-ups and operational folks act like kids (although some finance people we've known over the years seemed to feel that way). What we're talking about here is the *body of knowledge* in these two different areas of activity.

The accounting body of knowledge is defined, mature, and institutionalized. It all started some hundreds of years ago when some very bright Italian guy developed double-entry bookkeeping. Over the centuries, this fundamental set of techniques evolved into a defined body of knowledge, which in the U.S. we call "Generally Accepted Accounting Principles" (GAAP). It's institutionalized to the extent that it carries with it the force of law; CFOs who don't do their jobs accordance with GAAP not only might get fired, they could wind up in the slammer.

On the other hand, truly effective tools for resource planning, scheduling, and control didn't start to evolve until the 1960s with the advent of Material Requirements Planning. MRP is to ERP as double-entry bookkeeping is to GAAP; they're both basic sets of techniques that work. Double-entry booking, used properly, enables people to accurately answer questions such as: "What do we own and what do we owe?" (what's left over is called net worth), and "What have we been selling and what was that cost?" (what's left over is called net profit, hopefully). These are fundamental questions that must be answered validly. Resource planning, used properly, enables people to properly answer questions such as: "What materials will we need and when will we need them?", "When can we ship these customer orders?", and "When will we need to add plant capacity?" These are fundamental questions that must also be answered validly.

So why is accounting mature and resource planning immature? Two reasons:

Accounting has been around a lot longer—about four centuries versus four decades for resource planning. GAAP has had much longer to get "settled in": defined, codified, and institutionalized.

Accounting deals with facts, with what has happened. It's primarily historical. When things happen, we record them. On the other hand, resource planning deals with the future—"when will we need this and that, when can we ship, when should we expand?" The future, unlike the past, is subject to change. Therefore, the plans within resource planning need to be updated, recalculated, and refreshed routinely to cope with changing conditions.

This latter point helps to explain why MRP didn't arise until the 1960s—it had to wait on the digital computer. Accounting can be done manually; it has been for years. Resource planning *that works* can't be done manually except in the simplest of businesses; it requires a computer.

Specifically, the reasons why most companies will have an easier time implementing the accounting tools are:

1. The magnitude of the changes is often much less. As we said, current accounting processes work. Often, much of what's involved is moving the accounting applications from their legacy software to the new Enterprise System. Are changes involved in this? Certainly.

This implementation provides an ideal time to do a number of accounting-oriented activities better, faster, and cheaper. Almost always, the legacy accounting system has cumbersome pieces that people are very eager to eliminate. The ability to handle consolidations far more easily is, for many companies, a significant benefit, and so is closing the books more quickly, with less heavy lifting. But these are not core changes to the fundamental logic of the processes.

2. Finance and accounting processes tend to be more stable and straightforward, as we just said, because they deal with facts. Since current accounting processes work, then new accounting processes can be implemented in parallel. The essence of a parallel implementation is to compare the output from the new system to the old and, when the new system is giving consistently correct results, drop the old. As we'll see in Chapters 11 and 12, the parallel approach is *not* practical for planning and scheduling because, for most companies, their current processes here simply don't work. Parallel implementations generally are easier than the alternatives.

All of this adds up to good news for you folks on the financial side of the business. You'll have a good deal of work to do on this implementation, no doubt about it, but it won't be quite as challenging for you as for the people on the operational side.

Finance and accounting people have an important role to play whether you're implementation is ERP/ES or ERP only. In addition to implementing their own new processes, they have roles to play on the ERP steering committee, the project team, and spin-off task forces. They will need to devote some time to getting educated on ERP, via the series of business meetings we referenced in Chapter 7. It's necessary for them to understand the logical structure of ERP, the benefits to be achieved from running the business with only one set of numbers, and the competitive advantage that highly effective ERP can provide.

TIMING

The question arises: in a combined ERP/ES implementation, when should the new finance and accounting systems be implemented? Well, the answer here is "it depends." Let's first look at the broad choices:

- Implement all or most of the new financial and accounting systems prior to beginning implementation of the new planning and scheduling processes.

- Implement the new planning and scheduling processes first and have the accounting side follow.

- Implement the new financial and accounting systems simultaneously with those for planning and scheduling.

There are some downsides to each of these options. The first choice, implementing accounting first, will delay the planning and scheduling implementation and hence the benefits. One more time: being able to close the books better, faster, and cheaper can be quite helpful but it does not generate substantial competitive advantage. What can generate substantial competitive advantage is the ability to ship on time virtually all the time, using minimum inventories, and making possible maximum productivity at the company's plants and those of its suppliers. Because most of the benefits from ERP come from these areas, and because the cost of a one-month delay can be quite large, this approach can be expensive.

The second alternative—do planning and scheduling first—solves that problem. However it can be cumbersome, because it means that for a time the legacy accounting systems will be fed by the new ERP transactions. These legacy systems will need to be modified, or temporary software bridges be built, to make this possible. (Of course, the reverse of this problem applies to the first choice: The legacy planning and scheduling systems will need to feed the new ERP accounting systems.)

The third option, implementing all of these new tools simultaneously, can be a very attractive way to go. It may, however, create a workload problem—perhaps too much of a load on the information systems resource and also possibly giving the project team more to manage than they're able to cope with.

This third option is the most attractive to us, if—and it's a big "if"—the resources can handle it. It's the fastest and the best way to go. On the other hand, if resources are a problem, then your question is which one to do first. A few years ago, around the turn of the millennium, most companies implemented the accounting side first. Why? Y2K. That's gone away, so we expect more companies to

Figure 9-3
Decision: to implement the new finance/accounting systems before, after, or simultaneously with the new resource planning processes.

Are resources available to do them simultaneously?

If yes, do that.

If no, is there a compelling reason to implement finance/accounting first?

If yes, do that.

If no, do resource planning first.

---

choose the second alternative—do planning and scheduling first. At the end of the day, however, the company must have bulletproof processes for finance and accounting. If that means implementing those applications first, so be it. Figure 9-3 summarizes the decision process.

Q & A WITH THE AUTHORS

MIKE: Did you ever get a "push-back" from people about this process definition step, saying they don't need to do this because they already know their processes?

TOM: Yes, and my response is no one really knows what they don't know. It's essential to get your heads into process definition because this establishes the specifics of how you're going to run the business in the future. At the risk of getting a bit "preachy" here, I'll say that there is a responsibility and a trust placed in the people doing this: They owe their very best efforts to all the company's stakeholders—fellow employees, stockholders, customers, suppliers, and the community.

NOTE

[i] Robert Townsend, *Up the Organization* (New York: Alfred A. Knopf, 1978), p. 11.

IMPLEMENTERS' CHECKLIST

Function: Demand Management, Planning, and Scheduling Process Definition; Finance and Accounting Process Definition and Implementation

Task	Complete Yes	No
1. Process definition statements completed for all sales processes to be impacted by ERP.	____	____
2. Process definition statements completed for all distribution processes to be impacted by ERP.	____	____
3. Process definition statements completed for all purchasing processes to be impacted by ERP.	____	____
4. Process definition statements completed for all manufacturing processes to be impacted by ERP.	____	____
5. Timing of finance and accounting implementation determined and reflected accordingly in the project schedule.	____	____
6. Detailed project schedule established by the project team, naming names, in days or weeks, and showing completion of ERP project in less than two years.	____	____
7. Detailed project schedule being updated at least weekly at project team meetings, with status being reported at each meeting of the executive steering committee.	____	____
8. Changes to finance and accounting processes identified and related software issues, if any, taken care of.	____	____

Task	Complete	
	Yes	No
9. Decision on when to implement new finance and accounting processes made.	____	____
10. Master schedule policy written, approved, and being used to run the business.	____	____
11. Material planning policy written, approved, and being used to run the business.	____	____
12. Engineering change policy written, approved, and being used to run the business.	____	____
13. Finance and accounting applications implemented using a parallel approach.	____	____

Chapter 10

Data Integrity

An immutable law of nature states: garbage in garbage out. To the best of our knowledge, that law has not yet been repealed. So why do so many companies behave as though it has? Why do so many companies spend enormous amounts of money on software, but fail to invest a small fraction of that amount on getting the numbers accurate? Go figure.

It's essential to build a solid foundation of highly accurate numbers before demand management, master scheduling, and the other planning and scheduling tools within ERP can be implemented successfully. Accurate numbers *before,* not during or after.

Large quantities of data are necessary to operate ERP. Some of it needs to be highly accurate; some less so. Data for ERP can be divided into two general categories: *forgiving* and *unforgiving.* Forgiving data can be less precise; it doesn't need to be "accurate to four decimal places." Forgiving data includes lead times, order quantities, safety stocks, standards, demonstrated capacities, and forecasts. Unforgiving data is just that—unforgiving. It has little margin for error. If it's not highly accurate, it can harm ERP quickly, perhaps fatally, and without mercy.

Examples of unforgiving data include inventory balances, production orders, purchase orders, allocations, bills of material, and routings (excluding standards). The typical company will need to spend far more time, effort, blood-sweat-and-tears, and money to get the unforgiving data accurate. The forgiving data shouldn't be neglected,

Figure 10-1

ERP PROVEN PATH

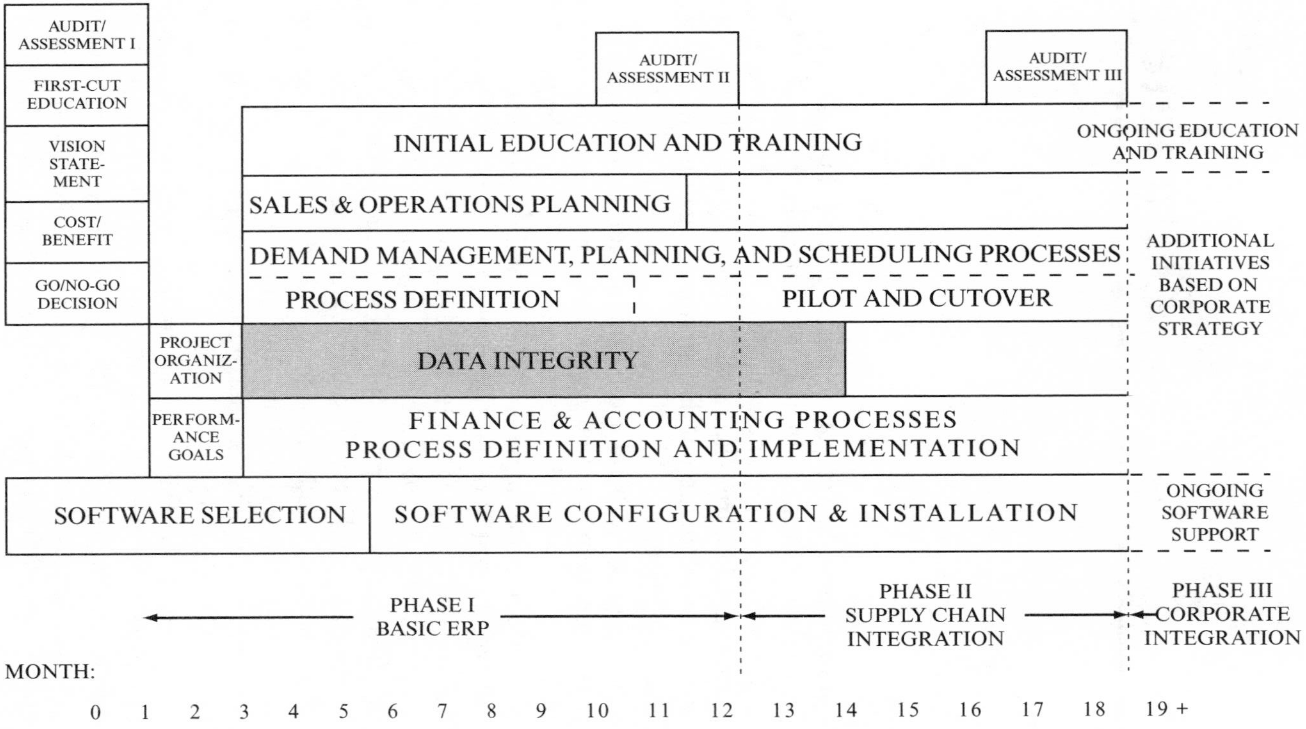

but kept in its proper perspective. It needs to be reasonable. The unforgiving data needs to be precise.

UNFORGIVING DATA

Inventory Balances

First, a disclaimer: The best way to have highly accurate inventory records is not to have any inventory. Short of that, have as little as you absolutely need. However, the role of the warehouse manager is not to specify the level of inventory; rather, he or she receives what arrives and issues what's requested. Therefore, given some amount of inventory, it's the responsibility of the people in the warehouses and stockrooms to get and keep the records at a high level of accuracy.

The on-hand inventory balances in the computer must be 95 percent accurate, at a minimum. Do not attempt to implement the planning and scheduling tools of ERP (master scheduling, Material Requirements Planning, Distribution Requirements Planning, plant scheduling, supplier scheduling) without this minimum level of accuracy.

The inventory balance numbers are vitally important because they represent the starting number for these planning processes. If the balance for an item is not accurate, the planning for it will probably be incorrect. If the planning is incorrect for a given item, such as a finished product or a subassembly, then the erroneous planned orders will be exploded into incorrect gross requirements for all of that item's components. Hence, the planning will probably be incorrect for those components also. The result: large amounts of incorrect recommendations coming out of the formal system, a loss of confidence by the users, a return to using the hot list, and an unsuccessful implementation of ERP.

What specifically does 95 percent accuracy mean? Of all the on-hand balance numbers inside the computer, 95 percent should match—on item number, quantity, and location—what is physically in the stockroom or the warehouse.

"But that's impossible!" people say. "What about all the nuts and bolts and shims and washers and screws and so forth? These are tiny little parts, they're inexpensive, and we usually have thousands of any given item in stock. There's no way to get the computer records to match what's actually out there."

Here enters the concept of counting tolerance. Items such as fasteners are normally not hand counted but scale counted. (The stock is weighed, and then translated into pieces by a conversion factor.) If, for example, the scale is accurate to plus or minus 2 percent, and/or the parts vary a bit in weight, then it obviously isn't practical to insist on an exact match of the count to the book record. In cases where items are weigh counted (or volume counted, such as liquids in a tank), companies assign a counting tolerance to the item. In the example above, the counting tolerance might be plus or minus 3 percent. Any physical count within plus or minus 3 percent of the computer record would be considered a hit, and the computer record would be accepted as correct.

Given this consideration, let's expand the earlier statement about accuracy: 95 percent of all the on-hand balance numbers inside the computer should match what is physically on the shelf inside the stockroom, within the counting tolerance. Don't go to the pilot and cutover steps without it.

There are a few more things to consider about counting tolerances. The method of handling and counting an item is only one criterion for using counting tolerances. Others include:

1. The value of an item. Inexpensive items will tend to have higher tolerances than the expensive ones.

2. The frequency and volume of usage. Items used more frequently will be more subject to error.

3. The lead-time. Shorter lead times can mean higher tolerances.

4. The criticality of an item. More critical items require lower tolerances or possibly zero tolerance. For example, items at higher levels in the bill are more likely to be shipment stoppers; therefore, they may have lower tolerances.

The cost of control obviously should not exceed the cost of inaccuracies. The bottom line is the validity of the material plan. The range of tolerances employed should reflect their impact on the company's ability to produce and ship on time. Our experience shows

Class A users employ tolerances ranging from 0 percent to 5 percent, with none greater than 5 percent.

The question that remains is how a company achieves the necessary degree of inventory accuracy. The answer involves some basic management principles. Provide people with the right tools to do the job, teach people how to use the tools (called education and training, right?), and then hold them accountable for results. Let's take a look at the specific elements in getting this job done.

1. *A zero-defects attitude.*

This is the people part of getting and maintaining inventory accuracy. The folks in the stockroom need to understand that inventory record accuracy is important, and, therefore, they are important. The points the company must make go something like this:

 a. ERP is very important for our future. It will make the company more prosperous and our jobs more secure.

 b. Having the planning and scheduling tools within ERP working well is critical for successful ERP.

 c. Inventory record accuracy is an essential part of making those tools work.

 d. Thus the people who are responsible for inventory accuracy are important. How well they do their jobs makes a big difference.

2. *Limited access.*

This is the hardware part of getting accuracy. In many companies, limited access means having the area physically secured—fenced and locked. Psychological restrictions (lines on the floor, signs, roped-off areas) have also been proven to be effective.

This need for limited access is not primarily to keep people out, although that's the effect. The primary reason is to *keep accountability in.* In order to hold the warehouse and stockroom people accountable for inventory accuracy, the company must give them the necessary tools. One of these is the ability to control who goes in and out. That means limiting access exclusively to those who need to be there.

Only then can the warehouse and stockroom people be in control and legitimately be held accountable for results.

Let us add a word of caution about implementing limited access. It can be an emotional issue. In the world of the informal system, many people (group leaders, schedulers, buyers, etc.) spend a lot of time in the stockroom. This isn't because they think the stockroom's a great place to be. They're in the stockroom trying to get components, to make the product, so they can ship it. It's called expediting, and they do it in self-defense.

If, one fine morning, these people come to work to find the warehouses and stockrooms fenced and locked, the results can be devastating. They've lost the only means by which they've been able to do the most important part of their jobs—get product shipped.

Before installing limited access, do three things:

1. *Tell 'em.* Tell people in advance that the stockrooms and warehouses are going to be secured. Don't let it come as a surprise.

2. *Tell 'em why.* The problem is *not* theft. It's accountability. It's necessary to get the records accurate, so that ERP can work.

3. *Tell 'em Job 1 is service*—service to the production floor, service to the shipping department, and ultimately service to the customers.

In a company implementing ERP, priority number one is to run the business; priority number two is implementation. Therefore, in the stockrooms and warehouses, priority one is service and priority two is getting the inventory records accurate. (Priority number two is necessary, of course, to do a really good job on priority number one.) Make certain that everyone, both in and out of the warehouses and stockrooms, knows these things *in advance.*

Talking about priorities gives us the opportunity to make an important point about inventories in general: Have as little as possible to get the job done. With inventories, less is truly more. However, you simply can't wave a magic wand, lower the inventories, and expect everything to be okay. What's needed is to *change processes,* so that inventory is no longer needed to the extent it was. Now, the folks in the warehouse are not the prime drivers of these kinds of process changes; it's the people on the plant floor and in purchasing and elsewhere throughout the company who should have as a *very high pri-*

ority this important issue of changing processes to lessen the need for inventories. More on this in Chapter 16.

3. A good transaction system.

This is the software part of the process. The system for recording inventory transactions and updating stock balances should be simple and should, to the extent possible, mirror the reality of how material actually flows.

Simple implies easy to understand and easy to use. It means a relatively few transaction types. Many software packages contain lots of unnecessary transaction codes. After all, what can happen to inventory? It goes into stock and out of it. That's two transaction types. It can go in or out on a planned or unplanned basis. That's four. Add one for a stock-to-stock transfer and perhaps several others for inventory adjustments, backflushing,[1] and miscellaneous activities. There are still probably less than a dozen different transaction types that are really needed. Just because the software package has 32 different types of inventory transactions doesn't mean the company needs to use them all to get its money's worth. Using too many unnecessary transaction types makes the system unduly complicated, which makes it harder to operate, which makes it that much more difficult to get and keep the records accurate. Who needs this? Remember, warehouse and stockroom people will be using these tools, not Ph.D.s in computer science. Keep it simple. Less is more.

The transaction system should also be a valid representation of reality—how things happen in the real world. For example: inventory by location. Many companies stock items in more than one bin in a given stockroom and/or in more than one stockroom. Their transaction systems should have the capability to reflect this. Another example: quick updates of the records. Inventory transaction processing does not have to be done in real time. However, it should be done fairly frequently and soon after the actual events have taken place. No transaction should have to wait more than 24 hours to be processed. Backflushing won't work well at all with these kinds of delays. Nor will our next topic: cycle counting.

---

[1] This is a technique to reduce component inventory balances by calculating component usage from completed production counts exploded through the bill of material. Also called post-deduct.

4. Cycle counting.

This is the mechanism through which a company gains and maintains inventory record accuracy. Cycle counting is fundamentally the ongoing quality check on a process. The process being checked is: Does the black box match the real world? Do the numbers inside the computer match what's physically in the warehouse?

Cycle counting has four specific objectives:

a. To discover the causes of errors, so that the causes can be eliminated. The saying about the rotten apple in the barrel applies here. Get it out of the barrel before it spoils more apples. Put more emphasis on prevention than cure. When an inventory error is discovered, not only fix the record but—what's far more important—eliminate the cause of the error. Was the cause of the error an inadequate procedure, insufficient security, a software bug, or perhaps incomplete training of a warehouse person? Whenever practical, find the cause of the error and correct it so that it doesn't happen again.

b. To measure results. Cycle counting needs to answer the question: "How are we doing?" It should routinely generate accuracy percentages, so the people know whether the records are sufficiently accurate. In addition, some companies routinely verify the cycle counting accuracy numbers via independent audits by people from the Accounting department, often on a monthly basis. In this way, they verify that the stockroom's inventory records are as good as the stockroom people say they are.

c. To correct inaccurate records. When a cycle count does not match the computer record, the item should be recounted. If the results are the same, the on-hand balance in the computer must be adjusted.

d. To eliminate the annual physical inventory. This becomes practical after the 95 percent accuracy level has been reached on an item-to-item basis. Although doing away with it is important, it's not primarily because of the expense involved. The problem is that most annual physical inventories make the records less accurate, not more so. Over the years, their main purpose has been to verify the balance sheet, not to make the individual records more accurate.

Consider the following scenario in a company implementing ERP.

The stockroom is fenced and locked; the computer hardware and software is operating properly; and the people in the stockroom are educated, trained, motivated, and enthusiastic. Inventory record accuracy is 97.3 percent. (Remember, this is units, not dollars. When the units are 95 percent to 99 percent accurate, the dollars are almost always in the 99 percent plus accuracy range. This is because plus and minus dollar errors cancel each other out; unit errors stand alone.)

It seems counterproductive to open the gates to the stockroom one weekend, bring in a bunch of outsiders, and have them running up and down the aisles, climbing up and down the bins, writing down numbers, and putting them into the computer. What happens to inventory accuracy? It drops. What happens to accountability? There's not much left. What happens to the morale of the people in the stockroom? It's gone—it just flew out the open gates.

Avoid taking annual physical inventories once the records are at least 95 percent accurate. Most major accounting firms won't insist on them. They will want to do a spot audit of inventory accuracy, based on a statistically valid sample. They'll probably also want to review the cycle counting procedures, to audit the cycle count results, and to verify the procedures for booking adjustments. That's fine. But there should be no need to take any more complete physical inventories, not even one last one to confirm the records. Having accounting people doing a monthly audit of inventory accuracy (as per paragraph b above) can facilitate the entire process of eliminating the annual physical inventory. This comes about because the accounting folks are involved routinely, and can begin to feel confidence and ownership of the process.

An effective cycle counting system contains certain key characteristics. First of all, it's done *daily*. Counting some parts once per month or once per quarter won't get the job done.

A critically important part of cycle counting is the control group. This is a group of about 100 items—less in companies with relatively few item numbers—that are counted every week. The purpose of the control group gets us back to the first objective of cycle counting: discovering the causes of errors. This is far easier to determine with parts counted last week than with those checked last month, last quarter, or last year.

Ease of operation is another requirement of an effective system. It's got to be easy to compare the cycle count to the book record, easy to reconcile discrepancies, and easy to make the adjustment after the error has been confirmed.

Most good cycle counting systems require a confirming recount. If the first count is outside the tolerance, that merely indicates the probability of an error. A recount is necessary to confirm the error. With highly accurate records, often it's the cycle count that's wrong, not the record.

Last, a good cycle counting system should generate and report measures of accuracy. A percentage figure seems to work best—total hits (good counts) divided by total counts. (Excluded from these figures are counts for the control group; within a few weeks, the control group should be at or near 100 percent.) Report these measures of accuracy frequently, perhaps once per week, to the key individuals—stockroom people, project team, steering committee. Post them on bulletin boards or signs where other people can see them.

Get count coverage on all items, and 95 percent minimum accuracy, before going live with the planning and scheduling tools. In many companies, cycle counting must be accelerated prior to going on the air in order to get that coverage. The company may need to allocate additional resources to make this possible.

Once the stockroom has reached 95 percent inventory record accuracy, don't stop there. That's merely the minimum number for running ERP successfully. Don't be satisfied with less than 98 percent accuracy. Our experience has been that companies that spend all the money and do all the things necessary to get to 95 percent need only dedication, hard work, and good leadership to get in the 98 percent to 99 percent range. Make sure everyone knows that going from 95 percent to 98 percent is not merely an accuracy increase of 3 percent. It really is a 60 percent reduction in exposure to error, from 5 percent to 2 percent. ERP will operate a good deal better with only 1 or 2 percent of the records wrong than with 4 percent or 5 percent.

There are two other elements involved in inventory status that need to be mentioned: scheduled receipts and allocations. Both elements must be at least 95 percent accurate prior to going live.

Scheduled Receipts

Scheduled receipts come in two flavors: open production orders and open purchase orders. They need to be accurate on quantity and *order* due date. Note the emphasis on the word order. Material Requirements Planning doesn't need to know the operational due dates and job location of production orders in a job shop. It does need to know when the order is due to be completed, and how many pieces remain on the order. Don't make the mistake of thinking that plant floor control must be implemented first in order to get the numbers necessary for Material Requirements Planning.

Typically, the company must review all scheduled receipts, both production orders and purchase orders, to verify quantity and timing. Then, establish good order close-out procedures to keep residual garbage from building up in the scheduled receipt files.

In some companies, however, the production orders can represent a real challenge. Typically, these are companies with higher speeds and volumes. In this kind of environment, it's not unusual for one order to catch up with an earlier order for the same item. Scrap reporting can also be a problem. Reported production may be applied against the wrong production order.

Here's what we call A Tale of Two Companies (with apologies to Charles Dickens). In a certain midwestern city, on the same street, two companies operated ERP quite successfully. That's where the similarity ends. One, company M, made machine tools. Company M's products were very complex, and the manufacturing processes were low volume and low speed. The people in this company had to work very hard to get their on-hand balances accurate because of the enormous number of parts in their stockrooms. They had far less of a challenge to get shop order accuracy because of the low volumes and low speeds.

Their neighbor, company E, made electrical connectors. The product contained far fewer parts than a machine tool. Fewer parts in stock means an easier job in getting accurate on-hand balances. These connectors, however, were made in high volume at high speeds. Company E's people had to work far harder at getting accurate production order data. They had to apply proportionately more of their resources to the shop order accuracy, unlike company M.

The moral of the story: Scratch where it itches. Put the resources where the problems are.

Allocations

Allocation records detail which components have been reserved for which scheduled receipts (production orders). Typically, they're not a major problem. If the company has them already, take a snapshot of the allocation file, then verify and correct the numbers. In the worst case, cancel all the unreleased scheduled receipts and allocations and start over. Also, be sure to fix what's caused the errors: bad bills of material, poor stockroom practices, inadequate procedures, and the like. If there are no allocations yet, make certain the software is keeping them straight when the company starts to run Material Requirements Planning.

Bills of Material

The accuracy target for bills of material is even higher than on inventory balances: 98 percent minimum in terms of item number, unit of measure, quantity per parent item, and the parent item number itself. An error in any of these elements will generate requirements incorrectly. Incorrect requirements will be generated into the right components or correct requirements into the wrong components, or both.

First, what does 98 percent bill of material accuracy mean? In other words, how is bill accuracy calculated? Broadly, there are three approaches: the tight method, the loose method, and the middle-of-the road method.

For the tight method, assume the bill of material in Figure 10-2 is in the computer:

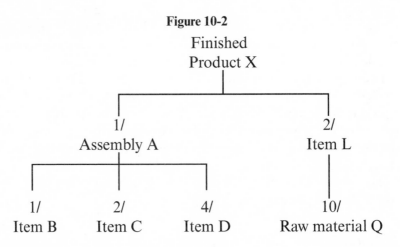

Figure 10-2

Finished
Product X

1/
Assembly A

2/
Item L

1/
Item B

2/
Item C

4/
Item D

10/
Raw material Q

Suppose there's only one incorrect relationship here—assembly A really requires *five* of part D, not four. (Or perhaps it's part D that's not used at all, but, in fact, four of a totally different part is required.) The tight method of calculating bill accuracy would call the entire bill of material for finished product X a miss, zero accuracy. No more than 2 percent of all the products could have misses and still have the bills considered 98 percent accurate.

Is this practical? Sometimes. We've seen it used by companies with relatively simple products, usually with no more than several dozen components per product.

The flip side is the loose method. This goes after each one-to-one relationship, in effect each line on the printed bill of material. Using the example above, the following results would be obtained:

Misses	Hits
D to A	B to A
	C to A
	A to X
	Q to L
	L to X

Accuracy: five hits out of six relationships, for 83 percent accuracy. Most companies would find this method too loose and would opt for the middle-of-the-road method. It recognizes hits and misses based on all single level component relationships to make a given parent. Figure 10-3 uses the same example:

Figure 10-3

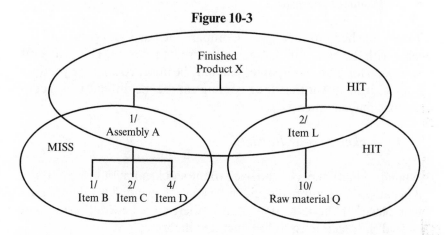

Accuracy: 67 percent. Overall, this approach is used most frequently. Select this method unless there are strong reasons to the contrary, and stick to it. Consistency is important; if the measurement is consistent, then you can determine if you're improving, on a plateau, or backsliding. Again, the overall bottom line is the validity of the master schedule and material plan.

Once the company has decided how to calculate bill of material accuracy, it'll need to determine the measurement approaches to be used, to both acquire accuracy initially and to monitor it on an ongoing basis. Here are some options:

1. Floor audit.

Put some product engineers into the assembly and subassembly areas. Have them compare what's actually being built to the bill of material. They should work closely with not only the foremen but also with the assemblers. Correct errors as they're discovered.

2. Office/factory review.

Form a team of people from the plant floor plus engineers, material planners, and perhaps cost people to review the bills jointly, sitting around a conference table. The question to be asked: "Is this the way we build it?" Again, correct errors as they're found.

3. Product teardown.

Take a finished product apart. Compare the parts and pieces on the table with the computer listing and correct the errors. This is a good approach for many companies, but may be impractical if the product is a jet airliner. Another shortcoming can be the difficulty in recognizing subassemblies.

4. Unplanned issues/receipts.

When production people go back to the stockroom for more parts, is it because they scrapped some or because they didn't get them in the first place? If the latter is the case, there may be a bill error that caused the picking list to be generated incorrectly.

If parts are returned to stock after the assembly of a product, perhaps they shouldn't have gone out to the plant floor in the first place. Again, the picking list may have been wrong because the bill was wrong. Correct the errors as they're discovered. This can be a good technique to monitor bill of material accuracy on an ongoing basis.

Certainly, some of these methods are inappropriate for some companies. Select one method, or a combination, and get started as soon as possible. Don't go on the air without 98 percent accuracy on all bills because MRP won't work well without accurate bills.

In addition to being accurate, the bills of material need to be complete, properly structured, and integrated.

1. Completeness.

Ideally, bills of material should include everything involved in making the product—things like raw materials, fasteners, packing materials, solder and flux, paint, and so forth. At a minimum, all the important stuff (like raw materials, purchased components, unique packaging materials, etc.) must be in the bills before turning on Master Scheduling and MRP.

The test is: Is this item a shipment stopper? If the unit in question is truly a standard item (nuts, bolts, paint, rivets, solder) that you can get off the shelf from the supply house down the street, then it's not a shipment stopper. Otherwise, it probably is. Therefore, all the shipment stoppers must be in the bills before you go live. However, don't delay the implementation to get all the non-shipment-stoppers on the system. They should be added as soon as it's practical, but don't let them be on the critical path.

2. Structure.

Structure has two meanings. First, bills must be properly structured to show stock points, phantoms, and so on.

Second, companies whose products have many options usually need to structure their bills into a modular format, creating what are called "planning bills." This enables effective forecasting, master scheduling, and customer order promising. (More on this later in this chapter.) Caution: Estimate the work load closely ahead of time.

Typically, it takes a good deal of time and effort to develop modular bills. Don't forget the principle of three knobs: the work to be done, the calendar time in which it needs to be done, and the resources available to do it.

3. Integration.

Some companies have a variety of different bill of material files. Engineering has one, but manufacturing has its own. The cost accounting department doesn't like either of those, so it maintains another one to fit its needs.

ERP represents a company-wide game plan, in units and dollars, so everyone is "singing from the same sheet of music." That's impossible if different departments have different hymnals. After all, the bill of material, along with the routings, represents the network around which ERP is built. The various bills must be integrated into a single, unified bill that serves the needs of all the different departments.[2]

Routings

Here's another example of why it's easier to implement ERP in a flow shop: The routings are often not very important. In many cases, they're not needed at all because, in a flow environment, the routing is defined by how the equipment is laid out. In a job shop, the routings are not physical; they're informational, and therefore they're essential for you job shoppers.

For those of you who need routings, there's good news and bad news. The bad news is that three key elements are unforgiving; they need to be at least 98 percent accurate. These three elements are the operations to be performed, their sequence, and the work centers at which they'll be done. Their accuracy is extremely important because they'll be used by the computer to locate jobs (in plant floor control) and to apply load (in capacity requirements planning). This

---

[2] This may not be as tough as it sounds. Much of today's software for ERP allows for flexible retrieval of bill of material information, tailored to the specific needs of each department. This can be done by intelligent coding capabilities within the bill of material (product structure) record.

is where most companies need to apply a fair amount of time and effort, typically by foremen and manufacturing engineers.

The good news is that the standards, the other key element within the routing, are forgiving. Extreme accuracy of the standards is not necessary for CRP and plant floor control. This is because they convert a variety of units—pieces, pounds, gallons, feet—into a common unit of measure: standard hours. Errors, plus and minus, tend to cancel each other out, and the law of large numbers has an effect. A good rule of thumb for standards is to try for accuracy of plus or minus 10 percent. Even if they're skewed to the high or low side, the efficiency factor can be used to translate the standard hours to clock hours.

Another good rule of thumb: If the standards today are good enough to calculate product costs, payroll, and efficiencies, then they'll be accurate enough for ERP. Companies that already have standards on a work-center-by-work-center basis typically find that they don't need to spend a great deal of time and effort in order to fix the ones that are obviously wrong. However, most of your time should be spent on the unforgiving elements.

Calculating routing accuracy is fairly straightforward. If, on a given routing, all of the operations, sequence numbers, and work centers are correct, that's a hit. Otherwise, it's a miss. The target is to get at least 98 hits out of every 100 routings checked.

Methods for auditing and correcting routings include:

1. *Floor audit.*

Usually one or more manufacturing engineers follows the jobs through the plant, comparing the computer-generated routing to what's actually happening. Here again, talk to the operators, the folks who are making the items. Virtually every element involves an operator to one degree or another. They know what's happening. A variation here is to check the jobs physically at a given work center. Does each job at a given work center have an operation in its primary routing or alternate that calls for that work center? If not, what's it doing there?

2. *Office/factory review.*

Normally involves people from production and from manufacturing engineering in a group, reviewing the computer-generated routings against their knowledge of the plant and any additional documentation available.

3. Order close-out.

As shop orders are completed and closed out, the actual reporting is compared to the computer-generated routing.

Not every one of these methods will be practical for every company. Some companies use a combination of several.

Companies that need plant floor control and CRP, but don't have routings and standards by work center, have a big job ahead of them, and can't afford to wait for phase II to begin. They should start just as soon as possible. This part of the project needs to be adequately resourced to do a big job—identify all the work centers, develop routings and standards—without delaying the implementation of the total system. Some companies have had to expand the manufacturing and engineering departments and/or obtain temporary industrial engineering help from outside the company. This is another case where that cost of a one-month delay number can help a lot with resource allocation/acquisition decisions.

Customer Orders

Last, but certainly not least, customer orders must be accurate. They usually are and, for that reason, we've listed them last. However, since the customer comes first, we'd better make sure that our customer order files match their purchase orders. Not usually a problem, but at a minimum take a spot check to ensure that everything's okay with what may be the most important set of data in the entire company.

The process of checking is usually simple. The customer service people pull a small sample, maybe 50 or 100 orders, call the customers and verify product, quantity, date, and anything else that may be important. If this audit turns up problems, the process may need to be expanded to a complete verification of the entire order file.

FORGIVING DATA

Virtually all forgiving data is made up of item and work center numbers. In these categories, four-decimal-place accuracy isn't necessary.

We're not aware of any ERP initiative that went down the drain because the order quantities were not calculated with sufficient precision or because the demonstrated capacities weren't within plus or minus 2 percent.

Item Data

Item data refers to the planning factors necessary for the planning and scheduling tools of master scheduling and MRP. Most of it is static and is stored in the computer's item master file. It includes things like lead times, order quantities, safety stock/time, shrinkage factors, scrap or yield factors (stored in the bill of material).

Getting the item data collected and loaded is a necessary step, but it's normally not a big problem. The people doing it should be primarily the same ones who'll be operating these planning systems: the master scheduler(s), material planners, and distribution planners. They'll need education, time to do the job, and some policy direction.

Wherever practical, use the numbers already available. Review them, make sure they're in the ballpark, and fix the ones that are obviously wrong. If the lead time for an item is too high or too low, change it to a reasonable number; otherwise, leave it alone. If the order quantity for a part is out of line, change it; if not, let it be. If an item routinely experiences some scrap loss in production, add in a scrap or shrinkage factor. Otherwise, leave that factor at zero.

The subject of using the numbers already in place leads to a larger issue. When implementing ERP, change only what's absolutely necessary to make it work. Don't make changes for incremental operational improvement unless they're also necessary for implementation. They'll be plenty of time later, after the system is on the air, to fine-tune the numbers and get better and better. There are two reasons for this—people and diagnosis:

1. Implementing Enterprise Resource Planning is a time of great change in a company. For most people, change is difficult. Introducing nonessential changes will make the entire implementation process more difficult than it needs to be.

2. Unnecessary changes also complicate the diagnostic process when something goes wrong. The greater the number of things

that were changed, the greater the number of things that could be causing the problem. This makes it correspondingly (perhaps even exponentially) harder to find the problem and fix it.

Work Center Data

The information involved here includes things like work center identification, demonstrated capacity, efficiency (or productivity) factors, and desired queues for the job shops.

Review the work center arrangement now being used. Ask whether the machines are grouped correctly into work centers and whether the operator skill groups are established properly. A key factor here—how does each foreman view the equipment and people in his or her department, in terms of elements to be scheduled and loaded?

Make whatever changes are necessary. The goal is to enable CRP, input/output, and shop dispatching to give the foreman the right information as to work load, priorities, and schedule performance. Realize that changes in work center identification will mean changes to the routings. A good bit of work may be involved. A computer program can often help in revising routings to reflect new work center assignments.

Start to gather statistics for each work center: demonstrated capacity, efficiency factors, and planned queue. This last element may represent a dramatic change. For most companies, planned queues will be smaller than they were under the informal system. Many companies determine their queues by considering "the range" and "the pain." Range refers to the variability of job arrival at the work centers; pain means how much it will hurt if the queue for a particular work center disappears, and it runs out of work.

The key players in these decisions are the foremen and the industrial engineers. Usually, the engineers develop the numbers, while the foremen are more involved with the qualitative information, such as grouping equipment for the best work center arrangement, the amount of pain suffered by the center that runs out of work, and so on. Foremen buy-in is critical here. Therefore, they, and their bosses, must call the shots. They, and their people, are the ones who'll be accountable for making it work.

Forecasts

Yes, Virginia, the sales forecasts fall into the forgiving category. And it's a darn good thing, too, because the forecasts will never be super accurate. This may be a tough pill for you long-term manufacturing people to swallow, but that's the way it is.

The reason your sales forecasts will never be highly accurate is that your marketing and sales people cannot predict the future with certainty. Okay? If they could, do you think they'd be working for a living, knocking themselves out 40 plus hours per week trying to get customers to order your product? Of course not. Where would they be if they could foresee the future with certainty? At the racetrack, of course. And if the track's closed? At home on their computers—trading in stock options and speculating on pork belly futures.

However, there's a flip side to this. In almost all companies who implement ERP, forecast accuracy improves substantially. This is done through more frequent reviews, on a more focused basis, with good communications and measurements. You marketing and sales folks should plan on working hard to improve the accuracy of your forecasts. Everyone, though, should recognize that the law of diminishing returns applies here: As forecast accuracy increases, there comes a point where each additional unit of effort does not generate a commensurate unit of greater accuracy.

This is where the forgiving nature of forecasts comes into play. Many companies have found their ability to cope with forecast error increases dramatically as they obtain:

1. *Improved demand management, order promising and master scheduling capabilities.* With closer links to the customers, they frequently can deal more with specific customer demand and rely less on purely forecasted projections.

2. *Reduced lead times.* Shorter lead times are one of the most important parts of running a manufacturing business well. The shorter the lead time—to enter the customer orders, to make the product, to buy the material—the less vulnerable a company is to forecast error. Consequently, the company is better able to ship what the customers want, when they want it. And isn't that what it's all about?

3. *The ability to forecast at a higher level.* A growing number of companies have found it really isn't necessary to do lots of forecasting at the individual item or stockkeeping unit (SKU) level. Rather, through the intelligent use of planning bills of material, they can forecast higher in the product structure. When Widget Model #123 comes in six different colors, all of which are applied in the finishing

operation, is it really necessary to forecast all six colors of Model #123? Probably not. Rather, whenever possible, forecast at the model level; this means one forecast rather than six. The law of large numbers will also apply—the one-model forecast will almost always be more accurate than the individual forecasts for each of the SKUs. Finish and paint to the customer orders as they're received. And the planning bills of material will be there to help them not run out of the different colors of paint.

Q & A with the Authors

MIKE: I can imagine you've seen some pretty impressive data accuracy efforts over the years. True?

TOM: Indeed. The most impressive was in a company that made highly complex machinery with many components, subassemblies, and piece parts. They had around 60,000 active part numbers. Because of management problems in their materials management group, their inventory accuracy efforts were lagging the rest of the project. They had about 55% percent accuracy in January and were scheduled to go live in April. Well, don't you know, they changed materials managers and got very focused on this problem. By mid-March, they had reached—and were maintaining—95 percent+ inventory accuracy in all four stockrooms. The pilot and cutover happened on schedule. It can be done.

IMPLEMENTERS' CHECKLIST

Task	Complete Yes	No
1. Inventory record accuracy, including scheduled receipts and allocations, at 95 percent or better.	___	___
2. Bill of material accuracy at 98 percent or better.	___	___

	Complete	
Task	Yes	No
3. Bills of material properly structured, sufficiently complete for MRP, and integrated into one unified bill for the entire company.	____	____
4. Routings (operations, sequence, work centers) at 98 percent or better accuracy.	____	____
5. Open production orders at 98 percent or better accuracy.	____	____
6. Open purchase orders at 98 percent or better accuracy.	____	____
7. Forecasting process reviewed for timeliness, completeness, and ease of use.	____	____
8. Item data complete and verified for reasonableness.	____	____
9. Work center data complete and verified for reasonableness.	____	____

Chapter 11

Going on the Air—
Basic ERP (Phase I)

Going on the air means turning on the tools, starting to run them. It's the culmination of a great deal of work done to date.

Back in Chapter 3, we discussed the proper implementation sequence:

- Phase I—Basic ERP

- Phase II—Supply Chain Integration

- Phase III—Extensions and Enhancements to support Corporate Strategy.

Let's take a moment and look at a new version of the Proven Path diagram, as shown in Figure 11-1. We've enlarged the section dealing with process definition, pilot & cutover—to show more specifics on the phase I and phase II implementations. We'll cover phase II—supply chain integration—in the next chapter. For now let's look at going on the air with the phase I tools of basic ERP.

These are Sales & Operations Planning, demand management, master scheduling, Rough-Cut Capacity Planning, and Material Requirements Planning. Further, in a flow shop, plant scheduling should be implemented here.

Recognize that some of the elements of ERP have already been im-

Figure 11-1

ERP PROVEN PATH–PHASE I ONLY

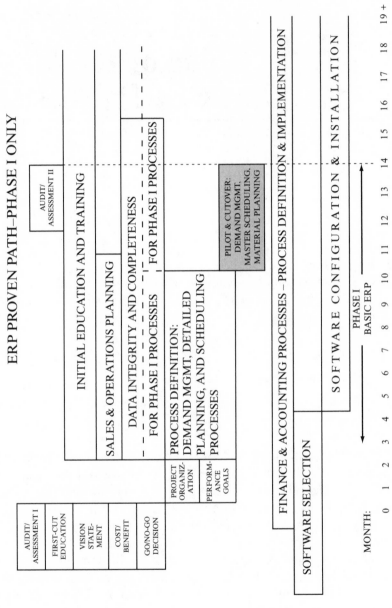

plemented. Sales & Operations Planning has been started, as much as several months ago. (See Chapter 8.) Supporting systems—bill of material processor, inventory transaction processor, perhaps new sales forecasting software—have, in most cases, already been installed.

Activating master scheduling (MS) and Material Requirements Planning (MRP) is another moment of truth during implementation. Virtually all the company's activities to date have been leading directly to activating master scheduling and MRP. Turning these on can be tricky, and we need to discuss at length how to do it.

THREE WAYS TO IMPLEMENT SYSTEMS

The Parallel Approach

There are, broadly, three different methods for implementing systems. First, the *parallel* approach. It means to start to run the new system while continuing to run the old one. The output from the new system is compared to the old. When the new system is consistently giving the correct answers, the old system is dropped. As we said in Chapter 9, this is the correct approach for accounting implementations.

There are two problems in using the parallel method for the planning and scheduling side of ERP. First of all, it's difficult. It's cumbersome to maintain and operate two systems side by side. There may not be enough staff to do all that and still compare the new system output to the old.

The second problem with the parallel approach is perhaps even more compelling than the first: it's *impossible.* The essence of the parallel approach is the comparison of the output from the new system against the old system. The new system in this case is basic ERP. But against *what* should its output be compared? The hot list? The order point system? The stock status report? The HARP[1] system? What's

---

[1] HARP is an acronym for Half-Baked Resource Planning. Many people who think they have ERP actually have HARP: monthly time buckets, requirements generated every month or so, etc. It's a primitive order launcher. It does happen to recognize the principle of independent/dependent demand, but otherwise bears little resemblance to ERP.

the point of implementing ERP if it's just going to deliver the same lousy information that the current system provides?

That's the problem with the parallel approach for ERP's planning and scheduling tools.

Big Bang

The inability to do a parallel leads some people to jump way over to the other side of the fence, and do what's called a *big-bang cutover*. We call it "you bet your company," and we recommend against it vigorously and without reservation.

Here's an example of a big-bang implementation, as explained by an unenlightened project leader:

> We've got master scheduling and MRP all programmed, tested, and debugged. We're going to run it live over the weekend. On Friday afternoon, we're going to back a pickup truck into the production control office and the computer room, throw all the programs, disks, tapes, procedures, forms, and so forth into the truck and take 'em down to the incinerator.

This gives new meaning to the phrase "burning one's bridges." A big-bang cutover (also called "cold turkey") carries with it two problems, the first one being that ERP may fail. The volume of output from the first live computer run of master scheduling and MRP may be so great that the users can't handle it all. By the time they work through about a quarter of that output, a week's gone by and then what happens? Master scheduling and MRP are run again, and here comes another big pile of output. The result: The users are inundated and your ERP effort has failed.

Folks, that's the least of it. The second problem is far more severe: You may lose your ability to ship product. Some companies who've done a big bang have lost their ability to order material and release production. The old system can't help them because they stopped running it some weeks ago, and the data isn't current. ERP isn't helping them; it's overwhelming them.

By the time they realize the seriousness of the problem, they often can't go back to the old system because the inventory balances and other data aren't valid any longer, and it might be a nearly impossible job to reconstruct it.[2]

A company that can't order material and release production will sooner or later lose its ability to ship product. A company that can't ship product will, sooner or later, go out of business.

Some organizations get lucky and muddle through without great difficulty. In other cases, it's far more serious. Although we're not aware of any company that has actually gone out of business for this reason, there are some who've come close. The people we know who've lived through a cold-turkey cutover never want to do it again. Never. *Don't do it.*

The Pilot Approach

The right way to do it is with a *pilot*. Select a group of products, or one product, or a part of one product, which involve no more than several hundred part numbers in all—and do a big bang on those. The purpose is to prove that master scheduling and MRP are working before cutting over all 5,000 or 50,000 or 500,000 items onto the system. The phrase MS/MRP working refers to two things: the technical side (does the software work properly?) and the users' side (do the people understand and believe what it's telling them, and do they know what to do?).

If master scheduling and MRP don't work properly during the pilot, it's not a major problem. Almost all the items are still being ordered via the old system, except for the few hundred in the pilot. These can be handled by putting them back on the old system or perhaps doing them manually. What's also necessary is to focus on why master scheduling and MRP aren't working properly and fix it. The people have the time to do that if they're not being inundated with output on 5,000 or 50,000 or 500,000 items.

What do we mean when we ask: "Is it working?" Simply, is it predicting the shortages? Is it generating correct recommendations to release orders, and to reschedule orders in and out? Does the master

---

[2] Even those cases when they can go back to the old system are very difficult. Why? Because they tried to implement ERP, and it didn't work. Now they're back to running the old system, not ERP, and they'll have to decide what to do now, where to go from here. A most unfortunate situation.

schedule for the pilot product(s) reflect what's actually being made? Can customer orders be promised with confidence using the available-to-promise function within master scheduling? Answering yes to those kinds of questions means it's working.

By the way, while we're talking about pilots, we should point out that it's generally a good idea to pilot as many processes as possible. So far in this book, we've talked about piloting Sales & Operations Planning, master scheduling, and MRP. Where practical, you should also pilot sales forecasting, inventory transaction processing, and bill of material creation and maintenance. Look for opportunities to pilot. Avoid big bangs—or even little bangs.

THREE KINDS OF PILOTS

Doing it right means using three different types of pilots—the computer pilot, the conference room pilot, and the live pilot.

1. The computer pilot.

This simply means checking out the hardware and software very thoroughly. It means running the programs on the computer, and debugging them. (Yes, there will be bugs in the software no matter how much you paid for it or how large the customer base.) This process should begin as soon as the programs are available.

Often, the computer pilot will deal initially with dummy items and dummy data. This should come with the software package. The dummy products are things like bicycles, pen and pencil sets, and the dummy data are transactions made up to test the programs. Then, if practical, run the new programs using real data from the company, using as much data as can readily be put into the system.

Next, do volume testing. Sooner or later, you'll need a program to copy your current data into the new formats required by the new software. Get that program sooner. Then copy your files over, and do volume testing. You're looking for problems with run times, storage, degradation of response times, whatever. Who knows, your computer may need more speed, more storage, more of both. (Doing one's homework at the onset of the project means recognizing these possibilities, and putting contingency money into the project budget to cover them if needed.)

In addition to hardware, other major objectives of the computer pilot are to ensure the software works on the computer and to learn more about it. The key players are the systems and data processing staff, usually with some help from one or more project team members.

2. *The conference room pilot.*

This follows the computer pilot. The main objectives of the conference room pilot are education and training: for the users to learn more about the software, to learn how to use it, and to manage their part of the business with it and make sure it fits the business. This process can also help to establish procedures and to identify areas that may require policy directions.

The key people involved are the users, primarily the folks in customer service, the master scheduler(s), the material planners, and probably some people from purchasing. They meet three to five times per week in a conference room equipped with at least one work station for every two people. The items involved are real-world items, normally ones that will be involved in the live pilot. The data, however, will be dummy data, for two reasons:

a. Live data shouldn't be used because the company's still not ready to run this thing for real. Everyone's still in the learning and testing mode.

b. It's important to exercise the total system (people, as well as software) as much as possible. Some of the dummy data for the conference room pilot should be created so it will present as many challenges as possible to the people and the software.

One technique that works nicely is for a key person, perhaps the project leader, to play Murphy (as in Murphy's Law—"whatever can go wrong, will go wrong"). As the conference room pilot is being operated, Murphy periodically appears and scraps out an entire lot of production or becomes a supplier who'll be three weeks late shipping or causes a machine to go down or generates a mandatory and immediate engineering change.[3]

---

[3] We can remember one project leader who had a sweatshirt made up. It was navy blue with MURPHY printed in red gothic lettering.

Murphy needs to determine if the players know the right responses to both major pieces of the system:

    a. The computer side—the hardware and the software. Do the people know how to enter and promise customer orders, how to update the master schedule, how to use pegging, firm planned orders, and the other technical functions within the software?

    b. The people part—and this gets at feedback. Do the planners know whom to give feedback to if they can't solve an availability problem on one of their items? Does the master scheduler know how and whom to notify in Customer Service if a customer order is going to be missed? Do the Customer Service people know to notify the customer as soon as they know a shipment will be missed?

This last point gets at the important ERP principle of "silence is approval." This refers to mandatory feedback when something goes wrong. In a Class A company, feedback is part of everyone's job: sales, planning, plant, purchasing, and suppliers. As long as things are going well, no one needs to say anything. However, as soon as people become aware that one of their schedules won't be met, it's their job to provide immediate feedback to their customer, which could be the next work center, the real end customer, or someone in between.

Presenting the people and the software with difficult challenges in the conference room pilot will pay dividends in the live pilot and cutover stages. One company we worked with used a slogan during their business meetings and conference room pilot: Make It Fail. Super! This is another version of bulletproofing. During the conference room phase, they worked hard at exposing the weak spots, finding the problems, making it fail. The reason: so that in the live pilot phase *it would work*.[4]

The conference room pilot should be run until the users really know the system. Here are some good tests for readiness:

---

[4] One of your authors used to fly airplanes for a living, and crashed many times. Fortunately, it was always in the simulator. The fact that he never crashed in the real world is due in large part to the simulator. The conference room pilot is like a simulator; it allows us to crash but without serious consequences.

a. Ask the users, before they enter a transaction into the system, what the results of that transaction will be. When they can routinely predict what will result, they know the system well.

b. Select several master schedule and MRP output reports (or screens) at random. Ask the users to explain what every number on the page means, why it's there, how it got there, and so forth. When they can do that routinely, they've got a good grasp of what's going on.

c. Are the people talking to each other? Are the feedback linkages in place? Do the people know to whom they owe feedback when things go wrong? The essence of successful ERP is people communicating with each other. Remember, this is a *people* system, made possible by the computer.

If the prior steps have been done correctly and the supporting elements are in place, the conference room pilot should not take more than a month or so.

Jerry Clement of the Oliver Wight group has a fine approach to dealing with this issue: "After the conference room pilot is virtually complete, I recommend running a full business simulation with both the outside and inside experts totally hands-off. If everyone executes with comfort, you're ready to install. I go one step further: I give the end users a veto over going live. If they don't feel we're ready, we must fix the issue before we go live. Think about hearing the end users saying, 'Hey, this stuff really works. What are we waiting for? Let's turn this baby on!' I hear that after a good conference room pilot when the end users really believed they counted."

3. The live pilot.

This is that moment of truth we mentioned earlier. It's when master scheduling and Material Requirements Planning go into operation for the first time in the real world. The objective of the live pilot is to *prove* master scheduling and MRP will work within the company. Until then, that can't be said. All that one could say up to that point are things like: "It should work," "We think it'll work," "It really ought to work." Only after the live pilot has been run successfully can the people say, "It works."

Before we get into the details of the live pilot, let's recap what we've covered so far by taking a look at Figure 11-2.

Figure 11-2
Three Types of Pilots

Type	Key People	Items/Data	Objectives
Computer	Systems people Project leader	Dummy/dummy Live/dummy Live/live	1. Learn more about the software. 2. Discover bugs. 3. Check for problems with run time, response time, and storage.
Conference Room	Customer svc. (Order entry) Master sched'r. MRP planners Systems analyst Project leader		1. Do further user education and training. 2. Build in feedback. 3. Verify that the software fits the business.
Live	Customer svc. (Order entry) Master sched'r. MRP planners Project leader		1. Use the system in the real world. 2. Prove that it works. 3. Obtain a sign-off from the users.

Selecting the Live Pilot

What are the criteria for a good live pilot? Some of the considerations are:

1. Size.

It requires enough items to get a good test of how the overall man/machine system performs, but not so many items as to get overwhelmed. Try to keep the total number of items (products, components, raw materials) to less than 500.

2. Product orientation.

The pilot should represent all the items for an entire product family (in the case of a simple product, such as clothing or cosmetics), a single product (moderately complex products, like some office equipment), or a part of a product (highly complex products, such as aircraft or machine tools). In the last example, the pilot might be one leg in the bill of materials or a modular planning bill for an option.

3. Good cross-section.

The pilot group should contain a good mix of finished products, subassemblies or intermediates, manufactured items, purchased items, and raw materials.

4. Relatively self-contained.

The fewer common parts contained in the pilot, the better. Items used in both the pilot product and others will not give a good test of MRP. MRP will not be aware of all the requirements for those items. The usual way of handling this is to post the MRP-generated requirements back to the old system. Some degree of commonality is almost always present (raw materials, in many cases), but try to pick a pilot where it's at a minimum.

5. Best planner.

If the company has material planners already and they're organized on a product basis, try to run the pilot on the product handled by the best planner. This is a people-intensive process, and it needs to have as much going for it as possible.

Look Before You Leap

Let's consider what has to be in place prior to the live pilot. One element is a successful conference room pilot, where the users have proven they understand the system thoroughly. The other key elements are data integrity, education, and training. Please refer to the Implementers' Checklist at the end of this chapter.

The project team should address the first six entries on the checklist. All must be answered yes. The project leader then reports the results to the executive steering committee and asks for formal permission to launch the live pilot. Only after that's received should they proceed.

Operating the Live Pilot

When everything's in place and ready to go, start running the pilot items on MS/MRP and stop running them on the old system. The objectives are to prove MS/MRP is working and to obtain user sign-off. Is it predicting the shortages, giving correct recommendations, and so forth? Are the users, the master scheduler(s), and the material planners making the proper responses and taking the correct action? Are the users prepared to state formally that they can run their part of the business with these tools? If the users are unwilling and/or unable to sign off on the system, then one of several factors is probably present:

- It's not working properly.
- They don't understand it.
- Both of the above.

In any of these cases, the very worst thing would be to proceed into the cutover phase—to put all the remaining items onto the new system. First, aggressively go after the problem: Either fix the element that's not working properly or correct the deficiency in education and training that's causing the user not to understand it, or both.

Run the live pilot for as long as it takes.

Don't go beyond the pilot stage until it's working and the users have signed off. This is one area where the aggressive implementation mentality must take a back seat. Everyone—executive steering committee, project team, users—should understand that the company won't go beyond the live pilot until it's been proven to work and until the users are comfortable with it.

Plan to run the live pilot for about a month, or longer if manufacturing cycles are long and speeds are slow. It's essential to observe how the man/machine system performs over a number of weeks to prove it really works. A week is not enough time, and a quarter is probably too long (for planning purposes) for most companies.

During the live pilot, don't neglect training. Get the other planning people as close to the pilot operation as possible, without getting in the way of the folks who are operating it. People not involved in the pilot need all the input they can get because they'll be on the firing line soon when the rest of the items are cut over to ERP.

The pilot must be successful to go to cutover, and visible success supports behavior change. Therefore, make sure the other planning folks can see the success.

CUTOVER

Once the live pilot is working well and the users are comfortable with it, it's time to cut over the rest of the items onto the master schedule and MRP.

There are two different ways to cut over. It can be done in one group, or the remaining items can be divided into multiple groups and cut over one at a time.

The multiple-group approach is preferable because it has the following advantages:

1. *It's less risky.* It represents a more controlled process.

2. *It's easier on the people.* If the first group to cut over belongs to planner A, then planners B and C should be deeply involved in helping planner A. It reduces planner A's workload, and also provides additional training for B and C. When planner B cuts over, planners A and C can help him or her.

The multiple-group approach, on the other hand, may not always be practical and/or necessary. In some companies, there is so much commonality of components that it's difficult to isolate groups. This means that during the cutover process, many items will be partially but not totally on the new system. The difficulties in passing requirements from the new system to the old (or vice versa) can easily outweigh the benefits gained from using multiple groups. In this case, the one-group approach would probably be best. It's usually better at this point to move ahead quickly rather than to spend lots of time and effort transferring requirements for common parts.

Sometimes the multiple-group approach may not be necessary. A company with only a few thousand items or less may conclude their entire population of items is small enough, and there's no real need to break it down any further.

A Word About Timing

Sometimes companies get hung up on a timing issue with cutover, specifically an accounting cutoff. Don't delay cutover for any appreciable amount of time—waiting for the beginning of the month, the beginning of the quarter, or (shudder) the new fiscal year. Rather, the systems folks should have any necessary bridging programs ready to go to feed data from the master schedule and MRP side of ERP into the accounting systems. In this way, cutover can occur as soon as practical and not be delayed waiting for the passage of time.

The Need for Feedback during Cutover

There's a potential dilemma here for you job shop people:

- This cutover is a phase I activity. The master scheduling and MRP planning tools are being made operational.

- However, closing the loop in a job shop is a phase II activity, which comes later. (Even in a flow shop, where plant scheduling can be made operational in phase I, supplier scheduling won't be fully implemented until phase II, for reasons we'll cover later.) How can master scheduling and MRP be made operational prior to that?

The answer is that there must be a form of loop closing even during phase I. It's essential. Without feedback from the plant and purchasing, the planning people won't be notified when jobs won't be completed on schedule. They must have that feedback, or they will not be able to keep the order dates valid. Therefore, the principle of silence is approval applies here, even at this early stage. This means that anticipated delay reporting from both the plant and purchasing must be implemented as part of phase 1. However, there's even a bit more to it than that for you job shop folks.

At this point, the company's beginning to operate with the formal priority planning system (MS/MRP) but doesn't yet have the priority execution system (the dispatching portion of plant floor control) in place. Given good feedback, order due dates can be kept valid and up to date, but the tools to communicate those changing priorities to the plant floor still aren't available. Further, without Capacity Requirements Planning, there's no specific, detailed visibility into future overloads and underloads at all the work centers on the plant floor.

A good approach here is to develop an interim, simple, possibly crude, plant scheduling system. Use it to get the job done until the full-blown plant floor control system is on the air. This interim system is usually manual, not computerized, and operates with order due dates and possibly a simplified back scheduling approach. (Example 1: Job A has a four-week lead time. It's due two weeks from now. It should be 50 percent finished. Is it 50 percent finished? If not, it should be given priority. Example 2: Back schedule from the order due date assuming all operations take the same amount of time. Set operation due dates accordingly.)

In addition, it's highly desirable to assign one or more plant people full-time to the project during this transition phase. This person's responsibility is to help the folks on the plant floor work on the right jobs. He or she maintains close contact with the interim plant scheduling system, with the material planners, and with the foremen. She finds out about the reschedules coming from the planners, makes sure the foremen are up to date, generates the anticipated delay report for the planners, helps break bottlenecks, and so forth.[5]

The last point, breaking bottlenecks, brings up another post-cutover issue: overloads. This can be a problem because, again, Capacity Requirements Planning isn't operational yet. Overloads are bad because the work won't get through on time. Underloads are al-

---

[5] This person can also make progress on plant floor cleanup activities during this period. Example: getting some of the large queues off the floor and back into the stockroom. The newly generated MRP priority information can help a lot in this job.

most as bad because people will run out of work and get a negative feeling about ERP.

This can be a major problem, and one that the project team needs to be aware of and follow very closely. Planning ahead can help a lot. Some companies have done a pre-cutover dry run or simulation to see what's likely to occur. Contingency plans can help a lot: plan A might be what to do in case of an overload; plan B for an underload.

Once again, that key plant person mentioned earlier can be a big help—by eyeballing the queues, talking to the foremen about their problems, talking to the material planners about what ERP shows is coming soon, breaking the bottlenecks, and making certain the plant doesn't run out of work. During this tricky transition period, do whatever possible to anticipate problems. Identifying them ahead of time can minimize their impact.

The buyers have a similar role to play with their suppliers. They need to follow up closely with their suppliers, learn which orders will not be shipped on time, and communicate these to the planners via the anticipated delay report.

There's also a potential capacity problem with suppliers. Since MRP is now involved in planning orders, the orders might not be coming out in the same pattern as before. The company could inadvertently be creating severe overloads or, just as bad perhaps, severe underloads at key suppliers. The buyers need to stay in close contact with these suppliers to solve these kinds of problems should they arise.

The three most important things the people can do during this period are:

1. Communicate

2. Communicate

3. Communicate

Talk to each other. Don't relax. Keep the groups—steering committee and project team—meeting at least as frequently as before, perhaps more so. Consider creating a spin-off task force to focus solely on these transitional problems, meeting perhaps every day.

Cutover is a very intense period. Plan to work long hours and to make additional resources available. The project leader should be present constantly—"carrying the water bucket" and helping the users in any way he or she can. That also applies to the assistant project leader, if there is one, the department head (P & IC manager or whatever), and the key system people. Don't overwhelm the planners. Rather, overwhelm the problems. Get through all of the output. Take all the necessary actions. Make it work.

THE POTENTIAL INVENTORY BLIP

What's the company's number one priority when implementing ERP? Is it to reduce the inventories? Nope, that's not even priority number two. The number one priority, of course, is to run the business. Number two is to implement Enterprise Resource Planning. Reducing inventories, during the implementation process, probably isn't even in the top five.

Should inventories start to drop during implementation? Toward the end, they should. But beware, *they may go up before they go down.* In a given company, there's about a 50–50 chance this will happen.

Here's why.

When the company starts to run master scheduling and MRP, its logic will identify a certain number of reschedule-ins and reschedule-outs. These would be for both open production orders and open purchase orders. Some will be needed sooner, some later. The logic of MRP will also recognize items that are needed but for which there is no scheduled receipt. It will recommend releasing a new order.

What the logic of MRP will *not* do is make recommendations about inventory already in the stockrooms and warehouses. It's in the on-hand balance; it can't be rescheduled out because it's already in stock. It'll probably be needed but not until later. This phenomenon will cause some companies, in the short run, to expedite more than they're able to de-expedite. That introduces the possibility of a temporary inventory rise. (See Figure 11-3.)

Figure 11-3
What Might Happen to Your Inventories

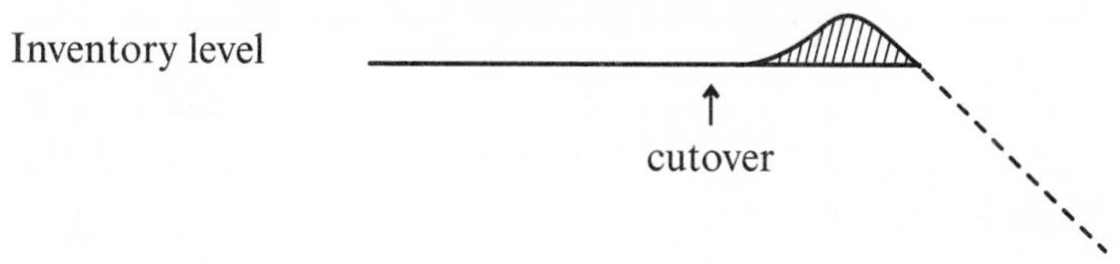

Be aware this may happen. It's not illegal, immoral, or fattening. It should be anticipated. Then, if it doesn't happen, so much the better.

DON'T STARVE THE SOURCES

Let's double back to a problem we touched on a short while earlier. Inventories that drop too quickly can also be a problem. A sharp drop in the inventory level may be an indication the implementation job is not being done properly.

The problem is the potential for "starving out" the plant and/or some key suppliers because less work is being released to them. This is most likely to happen in companies that had far too much inventory before implementation. After basic ERP is on the air, Material Requirements Planning will indicate there is far less need for parts or raw material. Therefore, few new orders are released to the plant and suppliers. These people, who have become accustomed to a regular flow of work over the years, now see few orders.

Consider how a plant foreman or key supplier would feel in this situation. After hearing all the talk about how great ERP is going to be, the first thing that happens is that orders dry up, and there's no work. ERP will have a lot of negative impressions to live down in this case, and these first impressions may be lasting ones.

My message is: Don't lose sight of this issue during cutover and risk starving the plant and/or the key suppliers. If necessary, be prepared to release work early to keep the flow of work going to them. The necessary adjustments to work loads and, therefore, inventories can be made gradually over a longer period, without turning these vital sources of supply against ERP.

THE INADVERTENT BIG BANG CUTOVER

Here's a potential booby trap. Some companies have accidentally backed into a big bang cutover, as follows:

1. They need to implement a new inventory transaction processing system in order to reach 95 percent inventory accuracy.

2. They need to do this prior to going on the air with master scheduling and MRP. This is proper since the records must be made accurate first.

3. The current inventory system contains *ordering logic;* it gives them signals of when to reorder. However, there is no ordering logic in the new inventory transaction processing module; its function is to maintain inventory balances. The ordering logic is contained within a module called MRP.

4. The company implements the new inventory processor and simultaneously discontinues using the old one.

5. The result is the company has lost its ability to order material and parts.

The wrong solution: Discover this too late, scramble, and plug in the new software module that contains the ordering logic (MRP). The result is to implement master scheduling and MRP across the board, untested, with the likelihood of inaccurate inventory records, bad bills, a suspect master schedule, and inadequate user education, training, and buy-in. The ultimate big bang cutover.

The right solution to this problem is to recognize ahead of time that it might happen. Then, make plans to prevent this inadvertent big bang from happening.

The alternatives here include running both the old and new inventory processors until master scheduling and MRP come up, writing some throw away programs to bridge from the new system to the old, or, worst case, developing an interim set of ordering logic to be used during this period.

PERFORMANCE MEASUREMENTS

Begin to measure performance at three levels:

1. Performance goals.

As soon as is practical, start to relate actual performance to the measurements identified in the performance goal step (Chapter 6). Make them simple and visible to all the people involved. Questions to ask:

• Is our performance improving?

• Are we getting closer to our goals?

- If not, why not? What's not working?

Remember, there's urgency to start getting results, to get the bang for the buck. In other words, "We paid for this thing—have we taken delivery?"

2. Operational measurements—ABCD Checklist.

This checklist is designed to help a company evaluate its performance and to serve as a driver for continuous improvement.

3. Technical measurements.

These cover the technical specifics of how the man/machine system is performing. Examples:

a. Number of master schedule changes in the near-term zone reserved for emergency changes. This should be a small number.

b. Master schedule orders rescheduled in, compared to those rescheduled out. These numbers should be close to equal.

c. Number of master schedule items overpromised.

d. MRP exception message volume, the number of action recommendations generated by the MRP program each week. For job shops, the exception rate should be 10 percent or less. For flow shops, the rate may be higher because of more activity per item. (The good news is that these kinds of companies usually have far fewer items.)

e. Late order releases, the number of orders released with less than the planning lead time remaining. A good target rule of thumb here is 5 percent or less of all orders released.

f. Production orders and purchase orders rescheduled in versus rescheduled out. Here again, these numbers should be close to equal.

g. Stock outs, for both manufactured and purchased items.

h. Inventory turnover—finished goods and raw materials, at a minimum. For job shops, tracking work-in-process inventory turns may be deferred until phase II.

i. User time required—the amount of time planning people and others must spend to perform their data input tasks (customer order entry, bill of material maintenance, etc.) compared to the times specified in the performance goals.

Except for inventory turns, most of these measurements are done weekly. Typically, they're broken out by the individual planner.

Here's one last point on this entire subject of measuring performance during this early stage. Walt Goddard said it very well:

My advice to the project team is to look below the surface. Frequently, at first glance, a new system looks like it's working well—the people are busy using it and hopefully saying good things about it. Yet, often this is on the surface and it has yet to get *into the bone and marrow of the company* [authors' italics]. A smart manager needs to probe. One of the effective ways of doing it is to sample the actions that a master scheduler or planner has taken to see if, in fact, he or she would have done the same thing. If not, does that person have a good explanation for the difference? Don't assume that things are okay but, rather, expect they're not. Then, you can have a pleasant surprise if things are in good shape.

AUDIT/ASSESSMENT II

This step is primarily an "in-process" check on the status and success of the implementation to date, and serves as a go/no-go decision point for phase II. The participants here are the same as in audit/assessment I, who we identified in Chapter 5 as "the executives, a wide range of operating managers, and, in virtually all cases, outside consultants with Class A credentials . . ." The process involves:

- formally reviewing what's been done so far,

- verifying that the performance goals are being met,

- tying its performance back to the vision statement and establishing that the vision statement is still valid or that it needs to be modified,

- identifying what, if any, of the phase I activities need to be modified or redone,

- assessing the company's readiness to press on with phase II of the implementation.

When all of the above points are positive, the audit/assessment team should present its findings to the executive steering committee with a recommendation to proceed to phase II.

This concludes our discussion of implementing basic ERP. Remember, at this point, many companies really don't have a complete set of tools. There's urgency to close the loop completely—to extend the power of ERP out into the total supply chain—and that'll be covered in the next chapter.

Q & A WITH THE AUTHORS

MIKE: Tom, we've talked about companies that have installed Enterprise Software but made no attempts to change their business processes—in other words, ES but no ERP. But I know a company that tried to do both ES *and* ERP at the same time. They got the software installed but failed miserably with ERP. Now they've got a mess on their hands and want to make ERP work. What should they do?

TOM: I'd say their situation is fundamentally the same as any other re-implementer. They tried to "do ERP" and it didn't work. Why not? Probably because they neglected the A item and the B item: little or no education, little or no attention paid to data integrity. In other words, they didn't follow the Proven Path. Everything we said about re-implementers back in Chapter 1 seems to apply to these folks. They need to re-implement, using the Proven Path. One decision they will need to make is whether to do a company-wide implementation or a Quick Slice, which we'll get into just a bit later.

IMPLEMENTERS' CHECKLIST

Function: Going on the Air—Basic ERP (Phase I)

Task	Complete Yes	No
1. Master scheduling/MRP pilot selected.	____	____
2. Computer pilot completed.	____	____
3. Conference room pilot completed.	____	____
4. Necessary levels of data accuracy—95 percent minimum on inventory records, 98 percent minimum on bills—still in place on all items, not merely the pilot items.	____	____
5. Initial education and training at least 80 percent complete throughout the company.	____	____
6. Executive steering committee authorization to start the live pilot.	____	____
7. Live pilot successfully operated, and user sign-off obtained.	____	____
8. Feedback links (anticipated delay reports) in place for both plant and purchasing.	____	____
9. Plant schedules (for flow shops) or interim plant floor control system (for job shops) in place and operating.	____	____
10. Executive steering committee authorization to cut over.	____	____
11. Cutover onto MS/MRP complete.	____	____
12. Performance being measured at all three levels: master scheduling, MRP, and plant floor.	____	____

Chapter 12

Going on the Air—Supply Chain Integration (Phase II)

The second major phase of going on the air involves extending the power of ERP into the total supply chain: the plants, the suppliers, the distribution centers, and the customers. We'll tackle them in that sequence. You'll see, however, more flexibility than in phase I. It's not quite as clear-cut in which order processes must be implemented.

Also, please keep in mind as we go through this set of steps that the ABCs of implementation fully apply: The people—inside and also outside the company—are the A item; the data is the B item; and the computer hardware and software represent the C item. This means that education and data integrity are essential, just as for phase I.

SUPPLY CHAIN INTEGRATION— INTERNALLY WITHIN THE PLANTS

With the implementation of master scheduling (MS) and Material Requirements Planning (MRP), many companies will have for the first time truly valid schedules of what's needed and when—in a constantly changing environment. The challenge here is to communicate these schedules to the plant(s), as frequently as needed and in a manner that best serves the people on the plant floor.

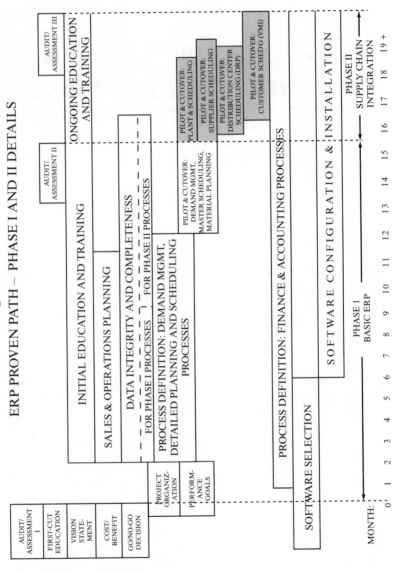

Figure 12-1

ERP PROVEN PATH – PHASE I AND II DETAILS

Here is another case where life in a flow shop is simpler than in a job shop. Implementing plant scheduling in a flow environment is normally far less difficult, so let's tackle that one first.

Flow Shops

Plant schedules for flow shops are most often derived directly from master scheduling and/or MRP. This is practical, because the nature of a flow form of organization is that material goes into the front end of the process (line, cell, work center, department) and comes out the other end as a finished product or component. This is not the case in a job shop, where a given job needs to travel to a number of different work centers before it is completed as a finished item. For more on this, please see Appendix B.

For flow shops, therefore, it's typically not a difficult matter to get the appropriate orders from MS/MRP and restate them as a schedule—finishing schedule, filling and packaging schedule, final assembly schedule, whatever—and make them available to the folks on the plant floor.

A brief pilot is appropriate here, and typically that's done by selecting an area, line, or cell within the plant and piloting that. This can help to verify that the schedules are being derived correctly from master scheduling or MRP, and that they're realistic and attainable.

Opportunity to Accelerate.

Now, the fact that this isn't difficult coupled with the flow shop environment leads to an opportunity to accelerate the implementation. Some flow shops might be able to implement plant scheduling during phase I and not wait until phase II. Here's why:

1. It may be *possible.* Let's say the pilot product line for MS/MRP is produced or at least finished in one and only one production resource, which we'll call Department X . If no other items are done there, then all of Department X's work load will be on the new system at the time of the pilot. Valid plant schedules for Department X can then be generated.

2. It may be *practical,* because the implementation work load for

plant scheduling—systems, education and training, data requirements—is typically not that large.

The same ground rules apply here as with any pilot and cutover: If at any time you can see that the new process is not working, don't add more items onto the process. Stop and fix what's wrong before proceeding.

As additional product groups come up on MS/MRP during cutover, the new plant scheduling processes can be kicked in at the same time. The result: As phase I wraps up with all items on master scheduling and MRP, plant scheduling has also been implemented for all items. We urge you flow shop people to look closely at this opportunity and to pursue it if it makes sense for you.

If for some reason, you can't do it this way, then we recommend that you tackle this as early as possible in phase II. Pilot the plant scheduling process in one production resource, prove that it's working properly, and then bring up the rest of the resources quickly.

A caveat: Don't bite off more than you can chew. Here and elsewhere throughout this chapter, we'll identify "opportunities to accelerate," to move phase II activities into phase I. But before you decide to do so, make sure that you have the resources of time, people, and mental energy to tackle the acceleration. This could be a significant issue for those of you who have multiple plants to deal with. If you decide you don't have the organizational bandwidth to do it in phase I, that's fine—leave it for phase II.

Feedback.

Another caveat: Don't forget feedback. In the last chapter, we stated the principle of "silence is approval": When something goes wrong and a schedule can't be met, people owe feedback up the line. When the plant—for whatever reason—can't hit a schedule, it must alert the scheduling people so that they can do damage control and develop plan B.

Feedback is not a software module; it won't come as part of your software package. This is a person-to-person communication process, which can be verbal, handwritten, and/or employing a computer message handling capability. Feedback also includes daily status meetings and the generation of anticipated delay reports. The feedback links established in phase I should be reviewed, tested, strengthened, made to work even better. The better the feedback, the better the closed-loop ERP processes will operate. Without feedback, there is no closed loop. As you bring up plant scheduling, make sure the feedback links are in place and working.

Job Shops

Now for the more difficult environment, the job shop, where there's more complexity and more elements to deal with. Let's talk first about two issues that concern the overall approach: sequence and timing. We recommend you implement in the following sequence:

1. Shop floor control (dispatching).

2. Capacity Requirements Planning.[1]

3. Input-output control.

Shop floor control comes first because it's urgent to communicate those changing priorities to the plant floor. Until it's possible to do that via the dispatching system, the company will have to live with the interim system. In all likelihood, that will be somewhat cumbersome, time consuming, and less than completely efficient.

Capacity Requirements Planning comes next. It's less urgent. Also, when Rough-Cut Capacity Planning was implemented as a part of basic ERP, the company probably began to learn more about future capacity requirements than ever before.

Input-output control has to follow CRP. Input-output tracks actual performance to the capacity plan. The capacity plan (from CRP) must be in place before input-output control can operate.

A Special Situation

Closing the loop in manufacturing becomes easy where the company has it all, or most of it, already. Some companies implemented shop floor control years before they ever heard of MRP II or ERP. This

---

[1] This refers to the specific technique known as (detailed) Capacity Requirements Planning. The other capacity planning technique, Rough-Cut Capacity Planning, has already been implemented in phase 1.

was frequently done in the mistaken belief that the causes of the problems—missed shipments, inefficiencies, excessive work-in-process inventories—were on the plant floor. Almost invariably, the *symptoms* are visible on the plant floor, but the *causes* get back to the lack of a formal priority planning system that works.

If most or all of the shop floor control/CRP tools are already working, that's super! In this case, closing the loop in manufacturing can occur just about simultaneously with cutover onto basic MRP. Several companies we've worked with had this happy situation, and it sure made life a lot easier.

A few words of caution. If you already have a shop floor control system and plan to keep it, don't assume that the data is accurate. Verify the accuracy of the routings, and the validity of the standards and work center data. Also, make certain that the system contains the standard shop floor control tools that have been proven to work (valid back scheduling logic, good order close-out tools, etc.). The Standard System[i] can often help greatly in this evaluation.

Plant Data Collection

Plant data collection means collecting data from the plant floor. (How's that for a real revelation?) However, it does not necessarily mean *automated* data collection (i.e., terminals on the plant floor with bells and whistles and flashing lights). In other words, the plant data collection process doesn't have to be automated to operate closed-loop MRP successfully. Some very effective plant floor control systems have used paper and pencil as their data collection device.

A company that already has automated data collection on the plant floor has a leg up. It should make the job easier. If you don't have it, we recommend that you implement it here—provided it won't delay the project. (If it'll slow down the project, do it later—after ERP is on the air.) Bar coding is particularly attractive here; it's simple, it's proven, and it's not threatening to most people because they see it in use every week when they buy groceries.

Pilot

We recommend a brief pilot of certain plant floor control activities. Quite a few procedures are going to be changing, and a lot of people are going to be involved. A two- to three-week pilot will help validate the procedures, the transactions, the software, and most importantly, the people's education and training.

It's usually preferable to pilot plant floor control with selected jobs rather than selected work centers. With these few selected jobs moving through a variety of work centers, one can usually get a good handle on how well the basics are operating.

Note the use of the word basics. The pilot will not be able to test the dispatch lists. Obviously, that won't be possible until after cutover, when all of the jobs are on the system and hence can appear on the dispatch lists in the proper sequence.

Cutover

Once the pilot has proven the procedures, transactions, software, and education and training, it's time for cutover. Here are the steps:

1. Load the plant status data into the computer.

2. Start to operate plant floor control and to use the dispatch list. Correct whatever problems pop up, fine-tune the procedures and software as required, and make it work.

3. Begin to run Capacity Requirements Planning. Be careful— don't go out and buy a million dollars' worth of new equipment based on the output of the first CRP run. Review the output carefully and critically. Get friendly with it. Within a few weeks, people should start to gain confidence in it and be able to use it to help manage this part of the business.

4. Start to generate input-output reports. Establish the tolerances and define the ground rules for taking corrective action.

5. Start to measure plant performance in terms of both priority and capacity.

6. Last, and perhaps most important of all, don't neglect the feedback links we mentioned earlier in the flow shop section of this chapter. Feedback is equally, perhaps even more, important to job shops.

FINITE SCHEDULING

Finite scheduling marries detailed plant scheduling and capacity planning into one powerful tool. Finite scheduling software, available from a sizable number of suppliers, calculates its recommended scheduling solution to the situation presented to it. Then it displays this solution and the relevant factors (stockouts, cost, inventory, changeovers, output, etc.) to the person controlling the software. When used intelligently, it enables plant schedulers to develop better schedules. It helps them to balance demand and supply at the most detailed, finite level.

These packages work well when they're tied directly to the company's ERP processes. In this environment, the near-term master schedule—typically between one and four weeks into the future—is downloaded into the finite scheduler and the scheduling person begins the interactive simulation process. The scheduler selects the solution that he or she prefers, and this schedule is then uploaded back to the master schedule and/or down to the plant floor system for execution. One significant benefit here is that the schedulers are equipped with a much greater ability to solve problems, by making available to them a clear picture of customer demand and resource supply at the most detailed level. Thus they're often better able to do a first-rate job of meeting customer needs with the most efficient use of resources.

That's finite scheduling. Now let's talk about when and how to implement it. First, should you implement finite scheduling at all? The answer is a definite "maybe." If you don't have complex scheduling problems, you'll probably get along fine without it. If your scheduling task is difficult, even moderately so, a good finite scheduling process can range from being a big help to being nearly indispensable.

For virtually all implementations, we recommend that finite scheduling be implemented later, in phase III. This is because implementing this tool will consume time and resources, and typically will not fit the project timing we've outlined. Implementing finite scheduling during phase II, or even worse phase I, can run the risk of delaying the entire ERP project—and that's a no-no. If you feel a need to implement finite scheduling very early, okay—do that first and then start the ERP project later. Recognize, however, that finite scheduling, like any other scheduling tool, requires valid dates of customer need—both external and internal. If you current master scheduling and material planning tools don't provide valid dates, please examine carefully how much finite scheduling can help you until you can get and keep those dates valid and current.

Implementing finite scheduling in phase III has the benefits of:

1. not delaying the overall ERP implementation.

2. making the finite scheduling implementation easier, because most of the data that finite scheduling needs has already been loaded and scrubbed as a part of the overall ERP project.

3. having a more knowledgeable and confident group of users, who have already achieved a big win (the successful ERP initiative) and are ready for more.

If you do it this way, you will give finite scheduling a substantially better chance for success. This is because of the favorable situation with the A item, the people, and the B item, the data. Select good finite scheduling software, the C item, and you'll be in very good shape. All that remains is to do a good job going on the air.

If possible, take a standard pilot-and-cutover approach. In flow shops, this is normally a very practical matter because, here again, flow shops tend to be much less "entangled" than job shops: The products run on line A, for example, aren't run anywhere else. Thus the pilot-and-cutover approach can work nicely.

In a job shop, it may not be quite so easy. The reason: any one work center in a job shop may be receiving jobs from a variety of other work centers. Further, upon completion, the jobs can go to a number of different work centers. For this reason, it's sometimes not possible to "disentangle" the job shop sufficiently to allow for a pilot and cutover.

Nor may a parallel approach be practical. As we've said, the essence of a parallel is to compare the new system's output against that of the current system. But that won't work, because the finite scheduling logic will be providing far different schedules than whatever is being generated today.

Therefore, an across-the-board cutover might be the only way to go. If so, be very careful. Using the conference room pilot approach, scrutinize the test output from the finite scheduling system as carefully and intensely as possible. Deeply involve the key players: plant management, supervisors, dispatchers, material planners, and master schedulers. Overwhelm the potential problems. Then when you go live with finite scheduling, keep the level of people involvement and intensity high and verify that the schedules do indeed make sense. Don't throw out the old system, whatever that may have been, but rather keep it ready in the event it needs to be reactivated. And be prepared to do just that, if the new system is not proving out. The potential difficulties in going on the air with finite scheduling in a job shop is yet another reason for this activity to wait for phase III.

Supply Chain Integration— Backwards to the Suppliers

It's time for a quiz. Now that we have the Internet, and B2B (business to business) transactions, and reverse auctions,[2] we can forget about all that stuff on supplier partnering, supplier teamwork, win-win relationships and so forth, right? Wrong. Forget about "all that stuff" at your peril. Yes, the Web has brought some new capabilities into the picture, but—sure enough—the fundamentals still remain and they are paramount.

John M. Paterson, a senior executive within IBM's purchasing operations, said this:

> The real value of Web services is in the integration of the supply chain rather than in being able to plug suppliers in and out based on price. Web-based services that tout spot buying and options are of little value to large manufacturers. (Authors' comment: and probably not great value for medium and small manufacturers either.) We want to develop continuity, quality, assured levels of supply from our OEMs. You don't develop lasting relationships with large suppliers from spot markets and option buys. . . .
>
> Our Web tools have enabled us to have a much more open relationship with our suppliers. Today, they have direct access to data on IBM . . . This is vital to creating the tightly coupled relationships on which we depend.[ii]

---

[2] A reverse auction consists of multiple sellers, with similar products, bidding against each other for a given customer's order. The supplier with the lowest price wins.

Figure 12-2

PURCHASED ITEM CHARACTERISTICS

CRITICALITY OF THE ITEM

	HIGH	*LOW*
C O S T *H I G H*	**II** Low Criticality High Cost	**III** High Criticality High Cost
O F		
T H E *L O W* **I T E M**	**I** Low Criticality Low Cost	**IV** High Criticality Low Cost

So should you buy everything from suppliers with whom you're tightly partnered? Not at all. There's definitely a role for spot markets and option buys, and it depends on the nature of the time you're buying. See Figure 12-2.

For items in quadrant III—high criticality and high cost—you probably don't want to buy these via "one-night stands" on the Web. These are items that cry out for long-term relationships with supplier partners who are closely tuned into the company's needs, products, markets, and so forth. In quadrant IV—high criticality with low cost—it's usually the same; cost of course is only one of a number of factors that determine an item's importance. The low-cost, low-criticality items in quadrant I are natural candidates for Web buying, as may be some of the items in quadrant II.

Yes, Virginia, supplier partnering is alive and well—even in this era of Web-based spot buying. On a dollar basis, most of a given company's purchased volume should come through a relatively few, highly important, closely-aligned suppliers. Well, an important element of supplier partnering is supplier scheduling, and that's what we'll talk about now.

Supplier scheduling is a phase II activity, because suppliers are somewhat like work centers in a job shop—any one of them can provide a range of items which go into many different product families. Therefore, it's usually necessary to have all, or at least most, products and components on MS/MRP to generate complete schedules for a given supplier. There are exceptions to this, and we'll examine them at the end of this section.

Here's a simplified look at supplier scheduling:

1. Establish long-term contractual relationships with suppliers.

2. Create a group of people (supplier schedulers) who are in direct contact with both suppliers and MRP, eliminating purchase requisitions for production items.

3. Give suppliers weekly or more frequent schedules, eliminating hard-copy purchase orders.

4. Get buyers out of the expedite-and-paperwork mode, freeing up their time to do the important parts of their jobs (sourcing, negotiation, contracting, cost reduction, value analysis, etc.).

In flow shops, supplier scheduling is usually the first thing that happens in phase II. For you job shop folks, supplier scheduling should be implemented either simultaneously with plant floor control, CRP, and input/output control or immediately after it. Most companies can do it simultaneously. Different people are involved: the foremen and some others for plant scheduling; the buyers, supplier schedulers, and suppliers for supplier scheduling.

If there is a resource conflict, it's often in the systems group. Perhaps there's simply too much systems work involved for both plant floor control and supplier scheduling to be done simultaneously. In this situation, close the loop in manufacturing first, then do purchasing. It's urgent to bring up the plant floor control system, so priority changes can be communicated effectively to the plant floor. Purchasing, even without supplier scheduling, should be in better shape than before. Basic ERP has been implemented, and probably for the first time ever, purchasing is able to give suppliers really good signals on what's needed and when.

Delaying supplier scheduling a bit is preferable to delaying plant floor control, if absolutely necessary. Try to avoid any delay, however, because it's best to be able to start in purchasing as soon as possible after the cutover onto basic ERP.

IMPLEMENTING SUPPLIER SCHEDULING

This process, as with every other part of implementing ERP, should be well managed and controlled. These are the steps:

1. Establish the approach.

The company has to answer the following kinds of questions: What will be the format of the business agreement? Will it be an open-ended format or for a fixed period of time? To whom will the supplier schedulers report: purchasing, production control, elsewhere? Will the company need to retain purchase order numbers even though they'll be eliminating hard-copy purchase orders?

2. Acquire the software.

There's good news and bad news here. The bad news is it may be necessary to write your own software for supplier scheduling. Many software packages don't have it. (Be careful: Many software suppliers claim to have a purchasing module as a part of their overall Enterprise System. What this usually means is their package can automate purchase requisitions and purchase order printing. Unfortunately, this is not the right objective. With supplier scheduling, the goal is to *eliminate* requisitions and hard-copy POs, not automate them. The good news is that writing the supplier scheduling programs is largely retrieval-and-display programming, drawn from existing files, which is typically less difficult.

3. Develop supplier education.

People who'll be involved with ERP need education about it. Suppliers are people (a potentially controversial point in some companies that treat their suppliers like dogs). Suppliers will be involved. Therefore, suppliers need education about ERP and supplier scheduling.

Most companies who've had success with supplier scheduling put together a one-day program for supplier education and training. The education part covers ERP, how material requirements planning generates and maintains valid due dates,[3] time fences, communications, feedback, and the concepts of customer/supplier partnerships and win-win.

The principle of silence is approval must be explained thoroughly and be well understood by key supplier people. This refers to the mandatory feedback from suppliers, as soon as they become aware that they will be unable to meet the supplier schedule. As long as the suppliers are silent, this means they will meet their scheduled deliveries. When something goes wrong, and they won't hit the schedule, it's their job to provide *immediate* feedback to their supplier scheduler.

The training part gets at the supplier schedule, how to read it, when and how to respond, when to provide feedback, and so forth.

4. Pilot with one or several suppliers.

Select one or a few suppliers and get their concurrence in advance to participate in the supplier scheduling pilot. A good supplier candidate for this pilot should supply substantial volume, should be cooperative, and ideally, would be located nearby. In the best of all possible worlds, this supplier would already be in supplier scheduling mode with one or more customers with Class A or B ERP but that's certainly not essential.

---

[3] Make certain that ERP is truly making that possible—that your due dates are now valid. Don't make the mistake of calling suppliers in and telling them how great ERP is if the dates on your purchase orders are no better than before. Let's make certain our own house is in order before we start to ask for major changes from suppliers.

Bring in their key people—sales manager, plant manager, key scheduling person, as well as the local sales person. Educate them, train them and, in the same session, cut them over onto supplier scheduling.

5. *Fine tune the process.*

Based on what's learned in this pilot, modify the approach if necessary, refine the education process, and tweak the software. Begin to measure the performance of your pilot supplier(s) and yourselves[4]— delivery performance, inventory levels, service to the plant floor, and so on.

6. *Educate and cut over the major suppliers.*

Go after the approximately 20 percent of the suppliers who are supplying about 80 percent of the purchased volume. Get their tentative concurrence in advance. Bring them into your company in groups of three to six suppliers per day. Or, if necessary, go to their plant. As in the pilot, educate them, train them, and cut them over on the same day.

If it isn't possible to get tentative concurrence in advance from a given supplier, attempt to convince them of supplier scheduling's benefits to them, as well as to the customer. Demonstrate how it's a win-win situation. Consider taking the one-day education session to their plant. If the supplier is still reluctant, involve your company president in direct contact with the supplier's president. (Carrying the water bucket is what presidents are for, right?) If all these efforts fail, give them ninety days or so to shape up. Show them some positive results with other suppliers already on supplier scheduling. If they're not cooperative by that time, start to look for a new supplier.

7. *Measure performance.*

As each supplier is cut over onto supplier scheduling, start to measure how well they *and* you are doing. Possibly for the first time ever,

---

[4] The suppliers can't perform well if you don't perform well. Just because a supplier isn't hitting the delivery dates doesn't mean that it's their fault; maybe your schedules aren't any good after all and you're constantly expediting around them.

a company can legitimately hold suppliers accountable for delivery performance—because probably for the first time ever, it can give suppliers valid due dates.

Also, begin tracking buyer performance and supplier scheduler performance. (For more details, see Chapter 15.) Communicate the measurements to everyone being measured. Raise the high bar—the level of expectation. When performance matches that, raise the bar again.

   8. Educate and cut over the remaining suppliers.

As soon as the major suppliers are on supplier scheduling, go after the remainder. The target should be 100 percent of all suppliers of production items on supplier scheduling. That will probably take longer than the several months implied on the Proven Path bar chart, but it's important to stick with it. It's also very helpful here if the company has already been successful in reducing the size of its supplier base, or is in the process of doing so.

Opportunity to Accelerate

There may be an opportunity to get started with supplier scheduling in phase I. Let's say you have a supplier who provides you with a limited number of items, all of which go into one product family. Well, if that family becomes the phase I pilot for master scheduling and MRP, then you could have a good opportunity to start supplier scheduling as a part of that pilot or shortly thereafter. Further, as additional product groups are cut over onto MS/MRP, there may be additional opportunities to bring certain suppliers up on supplier scheduling during phase I.

Supply Chain Integration— Forward to the Distribution Centers

Does your company make, for example, highly engineered-to-order widgets that go on spacecraft and jet fighters? If so, you probably don't stock them in warehouses all over the country and hence this section might not be highly relevant to you. On the other hand, if your company makes finished products that you stock in field warehouses or distribution centers, please read on.

First, a point about semantics. Elsewhere in this book, we talk about the undesirability of inventory: In general, the more you have the worse off you are. Then why, you may wonder, are we talking about warehousing inventory all over the country—and perhaps beyond? We like to make a distinction between warehousing and distributing. Warehouses typically are places where we keep a lot of stuff; distribution centers (DCs) receive product and—quickly, we hope—send it on its way to the customers. (Think about a Wal-Mart cross-dock DC for example: A high percentage of the product flowing in from manufacturers never hits the floor but goes right into trucks headed for the retail stores.) The DCs are necessary to receive and redistribute; hopefully, except for a few cases such as seasonality, they won't hold stock for very long.

The tool of choice here carries the acronym DRP, which stands for distribution requirements planning or, alternatively, distribution resource planning. Distribution *requirements* planning, which we'll call "little DRP," is a tool to schedule replenishment of inventory at remote locations such as distribution centers (DCs). It addresses when and how much of each product should be sent to which stocking points.

Distribution *resource* planning, "big DRP," adds the dimensions of freight planning (full carloads, truckloads), and space and manpower planning at the DCs. It's all of little DRP plus these extensions and enhancements.

DATA REQUIREMENTS

Much of the data needed for successful DRP is quite similar to that for other aspects of ERP. For little DRP you'll need a "bill of distribution," analogous to a bill of material at a plant, showing which products are stocked at which DCs. Also, for each product stocked at each DC, you'll need to have:

- Forecasts of future demand.

- Estimates of the replenishment lead time needed to get the product from its central stocking point to the DCs.

- The amount of safety stock or safety time needed to protect against stock outs at the DCs.

- On hand inventory balances.

- In-transit quantities.

For big DRP, in addition to the above, you'll need things such as:

- Product weight.

- Product size (cubic feet).

- Number of products per pallet.

- Staffing levels at each DC.

- Time estimates to receive and put away product.

- Time estimates to pick, pack, and ship product.

As with other parts of ERP, the distinction between forgiving and unforgiving data applies here. In DRP, the inventory records and the bills need to be highly accurate and that's typically the most challenging part of the data integrity task.

IMPLEMENTING DRP

Here we recommend not only the careful, controlled approach of pilot and cutover, but also to do a pilot within the pilot. The pilot should be one distribution center. The "mini-pilot" within that pilot should be a dozen or so products for that DC.

The purpose of the mini-pilot is to prove that little DRP is working, that it's giving the right recommendations as to when to replenish these products at the DC in question. That shouldn't take more than a few weeks, providing that the homework has been done correctly. Then it'll be time to cut over all products onto little DRP and to proceed to the full pilot.

This means running big DRP for the pilot distribution center: using the tool for effective freight planning and to develop future requirements for space and workforce at the DC. Once this pilot is working properly, then cutover the remaining DCs onto DRP. As this happens, you should notice that your master scheduling processes are working even better than before. This is because the demand coming from DRP into the master schedule is more valid and precise. Prior to DRP, most companies have to rely on national forecasts of demand for input to the master schedule and, of course, this is not the way it happens in the real world. The immediate demand on the plants is for the replenishment of the DCs, and that's what DRP is all about.

Opportunity to Accelerate

It may be possible to move "little DRP" up into phase I. As you pilot master scheduling, you may be able to pilot DRP on the same products. Ditto for cutover. In that way, all of little DRP will be implemented at the end of phase I, so that big DRP could come up quite early in phase II.

SUPPLY CHAIN INTEGRATION— FORWARD TO THE CUSTOMERS

We need to talk about two processes here: one called vendor managed inventories (VMI) and the other, collaborative forecasting.

Vendor Managed Inventories

VMI is also called continuous replenishment (CR). Some people use the latter term when referring to themselves shipping to their customers, while they'll use VMI for the process of their suppliers shipping to them. With either term, the process is much the same. We'll use VMI to refer to both approaches—outbound to customers and inbound to the buying companies.

VMI is supplier scheduling in reverse. It involves suppliers assuming responsibility for replenishing the inventory of their products at their customers' locations. It's seen by many companies using it as win-win. The customers win because they're guaranteed high service levels and low inventories by the supplier, plus they offload much of the administrative expense of the classic purchasing and inventory replenishment functions. The suppliers win because they have very good visibility into their customers inventory status, usage, and future production schedules—all of which helps to stabilize and smooth their own production schedules. A further benefit to suppliers is the element of incumbency that's created: A given supplier, doing a good job with VMI, can become a valuable asset to the customer and thus may be a leg up for the retention and expansion of future business.

VMI shares some strong similarities with not only supplier scheduling but also DRP. As with supplier scheduling, VMI crosses "company boundaries"—two totally separate organizations are typically involved. VMI (or CR or CRP) is similar to DRP in that it helps people to schedule the replenishment of remote inventories, using the time-phased logic inherent in resource planning. This raw logic really doesn't care if ownership of the products changes as they hit the remote location (VMI) or stays the same (DRP).

So much for the similarities. VMI means dealing with one's *customers* and that can make it a whole different ball game. You may have customers who don't want anything to do with VMI. Or maybe one of your customers wants you to do VMI with them before you're ready, say back in phase I or even sooner. Maybe the customer has an implementation methodology that just isn't sound. For most suppliers in most industries, it's the customers who call the shots. Thus you may not be able to implement VMI how and when you would like. For the most part, you will need to march to their tune.

In the perfect world, if a company has complete freedom of action, we believe it should follow a path similar to that for supplier scheduling:

1. Establish the approach.

2. Acquire the software.

3. Develop customer education.

4. Pilot with one customer.

5. Fine-tune the processes.

6. Educate and cut over the major customers.

7. Measure performance.

8. Educate and cut over the remaining customers, as appropriate.

Well, it's not a perfect world and it's very unlikely you'll have complete freedom of action. However, you may have some latitude and some degree of control; to the extent possible, try to follow the path outlined above. The closer you can get to that, the higher your odds for success.

COLLABORATIVE FORECASTING

Well, you certainly don't need to have a complete, closed-loop ERP capability within your company to do collaborative forecasting. Many companies have been doing so for years. But, for those of you who have not started a collaborative forecasting kind of process, phase II of your ERP initiative may be an ideal place to start. It's a sort of halfway point between business the same old way and VMI.

First, what does it mean? Here's a definition from Mike Campbell, president of Demand Management Inc., a software company that's active in this field:

> Collaborative forecasting is the sharing of forecasted requirements between supplier and customer with the goal of achieving a mutually agreeable forecast that will drive a replenishment planning system.

Some important words in this definition—"sharing," "between customer and supplier," "mutually agreeable"—imply the element of customer/supplier teamwork involved in this process.

Collaborative forecasting requires a high degree of sales force involvement, because it's done one-on-one with key customers. The forecasting sessions are typically done at the customer's location and include a review of both sales history and forecasts. To be effective, the process requires that the sales folks have easy entry to the sales forecast data base. Further, frequent performance statistics are vital, since the people in the sales department need to know quickly when actuals are deviating heavily from the forecast. This is necessary so they can involve the customer in developing the necessary corrections and alternative plans. The implementation path here is the same as that for VMI.

For the many companies not yet doing a formal collaborative forecasting process, phase II of the ERP implementation is an excellent time to get started. The benefits can be enormous.

Audit/Assessment III

Of all of the steps on the Proven Path, this one may be the easiest to neglect. However, it may also be the most critical to the company's long term growth and survival. The reason: audit/assessment III is the driver that moves the company into its next set of improvement initiatives. It's the entry point into phase III.

Under no circumstances should this step be skipped, even though the temptation to do so may be great. Why? Because the pain has gone away. We feel great! We're on top of the world! Let's kick our shoes off, put our feet up on the desk, and relax for a while.

Don't do it. Skipping audit/assessment III is high risk. Nothing more may be done; the phase III improvement initiatives may not be forthcoming. As a result, the company's drive for operational excellence will stall out, and you could be left in a competitively vulnerable position.

The first mission for audit/assessment III is to validate what's been implemented: the phase I processes of basic ERP and the phase II activities involving supply chain integration. Are they working as they should be? Are the benefits projected in the cost/benefit analysis being realized? What's the bad news, if any, in addition to the good— what's not working as well as we need it to?

In addition, audit/assessment III is the mirror image of audit/assessment I, which asks: "What should we do first?" Audit/assessment III asks: "What should we do next?" Answers to this question could be:

"For us, the next logical step is to implement superior Customer Relationship Management processes. We want to get very close and very intimate with our customers, and now is the perfect time to do it."

"We can and should get much more commercially active with the Internet. We now have a superb foundation to build on to do just that. We can now leverage our ERP/ES investment into a B2B competitive advantage."

"We need to become more nimble in manufacturing. Now that we've implemented ERP successfully and have things so well under control, we can use it as the foundation to launch a lean manufacturing/Just-in-Time initiative."

"We have to get better at new product launch. We're going to tie the power of our ERP tools together with a formal design for manufacturability (DFM) program. This will give us the capability to launch new products faster and better than our competitors."

"We can achieve substantial benefits by consolidating some aspects of the purchasing function. Our Enterprise Software and our first-rate ERP processes give us the opportunity to do just that and to generate significant savings."

"Integrating support functions across divisional boundaries will save us enormous amounts of money. We need to begin working on that aggressively."

In short, audit/assessment III should focus on what to do in phase III so that the total ERP/Enterprise Software effort will generate increasing benefits.

The participants in this step are the same as in audit/assessments I and II, (executives, a wide range of operating managers, and, in virtually all cases, outside consultants with Class A credentials) and the process employed is similar also.

The elapsed time frame for audit/assessment III will range from several days to several weeks. As with audit/assessment I, this is not a prolonged, multi-month affair. Rather, its focus and thrust is on what's not working well and what needs to be done now to become more competitive.

This concludes our discussion of the Proven Path as it applies to a company-wide implementation of ERP. Next, we'll look at an alternative and radically different method of implementation: Quick-Slice ERP.

Q & A WITH THE AUTHORS

TOM: Mike, you were involved in pioneering work with mass merchandisers and grocery retailers—companies like Wal-Mart and Kroger—in the areas of DRP and Vendor Managed Inventories. In a nutshell, what did you learn from that experience?

MIKE: First, VMI (Continuous Replenishment) works; it's very effective in improving shelf out-of-stocks and in reducing inventories. Second, the major obstacle to make it work is trust. The vendor's people must prove their ability and good intentions to truly manage the inventory of their product better than the customer. The best way to do this is to set mutually agreed upon goals for customer service and inventory with monthly reports to verify progress or highlight areas that work.

NOTES

[i] *Get Personal: An Interview with IBM's John M. Paterson,* APICS—The Performance Advantage, October 2000 Issue, Volume 10 No. 10.
[ii] Ibid.

IMPLEMENTERS' CHECKLIST

Function: Going on the Air—Supply Chain Integration (Phase II)

	Complete	
Task	Yes	No

PLANT SCHEDULING

1. Plant scheduling processes implemented (for flow shops). ____ ____

2. Routing accuracy of 98 percent minimum for all items achieved and maintained (for job shops). ____ ____

	Complete	
Task	Yes	No
3. Plant floor control pilot complete (job shops).	____	____
4. Plant floor control implemented across the board (job shops).	____	____
5. Dispatch list generating valid priorities (job shops).	____	____
6. Capacity Requirements Planning implemented (job shops).	____	____
7. Input-output control implemented (job shops).	____	____
8. Feedback linkages established and working (flow shops and job shops).	____	____
9. Plant measurements in place (flow shops and job shops).	____	____

SUPPLIER SCHEDULING

10. Supplier education program developed.	____	____
11. Supplier scheduling pilot complete.	____	____
12. Major suppliers cut over to supplier scheduling.	____	____
13. Supplier measurements in place.	____	____
14. All suppliers cut over to supplier scheduling.	____	____

DRP

15. Inventory records at distribution centers 95 percent accurate or higher.	____	____
16. Bills of distribution 98 percent accurate or higher.	____	____

Task	Complete	
	Yes	No
17. DRP mini-pilot run successfully on pilot products.	____	____
18. Big DRP pilot run successfully on pilot distribution center.	____	____
19. All products and distribution centers cutover onto DRP.	____	____

VENDOR MANAGED INVENTORIES AND COLLABORATIVE FORECASTING

20. VMI and/or collaborative forecasting implemented with customers where feasible and desirable.	____	____

PART III

Quick-Slice Implementation

Chapter 13

Quick-Slice ERP— Overview

Note: This chapter and the next could be the most important part of this book for many of you. You may be in this category if you work for one of the many companies that have a) installed an Enterprise System (ES), b) spent enormous amounts of time, money, blood, sweat, and perhaps a few tears, and c) don't have much to show for it. It's as though you paid a huge sum of money for a very exotic car—say a Rolls Royce or maybe a Lamborghini—but never took delivery. Well, let's look at how to get that baby out of the showroom and onto the road. (There are other reasons to consider a Quick-Slice implementation, and we'll look at those also in just a bit.)

Back in Chapter 2 we talked about the principle of the three knobs: the amount of work to be done, the time available in which to do it, and the resources that can be applied. We said that any two of those knobs can be held constant by varying the third.

In a company-wide implementation of ERP, the amount of work and time available are considered constants. The approach is to vary the resource knob. This will enable the project to be done correctly (the work knob) and completed quickly (the time knob). The approach, says Roger Brooks of the Oliver Wight organization, is to "never change the schedule; never change the load; simply add more horse."

Roger goes on to say that this may not always be possible. In fact, even when possible, it may not always be the best way. This is where Quick-Slice ERP enters the picture. This approach involves:

1. Selecting a high-impact product line—a very important slice of the business.

2. Implementing as many of the ERP functions as possible for that product.

3. Completing the pilot in a very short time, about 120 days.

Hence the label Quick-Slice ERP.

WHERE QUICK SLICE APPLIES

There are quite a few cases where the Quick-Slice implementation approach makes a lot of sense. See if any of these fits your situation.

1. ES software installed without process improvement.

We mentioned this one at the beginning of this chapter. Here's the problem: what are the chances of getting the people all geared up and excited about a company-wide ERP implementation, after they've gone through all the agony and angst of installing the Enterprise Software system? Once again, two chances: slim and none. These folks are burned out and will probably be that way for some time.

Quick-Slice ERP can give a major boost here. Quick success on a major slice of the business can go a long way toward rekindling enthusiasm. Nothing succeeds like success. Further, Quick-Slice ERP should be low cost here because the company already has software, which as we saw, is the largest cost element in implementation.

2. Re-implementers.

The company implemented ERP or MRP II some years ago but didn't do a good job of it. Now it wants to re-implement so it can get all the benefits of ERP. However, strong negative sentiment exists within the company; people are saying things like, "It didn't work the first time. Why should it work now? Let's not waste our time."

This is typical. In a re-implementation, one of the hardest things is to break through people's resentment and frustration, and it almost always makes for a more difficult job than a first-time implementation.

Note the similarities between this situation and the one above. In both cases, the people are frustrated and the software has been installed. If it's older software, it might not be very good. But, as we saw in Chapter 4, chances are very high that it will be good enough to get the job done.

3. Quick payback/self-funding.

Top management understands and wants ERP, but wants a quick payback for any one of a number of reasons:

- Funds are not available from corporate.

- The current year's budget has no provision for a major expenditure of this type.

- The senior managers are new and want to make their mark quickly and decisively.

- And/or the company's approach to major improvement projects is that they be self-funding.

This last point is a somewhat radical notion, not widely practiced. However, we feel that it represents perhaps the best way to mount major improvement initiatives within a manufacturing company. Pay as you go.

4. Middle management sells up.

Operating-level people understand the need for ERP and want it desperately. Top management doesn't see the need, nor are they interested in shelling out big bucks for what they might feel is a computer deal to order parts. They won't take the time to learn about ERP, nor will they authorize an audit/assessment. A Proven Path implementation on a company-wide basis is just not in the cards.

The solution here could be a Proven Path implementation on a Quick-Slice basis. Quick Slice is low dollars, low risk, high return, quick results. It just might get their attention.

It did at Engelhard Industries Chemical Group in Great Britain. The project leader there, Andy Coldrick,[1] made it happen on a Quick-Slice basis. In so doing, he and his team demonstrated to senior management the enormous power of what was then called Manufacturing Resource Planning. Once they saw it with their own eyes, they were convinced. They then proceeded to lead a company-wide implementation with Class A results.

5. *Jumbo-sized company.*

Companies[2] whose head count is well into the thousands typically have a more difficult time implementing ERP (or just about any other major improvement initiative, for that matter). The reason is, simply, more people—more layers in the organization, more communications interfaces, more competing initiatives underway, more opportunities for people not to get on board, more time required to make things happen, and so on.

The Quick-Slice approach dramatically reduces the size of the effort. One can "get one's arms around" an organization of a few dozen or even a few hundred people, and things can happen quickly. Obviously, the first slice would be followed by another and another and another.

6. *We're unique; we're different.*

Let's say the company is in a somewhat specialized industry; perhaps it makes widgets. The company thinks it may want to implement ERP, but it's not sure. The reason: No one in the widget

---

[1] One of the pioneers of Quick-Slice ERP and formerly managing director of Oliver Wight, UK.

[2] Specific business units, not necessarily entire corporations.

business has ever tried ERP. Management is reluctant to invest big bucks until they can see it working.

Quick-Slice ERP provides the opportunity to do this quickly and with very little cost.

7. *Bleeding from the neck.*

The company is in dire financial straits and needs help quickly: negative cash flow, red ink, rapidly eroding market share, whatever. Survival may be at issue. Although ERP may clearly be the answer, there might be too little time left for the company to take the 15 to 20 months necessary for a company-wide implementation. Quick Slice, on the other hand, gives major results in a short time.

One of the earliest documented implementations of this type occurred for exactly this reason.[i] The Quick-Slice approach saved the company.

8. *Others.*

There are probably other good reasons that mitigate for a Quick-Slice approach to implementation. One might be: "Why not?" Why not do it this way? It's fast; it's low dollars; it's low risk; it generates big results.

Here's what we recommend: When evaluating whether or not to do a Quick-Slice implementation, don't ask yourselves: "Why should we do it?" Ask yourselves: "Why not?" Start from there.

Are there any reasons not to do Quick Slice? Yes, there are a few:

1. *No logical slice.*

This could be a company whose products, components, raw materials and manufacturing processes are highly interwoven. There may be no valid way to "slice out" a product family.

2. *Unable to create flow manufacturing.*

This is the process analog of the prior case. There are a few companies—job shops—with such a multiplicity of work centers and

such low unit production volumes that creating cellular flow manufacturing may be next to impossible.

3. Two systems.

The company will be operating with the new ERP processes on the
slice product(s) and components, and with the current system on the
rest. This will continue until all of ERP has been implemented on all
of the business. It can be awkward. Further, some companies and industries have stringent reporting requirements to their customers,
their owners, regulatory agencies, and others; compliance may be
difficult when using two different sets of business processes for an extended time.

4. Very small company.

This is the flip side of the jumbo company mentioned earlier. In a
very small organization, the difference in elapsed time between company wide and Quick Slice may be very little. This could mitigate for
doing it all at once.

5. Lack of urgency.

Implementing Quick Slice is intense because of the time pressures
to get results quickly. If a strong sense of urgency isn't present, Quick
Slice won't be the best way to go. More on urgency in a moment.

6. Longer (maybe) to Class A.

Using Quick Slice will, at least in theory, take longer to reach Class
A ERP. Consider the following Quick-Slice implementation:

Step	Time
Implement first slice	4 months
Implement second slice	3 months[3]
Implement third slice	3 months

---

[3] We're assuming a bit of a learning curve effect here.

The company is now almost one year into implementation. They're getting enormous benefits from what they've done. However, they still don't have all of their products and components on the system, nor have they implemented all the functions of ERP. What they'll need to do at some point is to shift to a company-wide implementation to capture the missing items and functions, which may take another six to twelve months or more.

To us, this is acceptable; we'll opt for Quick Slice and perhaps a slightly longer time to reach Class A.[4] Others may not.

HOW CAN IT BE DONE SO QUICKLY?

Some of you may be thinking: "Only four months? Only 120 days? How can anything this major be accomplished in so little time?"

Good question. There are two main parts to the answer: first urgency and focus, and then work load.

Urgency and focus.

Shorter projects often require a deep sense of urgency among the team members, and Quick-Slice ERP is no exception. The Quick-Slice mind-set says: "We're going to concentrate on this slice; we're going to do it right; we're going to get it done in four months; and we're not going to let obstacles stand in our way, because we're going to run over 'em, run around 'em, or knock 'em down." The team needs to do anything and everything to get the job done quickly and correctly. This small group knows that deadlines will be met, that ingenuity is the norm, and that it will accomplish an extraordinary deed.

Urgency and focus are essential. If you're going to do Quick Slice, don't leave home without 'em.

Work load.

It's essential to turn down the work load knob because the time knob has been cranked down to about four months. This is why

---

[4] But perhaps not more time. As the first several slices are successful, momentum and enthusiasm can build. And this may result in the company-wide implementation on the rest of the products and functions going quite quickly.

Quick Slice focuses on only a small portion of the products and components. Virtually everything in a Quick-Slice implementation is scaled down, but there are three areas that really make the difference: education for the people (the A item, remember?), data integrity (the B item), and software (the C item). Typically, the critical path in a company-wide implementation is through one of these three. Let's take a look at each one.

1. Accelerated education for key people.

One of the time-consuming steps in a company-wide implementation is initial education—reaching all or virtually all the people in the company. Quick Slice acknowledges that can't happen; there's just not enough time.

Therefore, the Quick-Slice approach is to provide, at the outset, education for only those people who'll be directly involved with the slice. This is a small percentage of the total employment in the company, and can be done quickly.

2. Data integrity on slice items only.

Another time-consuming task in a company-wide implementation is to get all the data up to the high levels of accuracy required for ERP: inventory records, bills of material, formulas, routings, work orders, purchase orders, and more. It's a big job.

The Quick-Slice approach: Get data accuracy on only the slice products and components. You don't have time to do much more than that. Get the slice numbers right and worry about the rest later.

3. Software soon.

Urgency demands that the Quick-Slice implementation not get hung up on software, or hardware for that matter. It cannot be allowed to delay the project. If you already have software, fine. If not, don't despair. You can make it happen.

"Well," you may be thinking, "those are nice words, but how in the world do we do that? After all, there's a lot at stake: an Enterprise System is expensive; it's a major purchase decision; it has to be installed, interfaced, enhanced, and all that takes a good deal of time.

Our systems people will be hard pressed to get all of that done to fit with the timing for a company-wide implementation, much less Quick Slice."

My answer, one more time: It's up to you. How important is a Quick Slice implementation? We're back to urgency. If it's really important to you, you won't allow the software to delay the Quick-Slice implementation.

Make a quick decision on software—within a few days, not weeks or months. Forget about getting an ES. Focus on the low-cost, highly functional software that runs on personal computers. If need be, plan to use it on an interim basis only, for a year or so, until the enterprise software is installed. We'll talk more about this in the next chapter, which covers the details of Quick-Slice implementation.

In general terms, that's how it happens when companies do a Quick Slice on a Proven Path basis. Here's Roger Brooks again: "Time is the ultimate enemy. The longer the implementation takes, the more it will cost and the greater the 'window of risk.'"

Q & A WITH THE AUTHORS

MIKE: Have you ever seen a Quick-Slice implementation turn into a "slow slice"?

TOM: Unfortunately yes. The company did an insufficient "gut check" on the urgency and resource issues. They said the words but didn't really mean them. Without urgency and the resources to make things happen quickly, the project floundered and was subsequently abandoned.

NOTE

[i] Mark Kupferberg, *MRP and JIT: A Survival Strategy,* APICS 1987 Conference proceedings (Falls Church, VA: American Production and Inventory Control Society, p. 111).

Chapter 14

Quick-Slice ERP— Implementation

In implementing Quick-Slice ERP, the steps involved are much the same as in a company-wide implementation. Figure 14-1 shows the Proven Path adapted for Quick Slice. Several things to note:

- The time frame is compressed. We're talking about weeks instead of months.

- The finance and accounting step has been dropped.

- A new step has been added: physical process improvement.

We've already covered the accelerated time frame, and we'll discuss the other changes in just a bit.

The front-end steps—audit/assessment I through project organization—are done quite similarly to a company-wide implementation,[1] except that most of them will involve fewer people and be done more quickly.

---

[1] If you need to refresh your memory, you may want to take another look at Chapter 5, where these steps are discussed in detail as they relate to a company-wide implementation. Here, we'll mainly be discussing the differences between Quick Slice and company wide.

Figure 14-1

ERP PROVEN PATH–QUICK SLICE

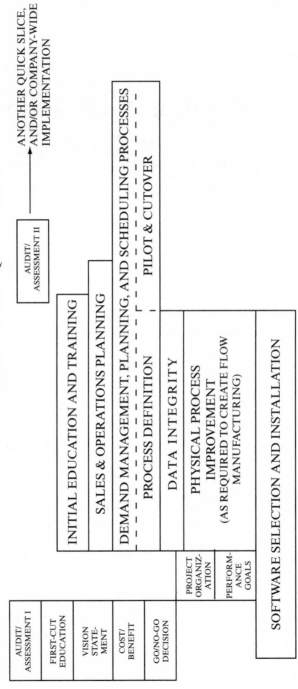

WEEK: 1 through 4 5 6 7 8 9 10 11 12 13 14 15 16 17 18 19 +

Audit/assessment I.

Of all these early steps in Quick Slice, audit/assessment I is most similar to company wide. At this point, it's unlikely that the company has decided to do Quick Slice. They may not know much about it, or may not have even heard of it. The job of this step is to set the direction. The participants in audit/assessment I include the executives, a number of operating managers, and one or several outsiders with Class A credentials. The process—fact finding, synthesis and report preparation, report presentation—are similar to company wide.

The one difference may be in timing. Back in Chapter 5, we pointed out that the elapsed time for this step could range from several days to about one month. Well, during the fact-finding stage, Quick Slice may emerge as a strong possibility. This is where the Class A consultants come in. If they're doing their jobs correctly, they'll recognize this. They should crank up the urgency lever and make a preliminary recommendation for Quick Slice, identifying one or several likely candidates for the slice product(s). This should happen at the conclusion of the fact-finding phase, so that the next step—first-cut education—can start early.

First-cut education.

For Quick Slice this should include all, or at least most, of top management. Unlike company wide, however, it does not involve all or most of the operating managers. Rather, it includes only those key people who will be directly involved with the slice: managers from the sales and marketing departments, the plant floor, planning, purchasing, systems, customer service, plus the likely full time project leader if already identified.

This step should finish quickly, ideally being completed at about the same time as the audit/assessment I wrap-up. When that happens, it opens up a real opportunity for the next steps, as we'll see in a minute.

Vision statement, cost/benefit analysis, go/no-go decision, performance goals, project organization.

These steps should be done together and, with few exceptions, can be completed in one or several days. Keep the vision statement brief (less is more, remember?). Do the cost/benefit study on a joint venture basis (see Chapter 5). It'll take less time than in company wide

Figure 14-2
Criteria for Selecting the Quick-Slice Product(s)

---

1. High Impact, High Visibility
   (A Pareto Class A product, not a B or a C)

2. Largely Self-Contained
   (The fewer components and work centers shared with other products the better)

3. Good People
   (With resistance to change at least no greater than normal)

4. Stability
   (No major changes pending, no deep structural problems present that would inhibit the Quick-Slice implementation)

5. Applicability
   (Lessons learned here apply to the rest of the company)

---

because there are fewer people and functions involved. Make a yes or no decision on Quick Slice: If yes, create a one-page written project charter, spelling out urgency as a primary requirement in the implementation process.

Establish the performance goals that you will achieve for the slice products and related elements. Included here is the selection of the slice products or family. Characteristics to look for in making this selection are shown in Figure 14-2. Chances are you'll have to compromise on one criterion or another, but get as close as you can.

Set up the steering committee, a complete one similar to company wide and with a designated torchbearer.[2] Create a project team but make it much smaller than in company wide, perhaps no more than the handful of managers mentioned above plus the full-time project leader.

Do you need a full-time project leader on a Quick-Slice implementation? Definitely.

---

[2] Unlike the torchbearer in a company-wide implementation (see Chapter 5), the Quick-Slice torchbearer should plan on being directly involved with the implementation more frequently, perhaps several times per day.

Why? After all, you may be thinking, it says earlier in this book that if you're dealing with a small business unit, less than 100 people, you can get by without a full-timer—so why do we need one? Because if you don't have one, it's almost certain you won't get this thing done in four months . . . or five months . . . or six. The issue is urgency.

The opportunity we referred to earlier is this: If you can finish your first-cut education while the audit/assessment report is being completed, then the following activities can take place within one several-day period:

- Presentation of the audit/assessment I report.

- Creation of the vision statement.

- Development of the cost/benefit study.

- Establishment of the performance goals.

- Creation of the steering committee, the project team, and the full time project leader.

You're killing several birds with one stone. You're accomplishing multiple tasks; you're getting maximum use out of your consultant; and you're saving him or her from having to make an extra trip to your company.

He or she should appreciate that. If your consultant's good, he or she will probably be busy, and you will need to see that person frequently during your first slice implementation. In general terms, you can figure on the consultant being with you at least three or four days per month for the first several months.

As we said earlier, an important part of the consultant's role is to help the company avoid the pitfalls and booby traps. This is even more critical in Quick Slice because there's less time to recover from a mistake than in a company-wide implementation.

Initial education.

This consists mainly of accelerated internal education for key people. A few folks may need to attend outside classes beyond those in first-cut education but probably not many. The participants in the series of internal business meetings are:

1. The project team.

2. The steering committee.

3. The other folks who'll be directly involved with the slice.

These are typically the three groupings for the meetings. Relative to company wide, the people are fewer and the time frame is compressed; the objectives, the process, and the media (videotapes, printed material[3]) are much the same, except that for Quick Slice some Lean Manufacturing/Just-in-Time material will be necessary for issues like cells, kanban, material storage at point of use, and others.

The series of business meetings for the project team can happen in four weeks or less, since they're accelerated and there are fewer of them. To save time, the other two groups can start a bit before the project team is finished.

Sales & Operations Planning.

Sales & Operations Planning should be implemented on all product families, not just the slice. There are important reasons for this:

1. Ease. It will be almost as easy to implement S&OP on all products as it will on the slice product(s) only.

2. Benefits. S&OP, of and by itself, will provide significant benefits prior to having any of the other ERP elements in place.

3. Early win. Quick Slice represents an early win. Implementing S&OP completely, within Quick Slice, is an *early,* early win. Early successes promote behavior change.

4. Balance. With so much attention on the Quick Slice, it's important to watch the rest of the products to ensure that resources aren't being drained from them. S&OP will facilitate minding that part of the store.

5. Motivator. Once all aspects of Quick Slice are implemented, an important difference will be apparent to the top management group

---

[3] Regarding media, however, the internal education materials will need to be tailored to cover only those elements necessary for the slice.

members. As they do Sales & Operations Planning on the slice products, they will have the confidence that their decisions will be translated logically, correctly, on a "rack-and-pinion" basis—to become the detailed schedules for the plant floor and the suppliers. That's what master scheduling and Material Requirements Planning do.

On the other hand, when they make S&OP decisions on the nonslice products, they won't have that assurance. They'll see a "disconnect" between what they decide and what may or may not happen in the plant and at the suppliers. This can serve as a strong motivator to the top management team to press on with additional slices and/or company-wide implementation. It helps to reduce complacency and, hence, the risk of stalling out after one or several successful slices.

Demand management, planning, and scheduling processes.

This nails down the details of what's going to be done and generates the detailed project schedule. This can happen concurrently with the series of business meetings for the project team.

The conference room pilot also is similar to that in a company-wide implementation. It involves fewer people, perhaps no more than three or four, and therefore, can take less time. Five sessions per day for several weeks should do the job; if more time is needed, perhaps the slice is too big and/or too complex.

Data integrity.

The key here is to "get data integrity on the slice products, components, and materials only. You don't have time to do much more than that. Get the slice numbers right and worry about the rest later."

Sure, if you can get some of the other inventory records or bills of material squared away while you're doing the slice items, fine—provided it doesn't slow you down. You simply can't allow yourselves to get into major activities here that are not necessary to bring up the slice.

Even though your data integrity focus needs to be largely or totally on the slice items, what you're doing will have indirect but important benefits for all other items as well:

• Learning how to get the records accurate. The learning curve applies; it'll be easier with the next bunch.

- Achieving an early win. Early successes promote behavior change.

What you need to make accurate are the on-hand inventory records, the open orders, the bills of material. The need to restructure bills is not likely, but it could be necessary in some cases. Make certain the item data, along with whatever work center data you may need, is reasonable and realistic.

The toughest data accuracy challenge for most companies in Quick Slice will be on-hand inventory balances. To get them accurate, we've seen companies do some creative things—all the time guided by the principle of urgency.

One example is what a company called their chicken wire stockroom. This was, in effect, a smaller stockroom within their unsecured primary stockroom. They cleared an area, fenced it in with chicken wire to obtain limited access, and proceeded to get the records accurate. In some companies, a painted line on the floor could have the same effect.

Another company had an accuracy problem with common items, ones used both in the slice product and elsewhere. Their solution: Stock 'em in two different locations and, to preserve integrity, add a letter (S for slice) to the slice item numbers.[4] In that way, the slice items were segregated in both the real world and the computer.

Finance and accounting processes.

In Quick Slice, implementing new finance and accounting processes usually doesn't happen, and that's why we've left it off of the Proven Path for Quick Slice. The name of the game is "use what you have." If you've already installed new Enterprise Software, you've most probably implemented new finance and accounting tools as a part of that effort. Great—you're a leg up, and you can proceed with your Quick-Slice ERP implementation knowing you're okay in that area.

If, on the other hand, you're still running legacy applications in the finance and accounting area, we urge you to stick with what you have

---

[4] This, of course, meant a minor modification to the slice bills of material, to call out the *S* items, not the regular. At that company, it was no problem.

for the time being. Here also, there's hardly ever enough time to make this transition within the Quick Slice time frame. The good news: Your current accounting applications work. They're giving the right answers. (It may be slower and more cumbersome than you'd like, but the fact remains that they work.) What's needed is simply to bridge the new ERP transactions into the current accounting systems. This will most likely require some temporary programming, but here also we feel strongly that this approach represents the "least worst choice." Or, maybe you'll wind up doing duplicate data entry if it's absolutely necessary. More on this issue in a bit when we talk about software.

The new finance and accounting processes can then be implemented later, when the implementation switches over from Quick Slice to company wide.

Physical process improvement.

Here's potentially a big difference between Quick-Slice and a company-wide implementation. In many slice implementations, particularly in job shops, a major process improvement step is mandatory. It involves the creation of flow manufacturing, by establishing manufacturing cells.[5]

In a job shop, assembly operations are almost always focused on a product basis. Fabrication, however, is done at functionally organized work centers, any one of which may be performing production operations on many different components that go into many different products. Most of the products will not be in the slice. Although not impossible, it will be difficult to implement Quick Slice successfully in that environment. It will be totally dependent on these functionally organized work centers that have little or no identification with the slice products and activities.

The solution is to create flow from the job shop, and the way this is done is with cells. This means to dedicate specific pieces of equipment to the manufacture of specific items and, typically, to arrange those pieces of equipment adjacent to each other in a flow arrangement. We call this a physical cell.

---

[5] For a detailed explanation of this issue, see William A. Sandras, Jr., *Just-in-Time: Making It Happen* (Essex Junction, VT: Oliver Wight Publications, Inc., 1989).

However, it's not always necessary to move equipment. In Appendix B we talk about conceptual cells, where the equipment does not get relocated. Instead, the equipment is linked together conceptually via kanban, which is also explained in Appendix B.

The message: Don't even think of having to delay the slice implementation if it'll take a lot of time to move equipment. Rather, use conceptual cells to get started, go on the air with the slice, and move the machines later.

One last point here concerns visibility. Make the slice equipment highly visible. Identify the physical cells and the machines belonging to the conceptual cells by putting up signs, banners, or flags, or even by painting the equipment a different color. Use the same color (green for go?) here, in the stockroom, and for the slice plant paperwork.

Software.

In a company-wide implementation, some activities that take quite a bit of time are:

• Software selection.

• Software interfacing.

• Software enhancements.

We have to find a way to shortcut the time required for these, or the Quick Slice will wind up being a Slow Slice. Push your urgency button a couple of times, and let's take a look at how to do that.

First, software selection. You either don't have software to support ERP, or you do—and today most companies are in this latter category. In this case, use what you have—even if you don't like it. Use it even if most people are going around saying, "Our software stinks."[6] Almost invariably, it will be good enough to support the slice.

If the somewhat unlikely event you don't have software for ERP, we urge you to buy one of the low-cost, PC-based packages we talked

---

[6] Maybe it does, but probably it doesn't. The reasons why most Class C and D users didn't get to Class A or B do not lie in the software. Typically, it's because the people part of the implemantation was not handled correctly.

about back in Chapter 4. Use it for at least the duration of the slice implementations, and then if you wish, convert over to a full-blown Enterprise System.

Second, do minimal (or even zero) interfacing of the new software with the current system, for example, the finance and accounting applications. Don't allow interfacing to get on the critical path. If necessary, do manual interfacing via duplicate data entry, use temporaries, do whatever to feed the slice data into the current accounting systems.

Third, make minimal (or even zero) enhancements to the software. Remember, this is not a company-wide implementation where there's time to do these kinds of things. We're dealing here with a limited number of people and items. Given a good set of software, plus enthusiasm and dedication on the part of the people directly involved, this typically is not a problem; they're willing to operate with a less than ideal set of screens and reports and transactions, in return for being part of a team that's making such major and rapid progress.

Pilot/cutover.

In Quick Slice, the pilot is the cutover; they're one and the same. The Quick-Slice pilot is the actual implementation itself. Let's see which of the ERP functions actually get implemented at this point, keeping in mind that Sales & Operations Planning has already been started. Figure 14-3 shows what will be implemented in this pilot/cutover step.

It indicates that supplier scheduling should be done where practical. It probably won't be practical to implement supplier scheduling on all slice purchased items, most of which come from suppliers who are also providing items for nonslice products. The dilemma is that the nonslice items can't be effectively supplier scheduled because:

1. They're not on ERP; hence, there are no planned orders; hence, a key element of supplier scheduling (visibility out beyond the quoted lead time) is missing.

2. They're on the current ERP system that's not working well; hence, the dates on the scheduled receipts and planned orders

Figure 14-3
ERP Functions Implemented During Quick Slice

Sales & Operations Planning
(On all product families)

Demand Management
(On the slice products)

Master Scheduling
(On the slice products)

Rough-cut Capacity Planning
(On the key resources)

Material Requirements Planning
(On the slice components and materials)

Plant Scheduling/Kanban
(On the slice products and components)

Supplier Scheduling
(On the slice components and materials, where practical)

---

are not valid; hence, a key element of supplier scheduling (valid dates on orders) is missing.[7]

However, where you can align a given supplier's items solely into the slice family, those items and that supplier should be supplier scheduled. Further, in some cases, it may be possible to work with a supplier on a split approach. That supplier could be supplier-scheduled for the slice items they're supplying but would continue to receive traditional purchase orders for the nonslice material.

The message here for you people in purchasing: Do as much supplier scheduling as you can in the slice, but realize that you probably won't be able to do 100 percent.

Still on the topic of scheduling, we need to talk about another kind of supplier: internal rather than external. Let's take the case of a company, largely a job shop, that is implementing Quick-Slice ERP.

---

[7] If all the dates are valid, why are you implementing ERP? You already have it, perhaps under a different name.

They've created flow, via cells, for their higher volume fabricated components. However, it's simply not practical to produce all of the slice components via cells; there may be many of them with too little volume to justify a cellular approach.

What to do? Treat the job as a supplier for those fabricated items that will continue to be made there. In effect, buy them from the job shop.

But this brings up another problem. How can we be sure that the job shop is going to deliver the slice items on time? After all, many of the jobs in the job shop are typically late. Well, there are several parts to the answer.

First, the dates on the slice components will be valid. This isn't the case for virtually all the other jobs.[8] Second, the people in the job shop need to understand those dates are valid and that they must complete slice jobs on time. Third, the plant paperwork accompanying the slice jobs should be easy to spot, perhaps bordered with the same color used to identify the slice cells (green for go?). And last, some clear direction and follow-up from the plant manager that the slice jobs will be done on time should be all it takes to make this happen.

Begin to measure results against the goals defined at the outset. In Quick Slice, this could include on-time shipments, lead time reduction, measures of productivity, cost reduction, inventory turns, and others. For the slice products, things should be significantly and visibly better on the plant floor and with customer service. If not, stop right here and fix whatever's not working. Do not, repeat, *do not* go beyond the first slice if the results aren't forthcoming. Things should also get visibly better, it is hoped, before too long, in the profit and loss statement and on the balance sheet.

Audit/assessment II.

The performance measurement step addresses the question: "Is it working?" The next question is: "What next—what do we do for an encore?"

The answer should come out of audit/assessment II and, most probably, will be to do another slice. If so, loop back to the front end

---

[8] Same comment as before: If all the dates are valid, you probably already have ERP, perhaps under a different name.

of the Proven Path and get started. Obviously, the first audit/assessment step shown on the chart no longer applies, having been replaced by audit/assessment II. First-cut education will probably involve no one, assuming that all the key players went through this process for the first slice.

However, and this is a big however, if one or more key people didn't get educated in the first slice (some top management people, maybe?), this is the ideal time to make that happen. The first slice is working, things are visibly better, and enthusiasm is high. Go for it!

A Quick-Slice implementation can result in a series of loops. The first slice is done and it's successful. Audit/assessment II leads the company to loop back and do the second slice. That's successful, and that leads to a third slice and possibly more. That's great; that's the way it should be.

At some point, after a number of slices, the need to shift to a company-wide implementation will become compelling. Several reasons:

1. The company continues to operate with two systems. Maybe as much as one-third or one-half of the products are now on Quick-Slice ERP, and this may represent well over 80 percent of the company's sales volume. However, many products/components are still on the old system.

2. The common parts problem is becoming difficult. Many of the materials and component items may go into both slice products and ones not on ERP. This can be cumbersome.

3. Not having all purchased items on ERP is inhibiting progress on supplier scheduling.

4. Even though much of the job shop may have been converted to cells during the slice implementations, some or much of it may need to remain in job shop mode for the long term. Dispatching and Capacity Requirements Planning normally won't work effectively without all the manufactured components on Material Requirements Planning.

5. The other phase II processes of Distribution Requirements Planning (DRP) and vendor managed inventories (VMI) are probably not getting much attention during the slices. Here again, they require most or all of the products to be up on ERP.

6. Similarly, the full financial interface can't happen until all products, manufactured components, purchased items, work centers, and routings are contained within ERP.

Sooner or later, if all goes well, the audit/assessment II step will lead you to shift to a company-wide approach to get all products and all ERP functions implemented. And, in some cases, it can be done simultaneously. Audit/assessment II could lead you to start a company-wide implementation at the same time that you're starting another slice.

Quick Slice without top management.

In the last chapter, we indicated that one reason to do a Quick Slice versus company wide is "middle management sells up" (i.e., top management doesn't want to be bothered and won't take the time to learn about ERP). In that situation, a company-wide implementation simply doesn't have much chance of getting beyond Class C. Quick Slice may be the only way to go, serving as a demonstration project to convince senior managers that ERP works and is very important. If conversation won't work, maybe a real life example will. (Build it and they will come.)

However, any implementation—company-wide or Quick-Slice—without active, visible, and informed top management leadership *is not a Proven Path implementation.* The odds for success drop, and that's the bad news. The good news is they drop less with Quick Slice.

What, then, are the differences in a Quick-Slice implementation without a top management team that's ERP knowledgeable? The answer to that question raises another: Can you persuade and lead and teach them to do Sales & Operations Planning? If yes, you've got a leg up and your slice implementation can probably proceed in a fairly standard fashion, with perhaps a few other exceptions. For example, top management may not want to participate in the steps that involve vision statement, cost/benefit, and performance goals. Do it without them. That's not ideal, but it sure beats doing nothing.

What if top management won't get involved with Sales & Operations Planning? You're still not dead in the water. What you will have to do, however, is to get their agreement that they'll keep their hands off of the slice family during and after the implementation. By this, we refer primarily to issues of demand management. If, for example, customer orders will be promised without regard to their impact on the plant and the suppliers, Quick Slice won't have much chance for success.

In cases like this, reconsider your options. Perhaps you could select a different product line for the first slice, maybe one of less significance to them. It might be easier to convince them to allow the slice team to manage the demand stream on a Class B product line rather than an A.

Regardless of how you do it—top management educated and involved, or top management not educated but involved, or top management completely uninvolved—it will be necessary to get schedule stability on the slice items. Build a fence around the slice products and components to keep out volatile, wildly erratic demand.

What about a torchbearer? If at all possible, get one. Isn't there at least one potential ERP enthusiast within the ranks of top management—or at a minimum, one who's open-minded and willing to get some education? If yes, then sign him or her up. Involve that person. An informed, knowledgeable torchbearer is as important in this situation as in a Proven Path implementation, maybe more so.

Similarly, how about professional guidance? Frequently, an uninterested top management team will be willing to spend the relatively few dollars required for an outside consultant; they just don't want to spend their time on ERP. In this case, go for it. Enlist the services of an experienced consultant with Class A credentials.

Now, in this scenario, you've got two heavyweights involved: the torchbearer and the consultant. The first slice still won't be Proven Path, but you've got a reasonable shot at success. If it goes well, top management should get on board. If they do, the second slice and subsequent company-wide implementation will be Proven Path. And they will work.

CONCLUSION

Quick-Slice ERP represents a major change in implementation methodology. As with company wide, it's proven; it's been shown to work in actual practice. It's not a free lunch, in that it has some minor drawbacks: two systems, possibly longer to reach Class A. However, Quick Slice offers the enormous advantage of significant early payback.

As we write this, a majority of ERP implementations continue to be company wide. That may change. The benefits from Quick Slice are so compelling that, at some point, it's quite possible that Quick Slice will become the primary implementation method.

Q & A WITH THE AUTHORS

TOM: Anything else you'd like to say about Quick Slice, Mike?

MIKE: Just one point: A major problem is in not learning enough from the first Quick Slice. Too often others in the company will pay little attention to the unit doing Quick Slice and thus the learning is lost. There needs to be a clear mechanism for others to be part of the Quick-Slice project in order to take that learning back to their parts of the business.

IMPLEMENTERS' CHECKLIST

Function: Quick-Slice ERP

This checklist serves the same purpose as the Implementers' Checklists for company-wide implementation in Chapters 5 through 12: to detail the major tasks necessary to ensure total compliance with the Proven Path. A company that can check yes for each task on this list can be virtually guaranteed of a successful implementation of Quick-Slice ERP.

Because this checklist spans a total Quick-Slice implementation, it's divided into monthly increments to serve as approximate guidelines on timing. These guidelines reflect the principle of urgency.

TASKS TO BE COMPLETED IN MONTH 1

Task	Complete	
	Yes	No
1-1. Audit/assessment I conducted with participation by top management, operating management, and an outside consultant with Class A experience.	_____	_____

Task	Complete	
	Yes	No
1-2. The general manager, key staff members, and key operating managers have attended first-cut education.	____	____
1-3. Vision statement and cost justification prepared on a joint-venture basis, with both top management and operating management from all involved functions participating and approved by general manager.	____	____
1-4. Written project charter created and formally signed off by all executives and managers participating in the justification process, citing urgency as a key element in the Quick-Slice implementation process.	____	____
1-5. Slice product(s) selected.	____	____
1-6. Full-time project leader selected from a key management role in an operating department.	____	____
1-7. Torchbearer identified and formally appointed.	____	____
1-8. Project team formed, consisting of key people who will be directly involved in the slice.	____	____
1-9. Executive steering committee formed, consisting of the general manager, all staff members, and the project leader.	____	____
1-10. Project team meeting at least twice per week, and executive steering committee meeting at least twice per month.	____	____

	Complete	
Task	Yes	No

1-11. Outside consultant, with Class A ERP/ MRP II experience, retained and on-site at least three or four days per month.   ____ ____

1-12. Detailed performance goals established, linking directly back to each of the benefits specified in the cost/benefit analysis.   ____ ____

TASKS TO BE COMPLETED IN MONTH 2

	Complete	
Task	Yes	No

2-1. Key members of project team to outsider-led ERP class (those who have not yet attended, if any).   ____ ____

2-2. Accelerated series of business meetings conducted for project team.   ____ ____

2-3. Process definition statements completed for all processes to be impacted by Quick Slice.   ____ ____

2-4. Software decision made; software and necessary new hardware installed.   ____ ____

2-5. Detailed project schedule established by the project team, naming names, dates, and showing completion of Quick-Slice project in less than five months.   ____ ____

2-6. Detailed project schedule being updated at least twice weekly at project team meetings, with status being reported at each meeting of the steering committee.   ____ ____

2-7. Sales & Operations Planning process initiated.   ____ ____

TASKS TO BE COMPLETED IN MONTH 3

Task	Complete Yes	No
3-1. Series of business meetings conducted for steering committee.	___	___
3-2. Series of business meetings conducted by project team people for all other persons involved with the slice.	___	___
3-3. Enthusiasm, teamwork, and a sense of ownership becoming visible throughout all groups involved in the slice.	___	___
3-4. Inventory record accuracy, including scheduled receipts and allocations, at 95 percent or better for all slice items.	___	___
3-5. All slice bills of material at least 98 percent accurate, properly structured, and sufficiently complete for ERP.	___	___
3-6. All item data for slice products and components, plus any necessary work center data, complete and verified for reasonableness.	___	___

TASKS TO BE COMPLETED IN MONTH 4

Task	Complete Yes	No
4-1. Executive steering committee authorization to implement master scheduling (MS) and Material Requirements Planning (MRP) on the slice products and components.	___	___
4-2. Master scheduling and MRP operating properly.	___	___

	Complete	
Task	Yes	No
4-3. Plant schedules, and kanban where appropriate, in place and operating properly for the slice items.	____	____
4-4. Feedback links (anticipated delay reporting) in place for both plant and purchasing.	____	____

TASKS TO BE COMPLETED IN MONTH 5

	Complete	
Task	Yes	No
5-1. Suppliers cut over to supplier scheduling as practical.	____	____
5-2. Performance measurements in place and being reviewed carefully by the steering committee and project team.	____	____
5-3. Audit/assessment II completed; next Quick Slice or other improvement initiative now underway.	____	____

PART IV

Beyond ERP
Implementation

Chapter 15

Operating ERP

Imagine the feelings of the winning Super Bowl team. What a kick that must be! They've reached their goal. They're number one.

Now, imagine it's six months later. The team, the coaches, and the team's owner have just held a meeting and decided to cancel this year's training camp. Their attitude is who needs it? We're the best in the business. We don't have to spend time on fundamentals—things like blocking, tackling, and catching footballs. We know how to do that. We've also decided not to hold daily practices during the season. We'll just go out every Sunday afternoon and do the same things we did last year.

Does this make any sense? Of course not. But this is exactly the attitude some companies adopt after they become successful ERP users. Their approach is: This ERP thing's a piece of cake. We don't need to worry about it anymore. Wrong, of course. No Class A or B ERP process will maintain itself. It requires continual attention.

There are two major objectives involved in operating ERP:

1. Don't let it slip.

2. Make it better and better.

It's easy to let it slip. Some Class A companies have learned this

Figure 15-1

ERP PROVEN PATH

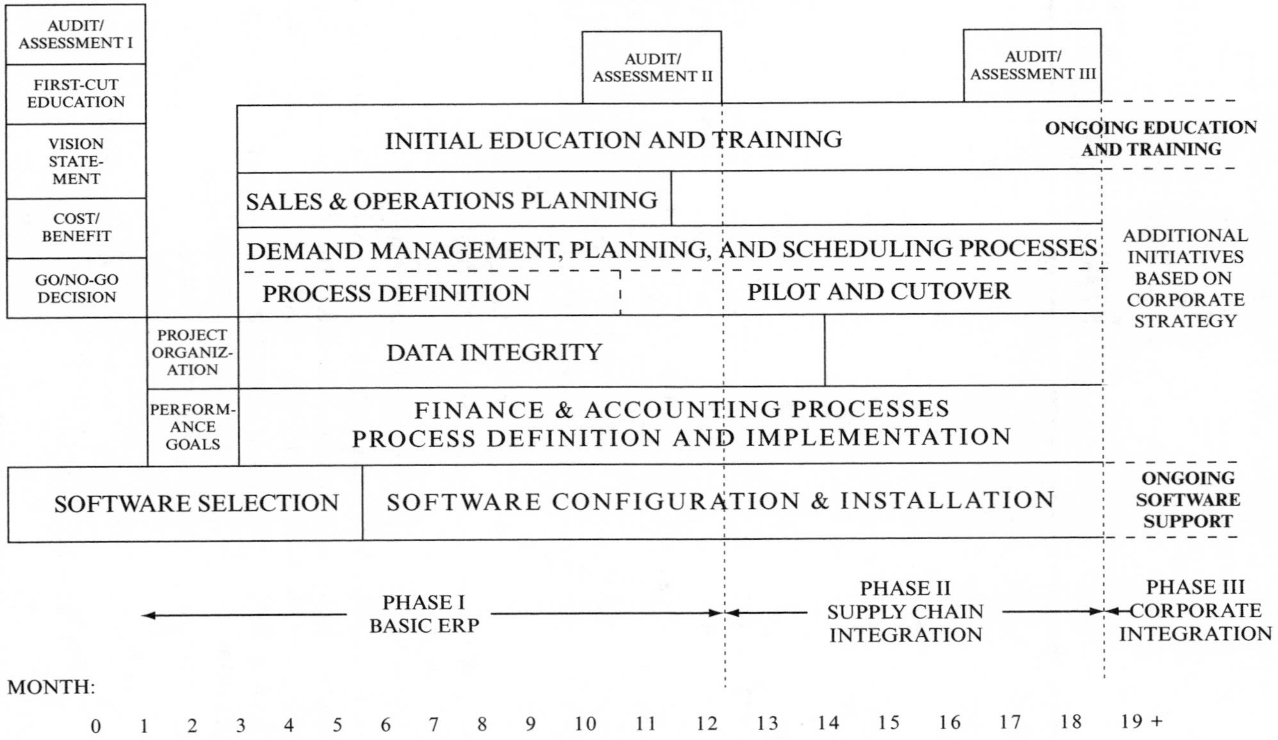

AUDIT/ASSESSMENT I

FIRST-CUT EDUCATION

VISION STATEMENT

COST/BENEFIT

GO/NO-GO DECISION

PROJECT ORGANIZATION

PERFORMANCE GOALS

SOFTWARE SELECTION

AUDIT/ASSESSMENT II

AUDIT/ASSESSMENT III

INITIAL EDUCATION AND TRAINING

ONGOING EDUCATION AND TRAINING

SALES & OPERATIONS PLANNING

DEMAND MANAGEMENT, PLANNING, AND SCHEDULING PROCESSES

PROCESS DEFINITION

DATA INTEGRITY

PILOT AND CUTOVER

ADDITIONAL INITIATIVES BASED ON CORPORATE STRATEGY

FINANCE & ACCOUNTING PROCESSES
PROCESS DEFINITION AND IMPLEMENTATION

SOFTWARE CONFIGURATION & INSTALLATION

ONGOING SOFTWARE SUPPORT

PHASE I
BASIC ERP

PHASE II
SUPPLY CHAIN INTEGRATION

PHASE III
CORPORATE INTEGRATION

MONTH:

0   1   2   3   4   5   6   7   8   9   10   11   12   13   14   15   16   17   18   19 +

lesson the hard way. They've "taken their eye off the ball," and assumed that ERP will maintain itself. In the process, they've lost a letter grade. They've slipped to Class B. (Companies who achieve Class B and make the same mistake can become Class C very quickly.) Then comes the laborious process of reversing the trend and re-acquiring the excellence that once was there. The flip side of these experiences is represented by the excellent ERP user companies. Their attitude is: "We're Class A, but we're going to do better next year than we did this year. We're not satisfied with the status quo. Our goal is to be even more excellent in the future than we are now."

How should a company address these issues? How can they not let it slip? What's involved in making it better and better?

Five important elements are involved:

- Understanding.
- Organization.
- Measurements.
- Education.
- Lean Manufacturing/Just-in-Time.

Let's look at each one.

UNDERSTANDING

In this context, understanding means lack of arrogance. In the example of the championship football team, things were reversed. They *had* arrogance; they *lacked* understanding. They also lacked any real chance of becoming next year's Super Bowl champions.

Operating at a Class A level is much the same. A company needs to understand that:

- Today's success is no guarantee of tomorrow's.
- People are the key.
- The name of the game is to win, to be better than the competi-

tion, and operating ERP at a Class A level is one of the best ways to do that.

ORGANIZATION

Don't disband the ERP project team and the executive steering committee. Keep these groups going. They're almost as important after a successful implementation as before. However, some changes in the way they operate should be made.

The ERP Operating Committee

After implementation is complete, the ERP project team should remain in place, with the following changes:

1. The group now has no full-time members; therefore, it's probably a bit smaller than it was. Its membership is now at or near 100 percent department heads.

2. Because ERP is no longer a project but is now operational, the name of the group might be changed to ERP operating committee or something along those lines.

3. Group meetings are held about once a quarter rather than once a week.

4. The chairmanship of the group rotates among its members, perhaps once or twice a year. First, a marketing manager might be the chairperson, next a manager from accounting, then perhaps someone from engineering or purchasing. This approach enhances the collective sense of ownership of ERP. It states strongly that ERP is a *company-wide* set of processes.

The group's job is to focus formally on the performance of the ERP processes, report results to top management, and develop and implement improvements.

Spin-off Task Forces

Just as during implementation, these temporary groups can be used to solve specific problems, capitalize on opportunities, and so forth.

The Executive Steering Committee

Following implementation, the executive steering committee should meet about once every six months.[1] It receives updates on performance from the ERP operating committee. Its tasks are much the same as during implementation: reviewing status, reallocating resources when necessary, and providing leadership.

MEASUREMENTS

Measuring the effectiveness of ERP performance requires both operational and financial measurements. Let's look at operational measurements first.

Operational Measurements—The ABCD Checklist for Operational Excellence[2]

Section 5 of the ABCD Checklist is the essential operational measurement of "how we're doing" operating ERP.

This part of the ABCD Checklist should be reviewed by the ERP operating committee formally, as a group, at least twice a year. Agreement should be reached on each of the 22 overview questions. For any answer that's lower than excellent, this group should focus on:

1. What's causing the no answer? What's going wrong? Use the checklist's detailed audit questions for diagnosis.

2. What's the best way to fix the problem? Does the problem exist only within one department? If so, that department manager should be charged with correcting the problem. On the other hand, if the problem crosses departmental boundaries, should the company activate a spin-off task force?

3. How quickly can it be fixed? (Set a date—don't let it drift.)

---

[1] This can happen in a separate meeting or as a part of a regularly scheduled executive staff meeting.

[2] The entire list of questions with instructions to their use is titled *The Oliver Wight ABCD Checklist for Operational Excellence* (New York, NY: John Wiley & Sons, 1992).

Each time the ABCD Checklist is reviewed, the results are formally communicated to the executive steering committee: the score achieved, the class rating (A, B, C, etc.), what the no answers are, what's being done about them, and what help, if any, is needed from top management.

Who does this communication? Who presents these results? The part time successor to the full-time project leader. In other words, the chairperson of the ERP operating committee.

Some companies do a formal re-certification once per year. Once a given business unit hits Class A, their challenge is, first, to stay there and, second, to get better and better. The Class A certification is good for only one year, and then it must be "re-earned." We endorse this approach. It's so easy to let things slip with so many things competing for attention. Re-certification helps to really focus attention once per year, and "get everyone's heads" back into ERP.

Operational Measurements—Other

Listed below is a series of detailed technical measurements, not explicitly covered in the ABCD Checklist, relating to the specific operation of certain ERP functions. This list will probably not be 100 percent complete for any one company, and, further, it contains some elements that may not apply in some organizations. We include them here to serve as a foundation for companies, to be used along with the ABCD Checklist, in developing their own measurements program.

In master scheduling, some companies measure:

1. Number of master schedule changes in the emergency zone. This should be a small number.

2. Master schedule orders rescheduled in compared to those rescheduled out. These numbers should be close to equal.

3. Finished goods inventory turnover for make-to-stock operations.

Typically, the first two of these measurements are done weekly, and the third monthly. In Material Requirements Planning, check on:

1. Number of stock outs for both manufactured and purchased items.

2. Raw material and component inventory turnover, again for both make and buy items.

3. Exception message volume. This refers to the number of action recommendations generated by the MRP program each week. For conventional (fabrication and assembly) manufacturers, the exception rate should be 10 percent or less. For process and repetitive plants, the rate may be higher because of more activity per item. (The good news is that these kinds of companies usually have far fewer items.)

4. Late order releases—the number of orders released within less than the planned lead time. A good target rule of thumb here is 5 percent or less of all orders released.

5. Production orders and supplier orders[3] rescheduled in versus rescheduled out. Here again, these numbers should be close to equal.

Except for inventory turns, most of these measurements are done weekly. Typically, they're broken out by the planner including, of course, the supplier schedulers.

In Capacity Requirements Planning, some companies track the past due load. Target: less than one week's work. Frequency: weekly.

In plant floor control, the following are frequently measured:

1. On-time production order completions, to the operation due date. A good measurement here is to track late jobs in (arriving) to a work center compared to late jobs out (completed). This recognizes that manufacturing departments shouldn't be penalized for jobs that arrive behind schedule. Some companies expand this to track total days of lateness in and out rather than merely members of jobs. This helps to identify people who may be making up some of the lost time even when jobs are completed late.

---

[3] Supplier orders refer to the firm orders (scheduled receipts) in the supplier schedule and, for those items not yet being supplier scheduled, conventional purchase orders.

2. Capacity performance to plan. Standard hours of actual output compared to planned output. A good target: plus or minus 5 percent.

The frequency of the above: weekly; the breakout: by manufacturing department. Please keep in mind these are ERP-related measurements only, and are not intended to replace measures of efficiency, productivity, and others.

For purchasing, we recommend measuring stock outs and inventory turns on purchased material by supplier and by buyer, as well as for the supplier schedulers as mentioned above. Here, also, don't neglect the more traditional important measurements on quality, price, and so forth.

For data, we recommend weekly reports on the accuracy of the inventory records, bills of material, and routings. The targets for all should be close to 100 percent.

Financial Measurements

At least once a year, the ERP operating committee should take a check on "how we're doing" financially with the ERP. Actual results in dollars should be compared to the benefits projected in the cost justification.

Just as with the operational measurements, a hard-nosed and straightforward approach should be used here: Is the company getting at least the benefits expected? If not, why not? Start fixing what's wrong, so the company can start to get the bang for the buck. Results are reported to the executive steering committee.

EDUCATION

Failure to establish an airtight ongoing education program is a major threat to the long-term successful operation of ERP. Ongoing education is essential because:

New people enter the company.

Plus, current employees move into different jobs within the company, with different and perhaps expanded responsibilities. Failure to educate these new job incumbents spells trouble. It means that sooner or later the company will lose that critical mass of ERP-knowledgeable people. The company then will be unable to operate ERP as effectively as before.

People tend to forget.

They need refresher education and training. To borrow a concept from the physical sciences, there's a half-life to what one learns. If that half-life is one year, people will remember about half of what they learned about ERP last year, 25 percent from two years ago.

Business conditions change.

For any given company, its operating environment three years from now will probably differ substantially from what it is today. Companies develop new product lines, enter new markets, change production processes, become subject to new governmental regulations, acquire new subsidiaries, find that they're operating in a buyers' market (not a sellers' market), or vice versa, and on and on and on.

Operating ERP means running the business with the ERP set of tools, which tends not to change.

However, business conditions *do change.* It's necessary periodically to match up the tools (ERP) to today's business environment and objectives. These may be quite different from what they were a few years ago when ERP was implemented.

What's needed is an ongoing process.

That is, one where people can review the tools they're using to do their jobs, match that up against today's requirements, and ask themselves, "Are we still doing the right things? How might we use the tools better? How could we do our jobs differently to meet today's challenges?" We're back to behavior change. (See Chapter 7.) It's necessary after implementation, as well as before. And the way to facilitate behavior change is via education.

Ongoing ERP education should be woven tightly into the operational fabric of the company. Minimum ERP educational standards should be established for each position in the company, and written into its job specification. New incumbents should be required to meet these standards within a short time on the job. How can ongoing ERP education be woven into the operational fabric of the company? Perhaps it can best be done by involving the folks in human resources. In the H.R. office, there are files for each employee. Checklists are maintained there to help ensure that employees have signed up for programs like health insurance, the blood drive, and the United Fund. Given these files and these checklists, the human resources department may be the best group to administer the ongoing ERP educational program, schedule people into classes, track attendance, and report and reschedule no-shows.

Let us add a word about ongoing education for top management. A change in senior management, either at the CEO level or on his or her staff, is a point of peril for ERP. If the new executive does not receive the proper education, then he or she will, in all likelihood, not understand ERP and may inadvertently cause it to deteriorate. New executives on board need ERP education more than anyone else. This requirement is absolute and cannot be violated if the company wants to operate ERP successfully over the long run. Here, also, this critically important educational requirement should be built directly into the executive's job specifications as a hard-and-fast rule with no latitude permitted.

LEAN MANUFACTURING

Lean Manufacturing (formerly called Just-in-Time) is arguably the best thing that ever happened to ERP. The reason? Because Lean Manufacturing, done properly, will not allow you to neglect your ERP processes.

Let's take the case of a company that first implements ERP successfully, and then attacks Lean Manufacturing.[4] Let's say the company allows ERP to slip, to deteriorate—perhaps by not keeping the inventory data accurate, or by not managing demand properly, or by

---

[4] This sequence isn't mandatory. Frequently, companies will go after Lean Manufacturing first. Some companies implement them simultaneously.

allowing the bills of material to get messed up, or by violating time fences in the master schedule, or all of the above. What will happen?

Well, before long, the problems created by not having excellent plans and schedules will begin to affect (infect?) the Lean Manufacturing processes. Poor plans and schedules will inhibit Lean Manufacturing from working nearly as well as it can and should. The reason: No longer will there be inventories, queues, and safety stocks to cover up the bad schedules. Stockouts are much more painful in this environment. Lean Manufacturing, in that case, will "send up a rocket" that there are major problems here. It will scream to get ERP back to Class A. And that's great.

But that's not all. Lean Manufacturing does more than keep ERP from slipping. It also helps it to get better and better. How so? By simplifying and streamlining the real world.

- As setup times drop, so do order quantities and, hence, inventories.

- As quality improves, safety stock can be decreased and scrap factors minimized.

- As flow replaces job shop, queues go down and so do lead times.

As these real world improvements are expressed into ERP, it will work better and better. As the real world gets simpler, data integrity becomes easier and planning becomes simpler.

SUMMARY

To those of you whose companies haven't yet started on Lean Manufacturing, we urge you to begin as soon as possible. You must do these things, and many others, in order to survive in the ultra-competitive worldwide marketplace of the twenty-first century.

ERP is essential but not sufficient. No one of these tools—Lean Manufacturing, Total Quality, Enterprise Resource Planning, Design for Manufacturability, CAD/CAM, Activity Based Costing, and all the others—is sufficient. They're all essential.

"How are we doing?" is one necessary question to ask routinely. Another is: "How can we do it better?"

Don't neglect this second question. The truly excellent companies seem to share a creative discontent with the status quo. Their attitude is: "We're doing great, but we're going to be even better next year. We're going to raise the high bar another six inches, and go for it."

There are few companies today who are as good as they could be. There are few companies today who even have any idea how good they could be. In general, the excellent companies are populated with individuals no smarter or harder working than elsewhere. They merely got there first, then stayed there (at Class A), and then got better and better.

With Class A ERP, a company can operate at an excellent level of performance—far better than before, probably better than it ever dreamed possible. High quality of life, being in control of the business and not at the mercy of the informal system, levels of customer service and productivity previously thought unattainable—to many companies today this sounds like nirvana. However, it's not good enough.

Are all Class A companies perfect? Nope. Are there things these companies could do better? Certainly.

The message is clear. Companies should not rest on their laurels after reaching Class A with ERP. Don't be content with the status quo. It's more important than ever to go after those additional productivity tools, those "better mousetraps," those better and more humane ways of working with people. Many of these projects can be funded with the cash freed up by the ERP-generated inventory reductions alone. Look upon your excellent ERP processes as an engine, a vehicle, a launch pad for continued and increasing excellence. And we'll talk more about that in the next chapter.

Q & A WITH THE AUTHORS

TOM: Mike, you've seen ERP operate inside a major corporation. In your opinion, what's the big issue that prevents some businesses from maintaining Class A status once they've reached it?

MIKE: Probably the biggest barrier to maintaining Class A is lack of understanding of ERP's business benefits. If Class A is seen as simply an artificial, project-focused goal, then other business priorities will overshadow ERP's needs for maintenance and improvement. The bottom-line business benefits in customer service, cash, profits, and sales need to be clearly connected to the level of performance signified by Class A.

IMPLEMENTERS' CHECKLIST

Function: Operating ERP

Task	Complete Yes	No
1. ERP project team reorganized for ongoing operation, with no full-time members and rotating chairmanship.		
2. Executive steering committee still in place.		
3. ABCD Checklist and financial measurements generated by project team at least twice per year and formally reported to executive steering committee.		
4. Ongoing ERP education program underway and woven into the operational fabric of the company.		
5. Lean Manufacturing/Just-in-Time processes initiated and successfully completed within the company and with suppliers.		

	Complete	
Task	Yes	No
6. Discontent with the status quo and dedication to continuing improvement adopted as a way of life within the company.	_____	_____

Chapter 16

The Strategic Future (Phase III)

SEE THE FUTURE

The fortune teller sings the familiar refrain—"Come and see the future." Are you tempted? Do you think that anyone can see the future or do you want to really know? Well, relax. We are not going to tell your fortune or your future. However, we are going to tell you that, with the tools provided by Enterprise Resource Planning, particularly in combination with Enterprise Software, you can now create a dramatically changed future for your company.

This is phase III on the Proven Path (Figure 16-1) and represents the brave new world of the future. Although ERP phases I and II are distinct and have endpoints, phase III is the ongoing effort to not only keep ERP alive but to capitalize on the full potential that now exists in the company.

The capabilities that you can create with ERP, particularly when coupled with Enterprise Software, are so dramatic that failure to move to a new corporate strategy may be failure indeed. For the first time, the supply chain can now be a key factor in creating corporate strategy instead of a limiting factor. This new, dynamic supply chain can deliver benefits that should prompt a complete revision of how the company does its business. In this chapter, we are going to give

Figure 16-1

ERP PROVEN PATH

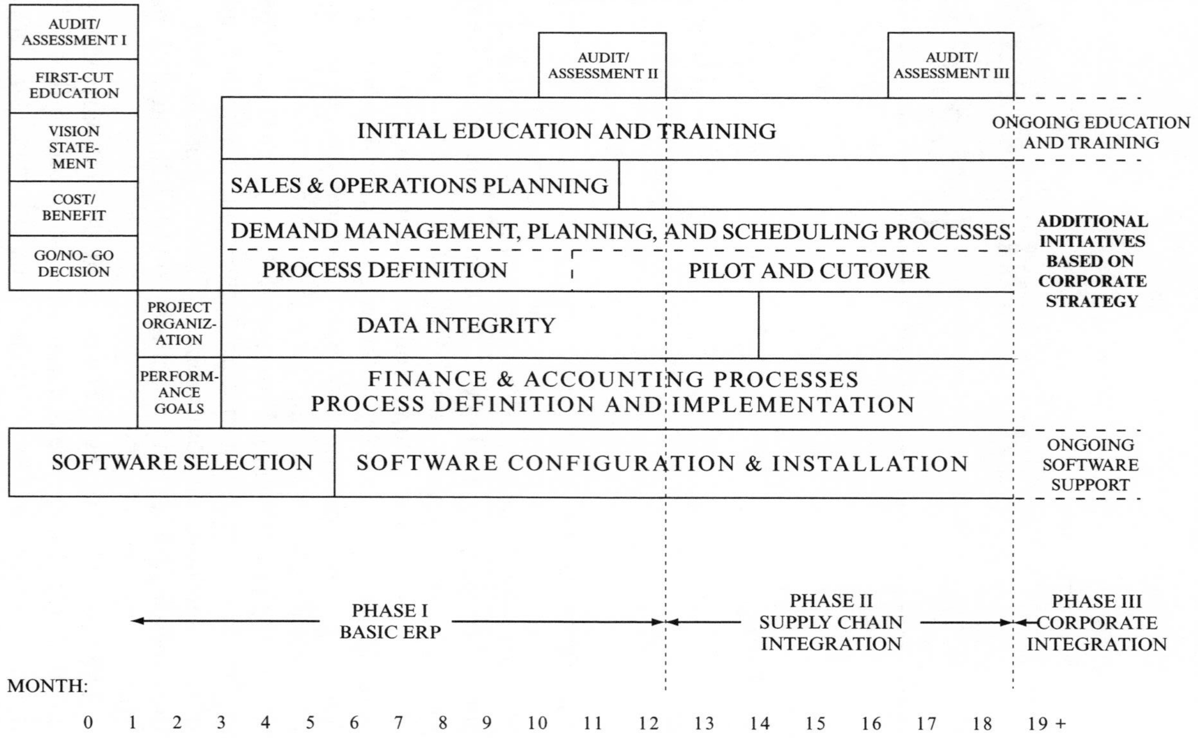

AUDIT/ ASSESSMENT I	FIRST-CUT EDUCATION	VISION STATE-MENT	COST/ BENEFIT	GO/NO-GO DECISION		PROJECT ORGANIZ-ATION	PERFORM-ANCE GOALS													

INITIAL EDUCATION AND TRAINING

AUDIT/ ASSESSMENT II

AUDIT/ ASSESSMENT III

ONGOING EDUCATION AND TRAINING

SALES & OPERATIONS PLANNING

DEMAND MANAGEMENT, PLANNING, AND SCHEDULING PROCESSES

PROCESS DEFINITION

PILOT AND CUTOVER

ADDITIONAL INITIATIVES BASED ON CORPORATE STRATEGY

DATA INTEGRITY

FINANCE & ACCOUNTING PROCESSES

PROCESS DEFINITION AND IMPLEMENTATION

SOFTWARE SELECTION

SOFTWARE CONFIGURATION & INSTALLATION

ONGOING SOFTWARE SUPPORT

PHASE I BASIC ERP	PHASE II SUPPLY CHAIN INTEGRATION	PHASE III CORPORATE INTEGRATION

MONTH: 0 1 2 3 4 5 6 7 8 9 10 11 12 13 14 15 16 17 18 19 +

you some examples of how corporate strategy might change and some ideas on how to sell the concept. Certainly, there are hundreds of possible strategic choices, so our thoughts are merely meant to trigger your own thought processes.

Keep in mind that we are talking about changes far in excess of the benefits that may have been used to justify installing ERP. We talked about these benefits and payout in Chapter 5. Those are effective and useful measures, but they do not recognize the opportunities to shift the corporate thinking to a bolder strategy. The reason for this additional major benefit is that ERP provides two currencies that are always in short supply: time and knowledge.

TIME AND KNOWLEDGE

An intriguing question here is "What assets or currencies will we always need in greater amounts?" A quick thought is that any company, like any individual, always needs more money. Isn't profit the engine that drives our business? The answer is yes and no. Your authors are not going to suggest that making money is bad. That's why this book has a price tag on the dust jacket. However, companies can make too much money. If margins are too high, there are several bad things that can happen. One is that more competition will enter the category and could drive pricing below acceptable levels. Another is that customers will become very upset when they realize that the products are carrying unseemly margins. Although having too much money is a business problem that would be fun to contemplate, it is possible to have too much for the long-term health of a business.

OK, if not money, then what? How about more assets (plants, buildings, vehicles, etc.)? Assets are necessary to produce or handle any product but clearly, accumulation of assets is an ineffective business strategy. The right asset at the right place at the right time is extremely important but excess assets are simply balance sheet baggage. Even a real estate developer can have too many assets if the market does not support the need for more offices or more houses.

We submit to you that no business ever has enough *time* or *knowledge*. If there were a way to bank these two elusive concepts, every company would be bragging in its annual report about the accumulation of time and knowledge. Time and knowledge are the untarnished currencies of the past, present, and future. Finding ways to move faster with more knowledge will always be in style and will provide the ability to generate more money, more assets, or any other important corporate measure. The million (billion?) dollar question is how to use time and knowledge to enable major business change.

We emphasize this topic because the new corporate strategy available with ERP is based on how you *choose to use* time and knowledge. You now have the knowledge of demand, capacity, and costs of decisions that make the supply chain transparent. This knowledge comes to you when you need it for long and short range planning and execution. The addition of ES makes this capability even more dramatic. Data flows instantaneously into the total system in a way that is now directly usable to shape and control the supply chain. No longer is the company limited by the supply chain. Now, the supply chain can be recreated to reshape the company.

How many times has each of us said: "If we only knew . . . ," or "If we only had a little more time . . . ?" ERP won't solve every such question in the company but the supply chain questions that are at the heart of costs, quality, and customer service should now be answered in a very different fashion.

ZERO INVENTORY

It's amazing that so many business people still consider inventory to be an asset. Well it is an asset on the balance sheet but is it an asset to the operation of the business? Some would say: "Of course, inventory is a great asset—how else can we meet customer demand?" Sadly, this question so permeates many companies that people are blinded to what we believe is a simple truth: *inventory is bad.*

Places where inventory is stored, warehouses, are evil places. Warehouses are places where products get damaged, become obsolete, and incur costs. In most cases, products don't get better in a warehouse and almost all products degrade some in storage. In other words, warehouses are not hospitals where products get better. (Note that we are ignoring products like whiskies, wines, and fine cheeses; storage is really part of the process for those delightful items.)

Bob Stahl has a good way of thinking about inventory: "Inventory is like having a fever. The higher the temperature, the worse the disease; the larger the inventory, the worse are the processes." Inventory is one of the least flexible assets owned by the company. Inventory of

Product A normally can't be used to ship to a customer who needs Product B. A single unit of inventory can be used to fill only one line on one order. Your desk may be more flexible than that!

Inventory has been used historically *to mask the absence of knowledge.* Not knowing what future demand fluctuations may be causes people to build inventory for protection. Not knowing production plans causes inventory to be created to protect for interruption of supply. In fact, these protections tend to build throughout the entire supply chain so that every link in the chain builds more protection. If the customer demand varies plus or minus 10 percent, the local DC may plan for plus or minus 15 percent. That prompts the central DC to plan on plus or minus 20 percent and the plant to plan for plus or minus 25 percent. By the time the suppliers see the impact, the plus or minus 10 percent variation looks like a cross-section of the Rocky Mountains. Without proper knowledge of demand throughout the supply chain, what looks like logical protection becomes a huge pile of useless assets that protect against variation that never existed.

For those who have been schooled in total quality thinking, you know that inventory also will hide product problems from quick correction. By the time that customers report a problem with a product, there may be weeks of inventory of the same product sitting in a warehouse waiting to be scrapped. With lower inventories, product quality problems will become visible—and fixable—sooner.

The same thing is true for new products. If your product line has periodic additions, improvements, or changes, then you're no doubt familiar with dumping obsolete inventory. The more product or raw material that sits in the supply chain—the greater the risk of obsolescence.

The answer for inventory is the responsive supply chain supported by the knowledge and time provided by ERP. The only way to even approach the concept of zero inventory is through greater knowledge of demand and supply. Just-in-Time production is certainly the ideal, but true JIT is normally not possible without the tools provided by ERP. Trying to run a Just-in-Time system is like playing Russian roulette if there is no communication and consensus of demand and capacity.

With zero inventory, distribution centers (DCs) become true distribution centers and not warehouses. A company may need to consolidate items for a customer and this is often done at a site near the major customer base. However, this DC should be largely a cross docking facility where the product never stops but simply moves from a supply truck to a delivery truck for a specific customer or customers. Every time you see a DC that is full of inventory, it is badly named. DC's need to be distribution points and not storage facilities.

Can companies with seasonal business ever operate without inventories? Probably not. In almost all seasonal businesses, it's not practical to have the production plan exactly match a sharply peaked sales plan. The cost of acquiring and maintaining the capacity to do that would be prohibitive, so what's needed is to "pre-build" some of the products to be sold during the peak selling season. This means inventory. However, the ERP business processes, particularly S&OP, can help quite a bit here, through better long and medium range planning and via quicker feedback during the selling season itself.

One last point is to start thinking about inventory beyond just your own balance sheet. The true inventory for your product also includes what is held at your customer, plus the materials held by your supplier. It does little good to reduce your own inventory if that reduction comes at the expense of adding more to customers or suppliers. Your balance sheet may improve momentarily but the true cost and flexibility of the total supply chain will probably not have changed.

The opportunity now is to attack the current supply chain logic and move well past the inventory savings used to justify ERP and ES. If zero inventory is too scary or appears to be too expensive for your operation, at least start with a big concept such as a 50 percent reduction. Think big about this because it will shape your entire company strategy. Releasing the cash tied up in inventory will make your stockholders smile, your costs go down, and will cure old age. (Okay, that last one may be an exaggeration, but at least you'll *feel* younger!)

INTERNET

With the supply chain in control via ERP, new ways to access the various parts of the supply chain using the Internet become a real strategy option. We receive lots of questions about the Internet as the answer to connecting your customers and suppliers. Typically, we are supportive since the Internet offers such great capability to link disparate operations and companies with real time connections. However, without the knowledge and time offered via ERP, the high speed of the Internet can simply raise expectations with limited ability to satisfy those expectations. With no control or knowledge of the supply chain, the Internet is like using a high-speed race car to deliver the mail—lots of wasteful starts and stops that nullify the speed between stops.

Far too many companies have pinned their hopes on an oversimplified view of the Internet as the short cut to make sense of their supply chain. There is no question that the Internet offers real potential to change the way that the supply chain works. The mistake is in assuming that simply building a cool web page will cure supply chain inefficiencies.

However, with ERP and perhaps ES, using the Internet as a business to business (B2B) connection makes real sense. B2B can make the supply chain transparent without having to re-wire the connections. The great breakthrough of the Internet is the ability to connect companies and pass massive amounts of data without point-to-point, electronic data interchange (EDI) links even though the software is different at each end of the connection. This technology not only permits a more open marketplace for purchases but also lets trading partners share information on critical decisions.

For the supply chain, the most obvious advantage is linking the supply chain from customers to suppliers. Demand and capacity can be illustrated and shared to provide the timely knowledge needed to meet customer needs at low cost. Instead of building an elaborate EDI capability, connectivity is created via a web page with links that let authorized suppliers and customers see the schedule and input their knowledge.

All of the data that is converted into knowledge by ERP processes—supplier scheduling, VMI, continuous replenishment—can be transmitted more quickly and with more clarity using the B2B Internet connections. Customers can provide real time demand information that can be visible through the entire supply chain. Just-in-Time production becomes real if the manufacturing system has visibility of demand virtually before orders are written. Suppliers can adjust their production plans at the same time to keep the supply chain as a flow system and not a storage system. Now ERP can provide more than the savings that were quoted to justify the installation. ERP enables the use of B2B to change the way the business operates.

One prediction is that ES will be transformed with the Internet. Remember, ES is really rapid transactional software that permits the transfer of data from any transaction directly to a central database. However, ES has been a difficult system to install with the need to examine every transaction and the routing of every piece of data. This requires a very complex installation that involves every workstation that handles a business transaction. The prediction is that the much of this rigid system could be replaced by use of the Internet.

The future of ES could well be "BinB" or Business in Business. There is no reason why each small segment of the internal supply chain and the rest of the company can't be treated like external suppliers and customers in today's B2B logic. The data can move in a way that is useful across the chain, even if the local software is not standardized. BinB could offer a much more user-friendly version of ES. Everything that we have said about the value of ERP and ES will still be true but the work to install and maintain ES will be much simpler.

Of course, this BinB logic may not even require the Internet, as we know it today. Certainly, the Internet provides the flexibility required for a changing business environment. But there could be new technologies just over the horizon that make the Internet seem sluggish. Don't bet against rapid and continuous technology change. Remember, a big complaint about Enterprise Software as it exists today is that it is as flexible as concrete—easy to change when poured, but like a rock later. The future for communications between companies and inside companies will be more flexible and much simpler.

CHOICES

Here are some examples that illustrate the kind of decisions that companies can make with the time and knowledge provided to them. Your business will probably have different options, so these are intended only as examples.

Example #1: Globalization

For companies that are operating across the world, the new capability is an unusual understanding of having the right products at the right place at the right time—worldwide. Without the burden of mystery forecasts or surprise supply, an entirely new organizational format is possible. Instead of regional or local profit centers that operate virtually independently of the rest of the company, there is a clear opportunity to create global profit centers with global supply chains.

A global profit center can be physically located anywhere in the world. Headquarters for one global product family could be in Europe while another is in Asia. Information flows with ES so quickly and deeply that location of the profit center headquarters can be anywhere that makes the most sense for the specific business. Suboptimizing around individual countries or geography makes no sense unless the product is limited to that geography.

A company can decide to have several profit center locations or can decide to have them all in one location. The information flow and the knowledge processes give the option of choosing where they provide the company with the greatest competitive advantage. It's unlikely that a given company's current profit center strategy is structured in a way that really utilizes the new capability offered by ERP and ES.

The global supply chain is now possible using the S&OP process in an entirely new way. The process is the same but the players are now located across the globe. Without ERP/ES, there was "no way" you could accumulate data about demand or supply that was dependable, predictable, or believable. ERP/ES provides the exciting capability of harnessing the right information in a way that is usable and actionable.

Think of the corporate advantage of being able to always produce your product line at the lowest cost location for each order every time. Not only will costs and inventories drop even further but customers also will be delighted with the new levels of service. A company now has the choice to build a new organization that brings products to market to meet customer needs with dazzling speed. Not only does this delight customers, but it reduces costs and improves cashflow.

Changing to a global profit center organization is not easy. People may have to relocate and/or change jobs. The design process will require serious thought and the execution needs to be systematic. However, the benefits may mean a competitive edge that can propel the company to new heights or, at least, may save the business from competitors that globalize faster.

Trying to run a worldwide business in today's global environment is frustrating and may be doomed to failure without taking advantage of ERP and ES. Speed is so limited with the old organization that it is unlikely that the rewards of a global enterprise will ever match the costs and confusion. Each company needs to decide how to use ERP and ES to forge their own global organization. The error would be standing pat. The opportunity is to think about what this new level of time and knowledge can let you do to provide the tools for a new organization.

Example #2: Geographic Redesign

Regardless of the profit center question, this new capability calls for a new look at the geographic location of distribution centers or offices. Very often the location of key facilities is based on historic assumptions, acquisitions, or strategies that no longer fit the business situation of today—much less take advantage of ERP and ES. Plants may be located on the coast because key raw materials used to come from overseas. Alternately, the plant locations may be in the center of the country because that is where the business started. Neither location strategy was wrong at the time it was made. However, the business environment has certainly changed and these locations may be increasingly obsolete.

Now with ERP and ES, a company has the chance to use this time and knowledge capability to shape a new geographic pattern. The knowledge of product location, availability, and demand frees any company from old locations. The location can now be independent of data flow or local control of inventory since the knowledge of key information is available broadly and at the right time.

The choice of DC location offers some good and simple examples. A product that is expensive to ship—bulky and low relative value—calls for short transportation chains. This kind of product mix would indicate that DC's and probably production should be located near customers. With the knowledge offered by ERP processes such as DRP, supplier scheduling, VMI, and so forth, the historic need to sit on top of a large DC so that all product can be controlled is no longer valid.

Conversely, a product that is relatively inexpensive to ship and perhaps difficult to produce can be distributed and produced from a central location. The need to stay close to customer demand is now handled with the knowledge and time provided by ERP/ES. Dependable, accurate information that highlights supply chain operation replaces the need to have expensive inventory scattered around the country.

In either case, the company has the opportunity to design the physical system based on the economics of that business and not the need for artificial control systems. This is a new capability that has not existed in the past and should change the corporate strategy around asset location.

Example #3: Customer Driven

This example may be the most dramatic of all and could have the biggest impact on any company's total business. The agile supply chain with real-time information availability opens the door for a true customer-driven strategy. We have seen examples of companies created around the concept of customer driven operation. Dell Computer and Amazon.com are examples from the 1990s of companies whose original strategy was based on consumer order fulfillment with the supply chain built to support that concept. Consumer orders would trigger production of the unit or assembly of the order with the supplier tied into the same information.

What is required to make this work in an existing business is an entirely new thought process. Remember our ERP diagram (Figure 1-5) back in Chapter 1? Essentially, the Demand side of Figure 1-5 can quickly be converted into the production orders for that day's operation. This information passes directly through to any upstream suppliers who can then provide the appropriate materials in time to meet that production. This information could be shared via EDI, but use of the Internet makes this a much more direct communication.

The magic that makes this happen is the ERP/ES capability that exists to match capacity with demand for the long term, and insures that the connections between operations and companies is simple, meaningful, and direct. Daily operations are driven entirely by today's orders with internal operations and outside connections enabled by the ERP/ES processes and systems. Long-term planning for capacity and predicting demand is the key role for the S&OP meeting that now becomes an entire supply chain process involving suppliers and any intermediate customers.

Besides the obvious benefits of virtually zero inventory and zero obsolescence, the marketing part of the organization receives immediate feedback on advertising or promotion efforts. The absence of the great flywheel of inventory means that any promotional activity can be seen virtually within the week that it happens. Do you want to see a marketing manager get excited? Tell that manager what this new strategy could provide in the way of immediate customer feedback.

With a customer-driven strategy, customers are delighted with quick delivery or availability of their order, the supply chain produces only what is required for each day's orders, and the enhanced knowledge of customer response will drive added sales. Let's not make this seem too easy. Of course, the supply chain needs to be redesigned. Internal operations need to be more flexible and agile, typically utilizing the processes of Lean Manufacturing. Suppliers need to develop equally responsive processes. Decision-making then can be at the point of need—production level for daily and executive level for long term. None of this is easy but making phase III a reality certainly can make it happen.

Selling ERP in Strategy

Even if a dramatic new corporate strategy is available with ERP/ES, how can that strategy be sold to the top managers of the company? This is a frequent question and a very important one. The techniques are similar to what you might do to sell any major change in the company. Each answer depends on the personalities and the needs of the business at the time, but here are a few ideas.

First, sell the vision. Most of us will focus on the tough work of the transition from one strategy to another. Everyone is conscious of the work that must be done and that mountain can seem insurmountable. However, if the vision is clear and exciting, the transition becomes a desired effort to reach a prize that is worth the effort. Express the vision of the new strategy in a way that everyone can understand. This should be as simple as possible. A single sentence using one-syllable words with action verbs has more impact than a long paragraph.

Next, dramatize the vision with facts that illustrate the degree of change. We have seen the use of these "factoids" change attitudes at all levels by helping people picture the impact. These factoids will rarely be the normal measures used in the company, but often they are the input to those measures. If at all possible, position these against the issues most important to the leader.

For example, let's say your company handles 100,000 customer orders per year. Saying that you have a 3 percent rate of missed shipments (late, incomplete, or both) conveys the facts. It does not, however, have the same impact as saying "we messed up 3,000 orders last year. That's 15 every day, about one every 30 minutes." That's the same basic data as 3 percent of 100,000 but a CEO might capture the picture of 3,000/15/30 and become excited by it. We have seen this very example become the heart of a major shift in strategy by a company wrestling with internal arguments about who was at fault. The CEO grabbed the 3,000 number and cut through the arguments to make sweeping changes.

Another example could be the cost of returned orders. Let's say the company typically incurs an annual transportation cost of around $60,000 for returned goods. Converting $60,000 to a factoid of 60 trucks has more mental impact. Not that the money is insignificant, but it may not carry the force of 60 trucks, more than one per week, bringing your products back to your dock. The same logic could apply to production outages caused by raw material or parts delivery. A 5 percent efficiency improvement would be welcome but translating that figure to the number of times a production line is shutdown can have greater impact.

A last piece of advice on selling a shift in corporate strategy is to avoid the "either/or" trap. This trap is characterized by someone saying that we can either do part of the strategy but not the other. Whenever you hear "either/or," look for a way to verify that you really do want to do both. In the early days of total quality work, we often heard people say: "Well you can either have higher quality or lower cost." Well, we know that total quality gives both lower cost and better quality.

You can have more DC's, lower cost, and lower inventory by using ERP. Zero inventory can deliver higher levels of customer service even though some will say "either/or." The choice is not B2B Internet or ERP—it must be both.

The degree of change that is offered by ERP/ES is so dramatic that people will have to be reminded that the results are equally dramatic. This requires a clear vision, a description of benefits that can be easily pictured in the minds of others, and choosing to deliver "both" of the choices.

This book is entitled *ERP: Making It Happen*. Your choice is to make sure that the company experiences the maximum benefit of making ERP happen. That means using ERP to reach new levels of corporate performance. What you are making happen is a new company that can grow and prosper well beyond this project.

Good luck and make it happen!

Appendix A

The Fundamentals of Enterprise Resource Planning

To be truly competitive, manufacturing companies must deliver products on time, quickly, and economically. The set of business processes known as Enterprise Resource Planning (ERP) has proven to be an essential tool in achieving these objectives.

Their capabilities offer a means for effectively managing the required resources: materials, labor, equipment, tooling, engineering specifications, space, and money. For each of these resources, ERP can identify what's required, when it's needed, and how much is needed. Having matched sets of resources at the right time and the right place is essential for an economical, rapid response to customer demands.

The logic of ERP is quite simple; it's in every cookbook. The Sales & Operations Plan says that we're having Thanksgiving dinner on the third Thursday in November. The master schedule is the menu, including turkey, stuffing, potatoes, squash, vegetables, and all the trimmings. The bill of material says, "Turkey stuffing takes one egg, seasoning, and bread crumbs." The routing says, "Put the egg and the seasoning in a mixer." The mixer is the work center where the processing is done.

333

Figure A-1

ENTERPRISE RESOURCE PLANNING

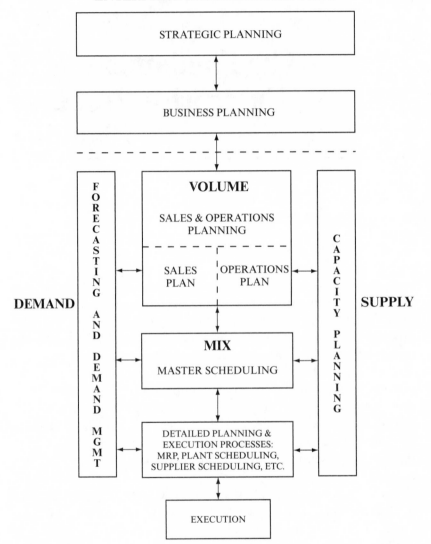

In manufacturing, however, there's a lot more volume and a lot more change. There isn't just one product, there are many. The lead times aren't as short as a quick trip to the supermarket, and the work centers are busy with lots of jobs. Thanksgiving won't get rescheduled, but customers sometimes change their minds and their orders may need to be resequenced. The world of manufacturing is a world of constant change, and that's where ERP comes in.

The elements that make up an ERP operating and financial planning system are shown in Figure A-1. We'll briefly walk through each to get an understanding of how ERP operates.

STRATEGIC PLANNING AND BUSINESS PLANNING

Strategic planning defines the overall strategic direction of the business, including mission, goals, and objectives. The business planning process then generates the overall plan for the company, taking into account the needs of the marketplace (customer orders and forecasts), the capabilities within the company (people skills, available resources, technology), financial targets (profit, cash flow, and growth), and strategic goals (levels of customer service, quality improvements, cost reductions, productivity improvements, etc.). The business plan is expressed primarily in dollars and lays out the long-term direction for the company. The general manager and his or her staff are responsible for maintaining the business plan.

SALES & OPERATIONS PLANNING

Sales & Operations Planning (S&OP) addresses that part of the business plan which deals with sales, production, inventories, and backlog. It's the operational plan designed to execute the business plan. As such, it is stated in units of measure such as pieces, standard hours, and so forth, rather than dollars. It's done by the same group of people responsible for business planning in much the same way. Planning is done in the aggregate—in broad categories of products—and the focus is on volume, not mix. It establishes an aggregate plan of attack for sales and marketing, engineering, manufacturing and purchasing, and finance.

Demand Management

Forecasting/Sales Planning

Forecasting/sales planning is the process of predicting what items the sales department expects to sell and the specific tasks they are going to take to hit the forecast. The sales planning process should result in a monthly rate of sales for a product family (usually expressed in units identical to the production plan), stated in units and dollars. It represents sales and marketing's commitment to take all reasonable steps to make sure the forecast accurately represents the actual customer orders to be received.

Customer Order Entry and Promising

Customer order entry and promising is the process of taking incoming orders and determining specific product availability and, for a make-to-order item, the product's configuration. It results in the entry of a customer order to be built/produced/shipped, and should also tie to the forecasting system to net against the projections. This is an important part of an ERP system; to look at the orders already in the system, review the inventory/backlog, available capacity, and lead times, and then determine when the customer order can be promised. This promise date is then entered as a customer commitment.

Rough-Cut Capacity Planning

Rough-cut capacity planning is the process of determining what resources (the "supply" of capacity) it will take to achieve the production plan ("demand" for capacity). The process relies on aggregate information, typically in hours and/or units, to highlight potential problems in the plant, engineering, finance, or other areas prior to the proposed schedule being approved.

Master Scheduling

Master scheduling addresses mix: individual products and customer orders. It results in a detailed statement of what products the company will build. It is broken out into two parts—how many and when. It takes into account existing customer orders, forecasts of anticipated orders, current inventories, and available capacities. This plan must extend far enough into the future to cover the sum of the lead times to acquire the necessary resources. The master schedule must be laid out in time periods of weeks or smaller in order to generate detailed priority plans for the execution departments to follow. The sum of what's specified in the master schedule must reconcile with the Sales & Operations Plan for the same time periods.

MATERIAL REQUIREMENTS PLANNING (MRP)

Material Requirements Planning starts by determining what components are required to execute the master schedule, plus any needs for service parts/spare parts. To accomplish this, MRP requires a bill of material to describe the components that make up the items in the master schedule and inventory data to know what's on hand and/or on order. By reviewing this information, it calculates what existing orders need to be moved either earlier or later, and what new material must be ordered.

CAPACITY REQUIREMENTS PLANNING (CRP)

Capacity Requirements Planning takes the recommended needs for manufactured items from MRP and converts them to a prediction of how much capacity will be needed and when. A routing that defines the operations involved is required, plus the estimate of time required for each. A summary by key work center by time period is then presented to compare capacity needed to capacity available.

PLANT SCHEDULING

Plant scheduling utilizes information from master scheduling and MRP to develop start and completion times for jobs to be run. The plant scheduling process can be as simple as lists derived directly from the master schedule or as complex as utilizing sophisticated finite scheduling software to simulate various plant schedules to help the plant and scheduling people select the best one.

Furthermore, a company must also monitor the flow of capacity by comparing how much work was to be completed versus how much has actually been completed. This technique is called input-output control, and its objective is to ensure that actual output matches planned output.

SUPPLIER SCHEDULING

Suppliers also need valid schedules. Supplier scheduling replaces the typical and cumbersome cycle of purchase requisitions and purchase orders. Within ERP, the output of MRP for purchased items is summarized and communicated directly to suppliers via any or all of the following methods: the Internet, an intranet, electronic data interchange (EDI), fax, or mail. Long term contracts define prices, terms, conditions, and total quantities, and supplier schedules authorizing delivery are generated and communicated at least once per week, perhaps even more frequently in certain environments. Supplier scheduling includes those changes required for existing commitments with suppliers—materials needed earlier than originally planned as well as later—plus any new commitments that are authorized. To help suppliers do a better job of long-range planning so they can better meet the needs of the company, the supplier scheduling horizon should extend well beyond the established lead time.

EXECUTION AND FEEDBACK

The execution phase is the culmination of all the planning steps. Problems with materials or capacity are addressed through interaction between the plant and the planning department. This is done on an exception basis, and feedback will only be necessary when some part of the plan cannot be executed. This feedback consists of stating the cause of the problem and the best possible new completion date. This information must then be analyzed by the planning department to determine the consequences. If an alternative cannot be found, the planning department should feed the problem back to the master scheduler. Only if all other practical choices have been exhausted should the master schedule be altered. If the master schedule is changed, the master scheduler owes feedback to sales if a promise date will be missed, and sales owes a call to the customer if an acknowledged delivery date will be missed.

By integrating all of these planning and execution elements, ERP becomes a process for effectively linking long-range aggregate plans to short-term detailed plans. From top to bottom, from the general manager and his staff to the production associates, it ensures that all activities are in lockstep to gain the full potential of a company's capabilities. The reverse process is equally important. Feedback goes from bottom to top on an exception basis—conveying unavoidable problems in order to maintain valid plans. It's a rack-and-pinion relationship between the top level plans and the actual work done in the plant.

FINANCIAL INTEGRATION

In addition to ERP's impact on the operations side of the business, it has an equally important impact on financial planning. By including the selling price and cost data, ERP can convert each of the unit plans into dollars. The results are time-phased projections of dollar shipments, dollar inventory levels, cash flow, and profits.

Incorporating financial planning directly with operating planning produces one set of numbers. The same data is driving both systems—the only difference being the unit of measure. Too often financial people have had to develop a separate set of books as they couldn't trust the operating data. Not only does this represent extra effort, but frequently too much guesswork has to be applied to determine the financial projections.

SIMULATION

In addition to information for operational and financial planning, simulations represent the third major capability of ERP. The ability to produce information to help answer "what if" questions and to contribute to contingency planning is a valuable asset for any manager to have. What if business increases faster than expected? What if business goes as planned, but the mix of products shifts sharply? What if our costs increase, but our prices do not? Do we have enough capacity to support our new products and maintain sales for current ones? These are common and critical issues that arise in manufacturing companies. A key part of the management job is to think through alternative plans. With ERP, people can access the data needed to help analyze the situation, play "what if," and, if required, initiate a better plan.

Plant Floor Organization Formats: Job Shop versus Flow Shop

There are two basic ways for companies to organize their production facilities: job shop and flow shop. Other terms you may have come across, such as batch or intermittent, are essentially subsets of job or flow. We don't need to concern ourselves with them here.

JOB SHOP

First, let's define job shop. Many people say a job shop is a place where you make specials. Well, it's true that specials can be made in a job shop but so can standard products. The issue is not so much the product but rather how the resources are organized. Let's try this one on for size:

> *Job shop:* a form of manufacturing organization where the resources are grouped by like type.

Other terms for job shop include functional form of organization or single-function departments. The classic example of this approach is a machine shop. Here all the lathes are in one area, the drills in another, the mills in another, and the automatic screw machines are in the building next door.

In a job shop, the work moves from work center to work center based on routings unique to the individual items being produced. In some job shops, there can be dozens or even hundreds of different operations within a single routing. Each one of these operations must be formally scheduled via a complex process known as back scheduling. These back-scheduled operations must then be grouped by work center, sorted by their scheduled operation completion dates, and communicated to the plant floor via what's called a dispatch list. This process is repeated once per day or more frequently.

Do job shops exist in other than metalworking? You bet. In a typical pharmaceutical plant, specifically that section making tablets and capsules, there are single-function departments for granulating, compressing, coating, capsule filling, and so on. The nature of the product would determine its routing. Tablets go to the compressing department; capsules don't. Some tablets got coated; some don't. Capsules get filled but not compressed.

This is a job shop, by the above definition. Note: They're not making specials. Their goal is to make the same products, to the same specifications, time and time again. The Food and Drug Administration prefers it that way.

Advantages typically attributed to the job shop form of organization include a higher rate of equipment utilization and enhanced flexibility.

FLOW SHOP

Flow shops are set up differently. Here's a definition:

> *Flow Shop:* a form of manufacturing organization where the resources are grouped by their sequence in the process.

Some refer to this as a process layout. Examples include oil refineries, certain chemical manufacturing operations, an automobile assembly line, a filling line in a consumer package goods plant, or a manufacturing cell.

Back to our previous example—the pharmaceutical plant making tablets and capsules. The filling and packaging operation is typically flow, not job shop. Each work center (line) consists of some very dissimilar pieces of equipment in a precise sequence: a bottle cleaner, a filler, a cotton stuffer, a capper, a labeler, a case packer, and so forth. Note: They don't have all of the cotton stuffers in one corner of the department, as the job shop layout would call for. This would be very slow, inefficient, and a waste of space.

Many flow shops don't use formal routing information inside the computer because the routing is defined by the way the equipment is located within the line or the cell. Where formal routings are maintained in this environment, they often consist of only one operation. In such a case, the routing might read "make the product" or "make the part."

In most situations in most companies, flow is superior to job shop:

- Products can be made much faster via a flow process than job shop. Hence, shorter lead times and better response to customers' needs.

- Inventories, both work-in-process and other, are much smaller. Hence, less space is required; fewer dollars are tied up; obsolescence is less likely.

- Less material handling is required. Hence, less risk of damage and, more important, non-value-adding activities are reduced with an attendant rise in productivity.

- Workers are more able to identify with the product. Hence, more involvement, higher morale, better ideas for improvement.

There are other benefits from flow, one of which is simplicity (see Figure B-1). Which is simpler? Which is easier to understand? Which is less difficult to plan and schedule? Which allows for more visual control and more immediate feedback?

The obvious answer, and the correct one, to all of these questions is: flow shop. Well, so what? Unless you're fully a flow shop today, what should you be doing? The answer is, wherever possible, you should be converting to flow, because if you don't and your competition does, you might be in trouble. And your competitors may be doing just that because, as a general principle, *the manufacturing world is moving to flow.* It's too good not to do it.

Figure B-1

Job Shop

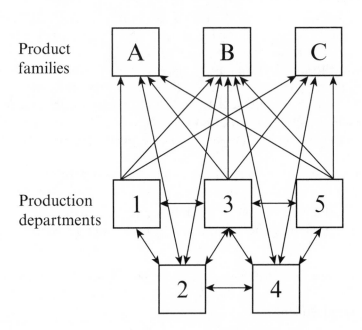

Product
families

Production
departments

And how do you convert from job shop to flow? Answer: Go to cellular manufacturing. More and more, we see companies migrating from job shop to flow via the creation of manufacturing cells (also called flow lines, demand pull lines, kanban lines, and probably some other terms that are just now being dreamed up).[1]

IMPLICATIONS FOR ERP IMPLEMENTATION

Flow is far simpler than job shop, all other things being equal. It's more straightforward, more visual and visible. It can use much simpler scheduling and control tools.

Flow requires fewer schedules, all other things being equal. To make a given item using flow normally requires only one operation

---

[1] For an excellent treatment of this topic, please see William A. Sandras, Jr., *Just-in-Time: Making It Happen* (Essex Junction, VT: Oliver Wight Publications, Inc., 1989).

Figure B-2

Flow Shop

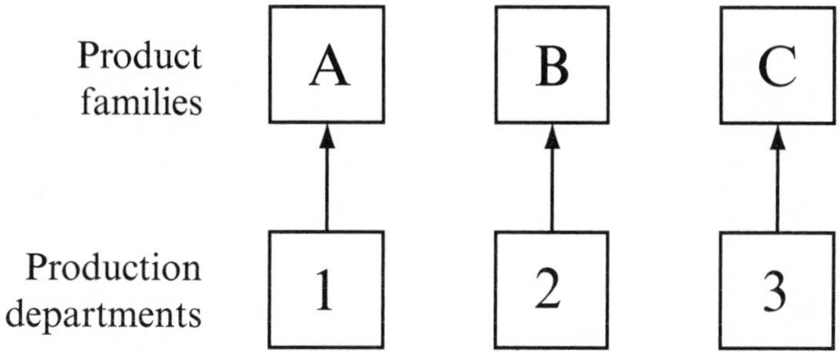

Product
families

| A | B | C |

Production
departments

| 1 | 2 | 3 |

to be scheduled. For example, the same item, made in a job shop and having a routing with ten operations, would require ten schedules to be developed and maintained via the back-scheduling process.

To sum up:

- Flow means FIFO—first in, first out. Jobs go into a process in a given sequence and, barring a problem, are finished in that same sequence.

- Flow means fast. As we said earlier, jobs typically finish far quicker in a flow process than in a job shop.

- FIFO and fast means simple schedules. These are frequently simple sequence lists derived directly from the master schedule or the material plan (MRP).

It's easier—and quicker—to implement simple tools. Therefore, implementing ERP in a pure flow shop should take less time, perhaps several months less, compared to an implementation in a job shop of similar size, and product complexity.

Sample Implementation Plan

This is an example of the first few steps in a detailed implementation plan. It's intended to give the reader a sense of how such a plan might look for a section of the plan that deals with inventory record accuracy.

Task	Responsible	Start		Complete	
		Sched	Act	Sched	Act
1. Measure 100 items as a starting point.	Nancy Hodgkins	11/1		11/8	
2. Map out limited access to warehouses and stockroom areas.	Nancy Hodgkins Tom Brennan	11/1		11/10	
3. Establish cycle counting procedures.	John Grier Nancy Hodgkins Maureen Boylan	11/3		11/10	
4. Begin cycle counting.	Nancy Hodgkins	11/13		(ongoing)	
5. Conduct ERP education for warehouse and stockroom personnel.	David Ball	11/5		11/20	
6. Conduct software training for warehouse and stockroom personnel.	Helen Weiss	11/8		11/23	

ERP Support Resources

APICS
5301 Shawnee Road
Alexandria, VA 22312-2317
800-444-2742
apics.org

Public classes, in-company classes, education materials, on-line bookstore.

Buker, Inc.
1425 Tri-State Parkway
Suite 120
Gurnee, IL 60031
800-654-7990
buker.com

In-company and public classes, education materials, consulting.

R.D. Garwood, Inc.
111 Village Parkway
Marietta, GA 30067
800-241-6653
rdgarwood.com

In-company and public classes, education materials, consulting.

Gray Research
270 Pinewood Shores
P.O. Box 70
East Wakefield,
NH 03830
603-522-5310
grayresearch.com

ERP consulting, ERP software evaluations, software for Sales & Operations Planning. The reference document, MRP II Standard System, is available from this Web site.

Richard C. Ling, Inc.
202 Walter Hagen Drive
Mebane, NC 27302
919-304-6459
BAPA@email.msn.com

Education and consulting
focused primarily on
Sales & Operations Planning.

Partners for Excellence
100 Fox Hill Road
Belmont, NH 03220
603-528-0840

In-company classes,
educational materials,
consulting.

Bob Stahl
6 Marlise Drive
Attleboro, MA 02703
508-226-0477
rstahl@aol.com

In-company classes,
educational materials,
consulting.

The Oliver Wight Companies
12 Newport Road
New London, NH 03257
800-258-3862
ollie.com

In-company and public classes,
education materials, consulting.

Glossary

Authors' note: A number of the definitions in this glossary are based on ones in the APICS dictionary.*

ABC CLASSIFICATION   A sorting of the items in an inventory in decreasing order of annual dollar volume or other criteria. This array is then split into three classes, called A, B, and C. Class A contains the items with the highest annual dollar volume and receives the most attention. The medium Class B receives less attention, and Class C, which contains the low-dollar volume items, is controlled routinely. The ABC principle is that effort saved through relaxed controls on low-value items will be applied to reduce inventories of high-value items.

ACTION MESSAGE   An ERP output that identifies the need for and the type of action to be taken to correct a current or a potential problem. Examples of action messages are Release Order, Reschedule Out, and Cancel.

ADVANCED PLANNING SYSTEM (APS)   A decision support tool that employs a) enhanced mathematical/statistical capabilities, b) a powerful simulation capability, and/or c) other advanced techniques to help provide superior plans and schedules.

ALLOCATION   In MRP, an allocated item is one for which a picking order

---

* James F. Cox III and John H. Blackstone Jr., eds., *APICS Dictionary,* ninth edition (Falls Church, VA: APICS 1998). Terms and definitions used with permission.

351

has been released to the stockroom but not yet sent out of the stockroom. It is an uncashed stockroom requisition.

ANTICIPATED DELAY REPORT   A report, normally issued by both manufacturing and purchasing to the master scheduling or material planning functions, regarding jobs or purchase orders that will not be completed on time, explaining why not, and telling when they will be completed. This is an essential ingredient of a closed-loop system.

APICS   Formerly the American Production & Inventory Control Society. Now identified as The Educational Society for Resource Management.

ASSEMBLE-TO-ORDER   A process where the final products are finished to customers' configurations out of standard components. Many personal computers are produced and sold on an assemble-to-order basis.

AUTOMATIC RESCHEDULING   Allowing the computer to automatically change due dates on scheduled receipts when it detects that due dates and required dates are out of phase. Automatic rescheduling is usually not a good idea.

AVAILABLE-TO-PROMISE (ATP)   The uncommitted portion of inventory and/or future production. This figure is frequently calculated from the master schedule and is used as the primary tool for order promising. *See* Capable-to-Promise.

BACKFLUSH   The deduction from inventory of the components used in production by exploding the bill of materials by the count of parent items produced. *See* Post-deduct Inventory Transaction Processing.

BACKLOG   All of the customer orders received but not yet shipped, irrespective of when they are specified for shipment.

BACK SCHEDULING   A technique for calculating operations start and due dates. The schedule is calculated starting with the due date for the order and working backward to determine the required completion dates for each operation. This technique is used primarily in job shops (see Appendix B).

BILL OF MATERIAL   A listing of all the subassemblies, intermediates, parts, and raw materials that go into a parent item, showing the quantity of each component required. May also be called formula, recipe, or ingredients list in certain industries.

BUCKETED SYSTEM   An MRP, DRP, or other time-phased system in which data are accumulated into time periods or buckets. If the period of accumulation were to be one week, then the system would be said to have weekly buckets.

BUCKETLESS SYSTEM   An MRP, DRP, or other time-phased system in which data are processed, stored, and displayed using dated records rather than defined time periods or buckets.

BUSINESS PLAN   A statement of income projections, costs, and profits usually accompanied by budgets and a projected balance sheet as well as a cash flow statement. It is usually stated in dollars. The business plan and the Sales & Operations Plan, although normally stated in different units of measure, should be in agreement with each other.

CAD/CAM   The integration of Computer Aided Design and Computer Aided Manufacturing to achieve automation from design through manufacturing.

CAPABLE-TO-PROMISE   An advanced form of available-to-promise (ATP). ATP looks at future production as specified by the master schedule. Capable-to-promise goes farther: It also looks at what could be produced, out of available material and capacity, even though not formally scheduled. This capability is sometimes found in advanced planning systems (APS).

CAPACITY REQUIREMENTS PLANNING   The process of determining how much labor and/or machine resources are required to accomplish the tasks of production, and making plans to provide these resources. Open production orders, as well as planned orders in the MRP system, are input to CRP which translates these orders into hours of work by work center by time period. In earlier years, the computer portion of CRP was called infinite loading, a misnomer. This technique is used primarily in job shops (see Appendix B).

CELLULAR MANUFACTURING   A method of organizing production equipment which locates dissimilar equipment together. The goal is to produce items from start to finish in one sequential flow, as opposed to a traditional job shop (functional) arrangement which requires moves and queues between each operation. *See* Group Technology, Flow Shop, Job Shop.

CLOSED-LOOP MRP   The second step in the evolution of ERP. This is a set of business processes built around Material Requirements Planning and also including the additional planning functions of production planning, master scheduling, and Capacity Requirements Planning. Further, once the planning phase is complete and the plans have been accepted as realistic and attainable, the execution functions come into play. These include the plant floor control functions of input-output measurement, dispatching, plus anticipated delay reports from both the plant and suppliers, supplier scheduling, and so forth. The term closed loop implies that not only is each of these elements included in the overall system but also that there is feedback from the execution functions so that the planning can be kept valid at all times. *See* Material Requirements Planning, Manufacturing Resource Planning, Enterprise Resource Planning.

COMMON PARTS BILL (OF MATERIAL)   A type of planning bill which groups all common components for a product or family of products into one bill of material.

CONTINUOUS REPLENISHMENT (CR)   Often called CRP for Continuous Replenishment Process or Program. The practice of partnering between distribution channel members that changes the traditional replenishment process from distributor-generated purchase orders, based on economic order quantities, to the replenishment of products based on actual and forecasted product demand.

CUMULATIVE LEAD TIME   The longest time involved to accomplish the activity in question. For any item planned through MRP it is found by reviewing each bill of material path below the item, and whichever path adds up the greatest number defines cumulative lead time. Also called aggregate lead time, stacked lead time, composite lead time, or critical path lead time.

CYCLE COUNTING   A physical inventory-taking technique where inventory is counted on a periodic schedule rather than once a year. For example, a cycle inventory count may be taken when an item reaches its reorder point, when new stock is received, or on a regular basis, usually more frequently for high-value fast-moving items, and less frequently for low-value or slow moving items. Most effective cycle counting systems require the counting of a certain number of items every work day.

DAMPENERS   A technique within Material Requirements Planning used to suppress the reporting of certain action messages created during the computer processing of MRP. Extensive use of dampeners is not recommended.

DEMAND   A need for a particular product or component. The demand could come from a variety of sources (i.e., customer order, forecast, interplant, branch warehouse, service part), or to manufacture the next higher level. See Dependent Demand, Independent Demand.

DEMAND MANAGEMENT   The function of recognizing and managing all of the demands for products to ensure that the master scheduling function is aware of them. It encompasses the activities of forecasting, order entry, order promising, branch warehouse requirements, interplant requirements, interplant orders, and service parts requirements.

DEMONSTRATED CAPACITY   Capacity calculated from actual performance data, usually number of items produced times standard hours per item plus the standard set-up time for each job. Sometimes referred to as earned hours.

DEPENDENT DEMAND   Demand is considered dependent when it comes from production schedules for other items. These demands should be calculated, not forecasted. A given item may have both dependent and independent demand at any given time. See Independent Demand.

DIRECT-DEDUCT INVENTORY TRANSACTION PROCESSING   A method of inventory bookkeeping which decreases the book (computer) inventory of an item as material is issued from stock, and increases the book inventory as material is received into stock. The key concept here is that the book record is updated together with the movement of material out of or into stock. As a result, the book record represents what is physically in stock. *See* Post-Deduct Inventory Transaction Processing.

DISPATCH LIST   A listing of manufacturing orders in priority sequence according to the dispatching rules being used. The dispatch list is usually communicated to the manufacturing floor via hard copy or CRT display, and contains detailed information on priority, location, quantity, and the capacity requirements of the manufacturing order by operation. Dispatch lists are normally generated daily or more frequently and oriented by work center. Used primarily in job shops (see Appendix B).

DISTRIBUTION CENTER (DC)   A facility stocking finished goods and/or service items. A typical company, for example, might have a manufacturing facility in Philadelphia and distribution centers in Atlanta, Dallas, Los Angeles, San Francisco, and Chicago. A DC serving a group of satellite warehouses is usually called a regional distribution center.

DISTRIBUTION REQUIREMENTS PLANNING   The function of determining the needs to replenish inventory at distribution centers. A time-phased order point approach is used, where the planned orders at the branch warehouse level are exploded via MRP logic to become gross requirements on the supplying source. In the case of multilevel distribution networks, this explosion process can continue down through the various levels of master DC, factory warehouse, and so on, and become input to the master schedule. Demand on the supplying source(s) is recognized as dependent, and standard MRP logic applies.

DISTRIBUTION RESOURCE PLANNING (DRP)   The extension of Distribution Requirements Planning into the planning of the key resources contained in a distribution system: warehouse space, manpower, money, trucks and freight cars, and so forth.

EFFICIENT CONSUMER RESPONSE (ECR)   A strategy in which the grocery retailer, distributor, and supplier trading partners work closely together to eliminate excess costs from the grocery supply chain. This is a global movement to enhance the efficiency of product introductions, merchandising, promotions, and replenishment.

ELECTRONIC DATA INTERCHANGE (EDI)   The computer-to-computer exchange of information between separate organizations, using specific protocols.

ENGINEER-TO-ORDER PRODUCT   A product that requires engineering design, and bill of material and routing development before manufacturing can be completed. Such products typically require master scheduling of average or typical items or expected activities and capacities, with many individual components being identified only after preliminary design work is complete.

ENTERPRISE RESOURCE PLANNING (ERP)   predicts and balances demand and supply. It is an enterprise-wide set of forecasting, planning, and scheduling tools, which:

- links customers and suppliers into a complete supply chain,
- employs proven processes for decision-making, and
- coordinates sales, marketing, operations, logistics, purchasing, finance, product development, and human resources.

It's goals include high levels of customer service, productivity, cost reduction, and inventory turnover, and it provides the foundation for effective supply chain management and e-commerce. It does this by developing plans and schedules so that the right resources—manpower, materials, machinery, and money—are available in the right amount when needed.

Enterprise Resource Planning is a direct outgrowth and extension of Manufacturing Resource Planning and, as such, includes all of MRP II's capabilities. ERP is more powerful in that it: a) applies a single set of resource planning tools across the entire enterprise, b) provides real time integration of sales, operating, and financial data, and c) connects resource planning approaches to the extended supply chain of customers and suppliers.

FINAL ASSEMBLY SCHEDULE (FAS)   Also referred to as the finishing schedule as it may include other operations than simply the final operation. For make-to-order products, it is prepared after receipt of a customer order, is constrained by the availability of material and capacity, and it schedules the operations required to complete the product from the level where it is stocked (or master scheduled) to the end item level.

FINITE LOADING   Conceptually, the term means putting no more work into a work center than it can be expected to execute. The specific term usually refers to a computer technique that involves automatic plant priority revision in order to level load operation-by-operation. Also called finite scheduling.

GROUP TECHNOLOGY   An engineering and manufacturing approach that identifies the sameness of parts, equipment, or processes. It provides for rapid retrieval of existing designs and facilitates a cellular form of production equipment layout.

HEDGE   1) In master scheduling, a quantity of stock used to protect against uncertainty in demand. The hedge is similar to safety stock, except that a hedge has the dimension of timing as well as amount. 2) In purchasing, a purchase or sale transaction having as its purpose the elimination of the negative aspects of price fluctuations.

INDEPENDENT DEMAND   Demand for an item is considered independent when unrelated to the demand for other items. Demand for finished goods and service parts are examples of independent demand.

INFINITE LOADING   *See* Capacity Requirements Planning.

INPUT-OUTPUT CONTROL   A technique for capacity control where actual output from a work center is compared with the planned output (as developed by CRP and approved by manufacturing). The input is also monitored to see if it corresponds with plans so that work centers will not be expected to generate output when jobs are not available to work on.

INTERPLANT DEMAND   Material to be shipped to another plant or division within the corporation. Although it is not a customer order, it is usually handled by the master scheduling system in a similar manner.

INVENTORY TURNOVER   The number of times that an inventory turns over during the year. One way to compute inventory turnover is to divide the average inventory level into the annual cost of sales. For example, if average inventory were three million dollars and cost of sales were thirty million, the inventory would be considered to turn ten times per year. Turnover can also be calculated on a forward-looking basis, using the forecast rather than historic sales data.

JOB SHOP   A functional organization whose departments or work centers are organized around particular types of equipment or operation, such as drilling, blending, spinning, or assembly. Products move through departments by individual production orders. *See* Flow Shop.

JUST-IN-TIME   In the broad sense, Just-in-Time is an approach to achieving excellence in manufacturing. In the narrow (and less correct) sense, Just-in-Time is considered by some as a production and logistics method designed to result in minimum inventory by having material arrive at each operation just in time to be used. *See* Lean Manufacturing.

KANBAN   A method for Just-in-Time production in which consuming (downstream) operations pull from feeding (upstream) operations. Feeding operations are authorized to produce only after receiving a kanban card (or other trigger) from the consuming operation. Kanban in Japanese loosely translates to "card." Syn: demand pull.

LEAD TIME   A span of time required to perform an activity. In a logistics context, the activity in question is normally the procurement of materials and/or products either from an outside supplier or from one's own manufacturing facility. The individual components of any given lead time can include some or all of the following: order preparation time, queue time, move or transportation time, receiving and inspection time.

LEAN MANUFACTURING   An approach to production that emphasizes the minimization of the amount of all the resources (including time) used in the various activities of the enterprise. It involves identifying and eliminating non-value-adding activities in design, production, supply chain management, and dealing with the customers.

LOAD   The amount of scheduled work ahead of a manufacturing facility, usually expressed in terms of hours of work or units of production.

LOGISTICS   In an industrial context, this term refers to the functions of obtaining and distributing material and product.

LOT-FOR-LOT   An order quantity technique in MRP which generates planned orders in quantities equal to the net requirements in each period. Also called discrete, one-for-one.

MAKE-TO-ORDER PRODUCT   The end item is finished after receipt of a customer order. Frequently, long lead-time components are planned prior to the order arriving in order to reduce the delivery time to the customer. Where options or other subassemblies are stocked prior to customer orders arriving, the term assemble-to-order is frequently used.

MAKE-TO-STOCK PRODUCT   The end item is shipped from finished goods off the shelf, and therefore, is finished prior to a customer order arriving.

MANUFACTURING RESOURCE PLANNING (MRP II)   The third step in the evolution of ERP. This is a method for the effective planning of the resources of a manufacturing company. It addresses operational planning in units, financial planning in dollars, and has a simulation capability to answer what if questions. MRP II is made up of a variety of functions, each linked together: business planning, Sales & Operations Planning, demand management, master scheduling, Material Requirements Planning, Capacity Requirements Planning, and the execution support systems for capacity and material. Output from these tools is integrated with financial reports such as the business plan, purchase commitment report, shipping budget, inventory projections in dollars, and so on. Manufacturing Resource Planning is a direct outgrowth and extension of closed-loop MRP. *See* Material Requirements Planning, Closed-Loop MRP, Enterprise Resource Planning.

MASTER PRODUCTION SCHEDULE (MPS)   *See* master schedule.

MASTER SCHEDULE (MS)   The anticipated build schedule. The master scheduler maintains this schedule and, in turn, it drives MRP. It represents what the company plans to produce expressed in specific configurations, quantities, and dates. The master schedule must take into account customer orders and forecasts, backlog, availability of material, availability of capacity, management policy, and goals.

MATERIAL REQUIREMENTS PLANNING (MRP)   The first step in the evolution of ERP. This is a set of techniques which uses bills of material, inventory data, and the master schedule to calculate requirements for materials. It makes recommendations to release replenishment orders for material. Further, since it is time phased, it makes recommendations to reschedule open orders when due dates and need dates are not in phase. *See* Closed-Loop MRP, Manufacturing Resource Planning, Enterprise Resource Planning.

MATERIALS MANAGEMENT   An organizational structure which groups the functions related to the complete cycle of material flow, from the purchase and internal control of production materials to the warehousing, shipping, and distribution of the finished product.

MODULAR BILL (OF MATERIAL)   A type of planning bill which is arranged in product modules or options. Often used in companies where the product has many optional features (e.g., automobiles, computers). *See* Planning Bill.

NET CHANGE MRP   A method of processing Material Requirements Planning on the computer whereby the material plan is continually retained in the computer. Whenever there is a change in requirements, open order, or inventory status, bills of material, or the like, a partial recalculation of requirements is made only for those parts affected by the change.

NET REQUIREMENTS   In MRP, the net requirements for an item are derived as a result of netting gross requirements against inventory on hand and the scheduled receipts. Net requirements, lot sized and offset for lead time, become planned orders.

ON-HAND BALANCE   The quantity shown in the inventory records as being physically in stock. (APICS)

OPEN ORDER   An active manufacturing order or purchase order. *See* Scheduled Receipts.

OPTION   A choice or feature offered to customers for customizing the end product. In many companies, the term option means a mandatory choice (i.e., the customer must select from one of the available choices). For example, in ordering a new car, the customer must specify an engine (option) but need not necessarily select an air conditioner.

ORDER ENTRY   The process of accepting and translating what a customer wants into terms used by the provider. This can be as simple as creating shipping documents for a finished goods product to a far more complicated series of activities including engineering effort for make-to-order products. A key element in the order promising process is customer order promising.

ORDER PROMISING   The process of making a delivery commitment (i.e., answering the question "When can you ship?") *See* Available-to-Promise.

ORDER QUANTITY   The amount of an item to be ordered. Also called lot size.

PEGGING   In MRP pegging shows, for a given item, the details of the sources of its gross requirements and/or allocations. Pegging can be thought of as live where-used information.

PERIOD ORDER QUANTITY   An order quantity technique in which the order quantity will be equal to the net requirements for a given number of periods (days or weeks) into the future. Also called days supply, weeks supply, fixed period.

PICKING   The process of issuing components to the production floor on a job-by-job basis. Also called kitting.

PICKING LIST   A document used to pick manufacturing orders, listing the components and quantities required.

PLANNER/BUYER   *See* Supplier Scheduler.

PLANNING BILL (OF MATERIAL)   An artificial grouping of items in bill of material format, used to facilitate master scheduling and/or material planning. A modular bill of material is one type of planning bill.

PLANT FLOOR CONTROL   A system for utilizing data from the plant floor as well as data processing files to maintain and communicate status information on shop orders (manufacturing orders) and work centers. The major subfunctions of shop floor control are: 1) assigning priority of each shop order, 2) maintaining work-in-process quantity information, 3) conveying shop order status information, 4) providing actual input and output data for capacity control purposes, 5) providing quantity by location by shop order for work-in-process inventory and accounting purposes, 6) providing measurements of efficiency, utilization, and productivity of manpower and machines. Syn: Shop Floor Control.

POST-DEDUCT INVENTORY TRANSACTION PROCESSING   A method of inventory bookkeeping where the book (computer) inventory of components is reduced only after completion of production of their upper level parent. This approach has the disadvantage of a built-in differential between the book record and what is physically in stock. Also called backflush.

PRODUCT STRUCTURE   *See* Bill of Material.

PULL SYSTEM   Usually refers to how material is moved on the plant floor. Pull indicates that material moves to the next operation only as needed by that next operation. *See* Kanban.

PUSH SYSTEM   Usually refers to how material is moved on the plant floor. Push indicates that material moves to the next operation automatically upon completion of the prior operation.

QUEUE   In manufacturing, the jobs at a given work center waiting to be processed. As queues increase, so do average lead times and work-in-process inventories.

QUEUE TIME   The amount of time a job waits at a work center before work is performed on the job. Queue time is one element of total manufacturing lead time. Increases in queue time result in direct increases to manufacturing lead time.

QUICK-SLICE   A method of implementing most of the ERP functions into a small slice of the business, typically one product or product line, in a very short time.

REGENERATION MRP   A method of processing Material Requirements Planning on the computer whereby the master schedule is totally exploded down through all bills of material to maintain valid priorities. New requirements and planned orders are completely regenerated at that time. *See* Net change MRP.

REPETITIVE MANUFACTURING   Production of discrete units, planned and executed via schedule, usually at relatively high speeds and volumes. Material tends to move in a sequential flow. *See* Flow Shop.

RESCHEDULING ASSUMPTION   A fundamental piece of MRP logic which assumes that existing open orders can be rescheduled in nearer time periods more easily than new orders can be released and completed. As a result, planned order receipts are not created until all scheduled receipts have been applied to cover gross requirements.

RESOURCE REQUIREMENTS PLANNING   *See* Rough-Cut Capacity Planning.

ROUGH-CUT CAPACITY PLANNING   The process of converting the production plan (from Sales & Operations Planning) and/or the master schedule into capacity needs for key resources: manpower, machinery, warehouse space, suppliers' capabilities and, in some cases, money. Product load profiles are often used to accomplish this. The purpose of Rough-Cut Capacity Planning is to evaluate the plan prior to attempting to implement it. Sometimes called Resource Requirements Planning.

ROUTING   Information detailing the manufacture of a particular item. It includes the operations to be performed, their sequence, the various work centers to be involved, and the standards for set-up and run times. In some companies, the routing also includes information on tooling, operator skill levels, inspection operations, testing requirements, and so forth.

SAFETY STOCK   A quantity of stock planned to be available to protect against fluctuations in demand and/or supply.

SAFETY TIME   A technique whereby material is planned to arrive ahead of the requirement date. This difference between the requirement date and the planned in-stock date is safety time.

SALES & OPERATIONS PLANNING (S&OP)   A business process that helps companies keep demand and supply in balance. It does that by focusing on aggregate volumes—product families and groups—so that mix issues (individual products and customer orders) can be handled more readily. It occurs on a monthly cycle and displays information in both units and dollars. S&OP is cross-functional, involving general management, the sales and marketing department(s), operations, finance, and product development. It occurs at multiple levels within the company, up to and including the executive in charge of the business unit. S&OP links the company's strategic plans and business plan to its detailed processes—the order entry, master scheduling, plant scheduling, and purchasing tools used to run the business on a week-to-week, day-to-day, and hour-to-hour basis. Used properly, S&OP enables the company's managers to view the business holistically and provides them with a window into the future.

SALES PLAN   The overall level of sales expected to be achieved. Usually stated as a monthly volume of sales for a product family (group of products, items, options, features, etc.). It needs to be expressed in units identical to the production plan (as well as dollars) for planning purposes. It should represent the sales and marketing department manager's commitment to take all reasonable steps necessary to make the sales forecast (a prediction) accurately represent actual customer orders received.

SCHEDULED RECEIPTS   Within MRP, open production orders and open purchase orders are considered as scheduled receipts on their due date and will be treated as part of available inventory during the netting process for the time period in question. Scheduled receipt dates and/or quantities are not normally altered automatically by the computer. Further, scheduled receipts are not exploded into requirements for components, as MRP logic assumes that all components required for the manufacture of the item in question have either been allocated or issued to the plant floor.

SERVICE PARTS   Parts used for the repair and/or maintenance of a product. Also called repair parts, spares.

SHOP FLOOR CONTROL   See Plant Floor Control.

SIMULATION   Within ERP, utilizing operational data to perform what-if evaluations of alternative plans, to answer the question: "Can we do it?" If yes, the simulation can then be run in financial mode to help answer the question: "Do we really want to?"

SUPPLIER SCHEDULER   A person whose main job is working with suppliers regarding what's needed and when. Supplier schedulers are in direct contact with both MRP and the suppliers. They do the material planning for the items under their control, communicate the resultant schedules to their assigned suppliers, do follow-up, resolve problems, and so forth. The supplier schedulers are normally organized by commodity, as are the buyers. By using the supplier scheduler approach, the buyers are freed from day-to-day order placement and expediting, and therefore have the time to do cost reduction, negotiation, supplier selection, alternate sourcing, and the like. Syn: Vendor Scheduler, Planner/Buyer.

SUPPLIER SCHEDULING   A purchasing approach which provides suppliers with schedules rather than individual hard-copy purchase orders. Normally a supplier scheduling process will include a business agreement (contract) for each supplier, a daily or weekly schedule for each supplier extending for some time into the future, and individuals called supplier schedulers. Also required is a formal priority planning system that works well, because it is essential in this arrangement to provide the suppliers with consistently valid due dates. Some form of supplier scheduling is essential for Just-in-Time purchasing. Syn: Vendor Scheduling.

SUPPLY CHAIN   1) The processes from the initial acquisition raw materials to the ultimate consumption of the finished product linking across supplier-user companies. 2) The functions inside and outside a company that enable the value chain to make products and provide services to the customer.

TIME FENCE   A point in time where various restrictions or changes in operating procedures take place. For example, changes to the master schedule can be accomplished easily beyond the cumulative lead time; whereas, changes inside the cumulative lead time become increasingly more difficult. Time fences can be used to define these points.

TWO-LEVEL MASTER SCHEDULE   A master scheduling approach for make-to-order products where an end product type is master scheduled along with selected key options, features, attachments, and common parts.

VENDOR SCHEDULER   *See* Supplier Scheduler.

VENDOR SCHEDULING   *See* Supplier Scheduling.

WORK-IN-PROCESS   Product in various stages of completion, including raw material that has been released for initial processing and completely processed material awaiting final inspection and acceptance as finished product or shipment to a customer. Many accounting systems also include semi-finished stock and components in this category.

Index